THE FILMS OF MIRA NAIR

THE FILMS OF
MIRA NAIR

DIASPORA VÉRITÉ

AMARDEEP SINGH

University Press of Mississippi / Jackson

Publication of this book has been generously supported by the Humanities Center at Lehigh University.

www.upress.state.ms.us

Designed by Peter D. Halverson

The University Press of Mississippi is a member of the Association of University Presses.

Copyright © 2018 by University Press of Mississippi
All rights reserved

First printing 2018

∞

Library of Congress Cataloging-in-Publication Data

Names: Singh, Amardeep, 1974– author.
Title: The films of Mira Nair : diaspora vérité / Amardeep Singh.
Description: Jackson : University Press of Mississippi, [2018] | Includes bibliographical references and index. |
Identifiers: LCCN 2018006723 (print) | LCCN 2018010238 (ebook) | ISBN 9781496819123 (epub single) | ISBN 9781496819130 (epub institutional) | ISBN 9781496819147 (pdf single) | ISBN 9781496819154 (pdf institutional) | ISBN 9781496819116 (hardcover : alk. paper) | ISBN 9781496821164 (pbk. : alk. paper)
Subjects: LCSH: Nair, Mira—Criticism and interpretation. | Motion picture producers and directors—Women—United States. | East Indian diaspora in motion pictures.
Classification: LCC PN1995.9.W6 (ebook) | LCC PN1995.9.W6 S574 2018 (print) | DDC 791.4302/32092—dc23
LC record available at https://lccn.loc.gov/2018006723

British Library Cataloging-in-Publication Data available

CONTENTS

Acknowledgments
- vii -

1. Mira Nair's Diaspora Vérité
- 3 -

2. "Our Hearts and Eyes Are Wide Open"
Mira Nair's Documentaries
- 30 -

3. The Aesthetics of Disillusionment
Salaam Bombay! (1988)
- 57 -

4. A Tale of Two "Chunaris"
The Critique of Bollywood in *Monsoon Wedding* (2001)
- 81 -

5. Into the Diasporic Mixing Bowl
Mississippi Masala (1991), *The Perez Family* (1995), and *My Own Country* (1998)
- 105 -

6. Feminist Period Pieces
Vanity Fair (2004) and *Kama Sutra: A Tale of Love* (1996)
- 133 -

7. "Every Day Since Then Has Been a Gift"
The Namesake (2006)
- 158 -

8. "I Had a Pakistani Once"
The Reluctant Fundamentalist (2013) and Nair's Post-9/11 Short Films
- 177 -

9. "Where Do You Belong?"
Returning to Uganda in *Queen of Katwe* (2016)
- 189 -

Mira Nair's Filmography
- 197 -

Notes
- 211 -

References
- 213 -

Index
- 221 -

ACKNOWLEDGMENTS

One of the lessons we learn in academic life is how dependent we are on a large cohort of other people—starting with our teachers and advisors; then, as we progress, peers, collaborators, and anonymous readers and reviewers; and, finally, students. To the extent we succeed, we do so with all of those people helping us along, often for little or no reward or recognition. This project would not have been possible without help and support from a wide community of people who have helped in ways large and small. To begin with, I'm grateful to the filmmaker herself for her support and encouragement early in the process. I'm also grateful to my friends and colleagues in the Lehigh University English Department for their friendship and support; Drown Hall has turned out to be a better intellectual home for me than I could have ever imagined. Nilanjana Bhattacharjya and Monika Mehta gave crucial advice and offered moral support when I encountered roadblocks along the way. I want to thank friends and family who watched and debated Nair's movies with me in recent years: Samian Kaur, Kate and Shapoor Pourshariati, Virender and Ravinder, Tejinder and Jagmohan, Harmeet and Ena, Baljeet and Raveena, Nandini Deo and Timothy Loftus, and lately, Puran Veer Singh and Simran Bani Kaur. Finally, I would like to thank Ania Loomba, Suvir Kaul, Priya Joshi, Amitava Kumar, Susan Stanford Friedman, and the South Asia Center at the University of Pennsylvania for their professional support over the years.

THE FILMS OF MIRA NAIR

Chapter 1

MIRA NAIR'S DIASPORA VÉRITÉ

Mira Nair is a filmmaker who uses a documentary realist sensibility to explore the lives and experiences of diasporic subjects. Nair, who made her first film in 1979, is best known for her crossover hits *Salaam Bombay!* (1988) and *Monsoon Wedding* (2001), but all told she has made (as of the present writing) twelve feature-length fiction films, five documentaries, and half a dozen short films. Taken together, her body of work gives her a unique status as an Indian diasporic artist with links to the Anglo-American as well as Indian cinema worlds as well as an ability to bridge the arthouse and the mainstream. While there is currently no shortage of critical engagement with Nair's most influential films, the disciplines of film studies and postcolonial media studies have perhaps not thus far taken adequate stock of the breadth of Nair's contribution to the representation of diasporic lives throughout her long career or discovered the essential unity of her filmic oeuvre. This study aims to correct that oversight with a comprehensive look at Nair's major works.

Both Nair's earlier and her more recent films are marked by her early exposure, first at Harvard University and then in the New York City film community of the early 1980s, to the cinéma vérité style of documentary realism. While Nair made a format shift from documentary to fiction film beginning in 1987, she has continued to remain invested in a documentary realist aesthetic since then. Nair has cultivated a filmmaking style that emphasizes naturalistic acting over melodrama, that minimizes the evidence of narrative or visual manipulation on screen, and that aims to document the lives of ordinary people from a diverse range of racial and class backgrounds. Nair has also always been invested in filming on location rather than in studio, using mobile, eye-level cameras wherever possible, and synchronous sound rather than overdubbing (even as the latter remains quite common in commercial Hindi cinema). Also, in making *Salaam Bombay!*, *Monsoon Wedding*, and, most recently, *Queen of*

Katwe, Nair has used amateur actors filmed in their own everyday settings for added realism. While these techniques are not universal in Nair's work, I will argue that they do largely define her approach to filmmaking at its best. In *The Films of Mira Nair: Diaspora Vérité*, I aim to show that the filmmaker uses documentary realism in order to show that the prospect of migration, dislocation, and even exile offers her characters a potential path to freedom from social and cultural repression. The phrase "diaspora vérité" in my title aims to encapsulate the way Nair uses documentary realist techniques to explore diverse experiences of migration and displacement in her films. I intend the phrase to be suggestive rather than technical—"diaspora vérité" alludes to the sources of Nair's aesthetic sensibility, but it also gestures towards the filmmaker's commitment to social justice, especially with respect to women and socially and economically marginalized groups.

Nair's films cannot be said to be wholly defined by any singular national or linguistic tradition in cinema; rather, they reflect a wide range of geographical and cultural contexts. Her polyglot films often stretch conventional limits on spoken language associated with national and language-specific cinemas, and they use transnational casts, crews, and production teams. Nair's films are also marketed and distributed internationally; while she is not alone in that, she *is* one of very few working filmmakers to be an established name amongst both South Asian and Euro-American filmgoing publics. Insofar as her work has so consistently focused on themes of migration, travel, and cross-cultural encounter—themes that have come to define the cultural landscape of the current globalization era—Nair might be one of a handful of diasporic film directors whose work has helped transform the scope of contemporary world cinema. Besides immediate Indian diasporic peers such as Gurinder Chadha and Deepa Mehta (whose films will be discussed in greater detail below in comparison to Nair's own work), other directors that come to mind as peers in Nair's case are Alejandro Gonzales Iñarritu, Alfonso Cuarón, Jane Campion, and the early Ang Lee. Close analysis of those filmmakers' quite heterogeneous works falls outside of our present scope, but what one sees in all their work is a deep interest in exploring the cultural and psychological effects of migration and displacement—social phenomena that are at the core of the current globalization era. It is not an accident that this short list of Nair's directorial peers is also heavy on individuals who have done much of their most influential work in countries other than the ones where they were born.

A central focus on the theme of diaspora is readily evident in several Nair films that are centrally focused on immigrants and refugees in the contemporary world. Some of the relevant titles have already been mentioned; a more inclusive list of Nair films that are self-evidently diasporic would include *So Far from India*, *Mississippi Masala*, *My Own Country*, *The Perez Family*, *Monsoon Wedding*, *The Namesake*, and *The Reluctant Fundamentalist*. Domestic (intranational) displacement is also centrally figured in *India Cabaret*, *Salaam Bombay!*, and *Kama Sutra: A Tale of Love*. Further, Nair's two commercial period pieces—her 2004 adaptation of William Thackeray's *Vanity Fair*, and her 2009 biopic *Amelia*, about the American aviator Amelia Earhart—also figure displacement in important ways. A quick look at that array of titles also immediately underscores the centrality of women's stories in Nair's works: from the above list, which includes several of Nair's documentaries, all but two of the films named have women as either protagonists or coprotagonists. And a surprising number of those films, from *Mississippi Masala* to *Vanity Fair*, feature female protagonists who face constraining familial pressure and social limitations—and use the possibility of departure and migration as a means of escape from traditional social structures.

Before we explore these aspects of Nair's approach to filmmaking in greater depth, a general introduction to the filmmaker and her works is in order. This will be organized below into a brief biographical sketch, followed by a more in-depth contextualization of Nair as a postcolonial and diasporic Indian artist, as a feminist filmmaker, and as a participant in an international art cinema culture.

Let us begin by briefly rehearsing Nair's general profile as a filmmaker. Nair is arguably the most accomplished filmmaker in the current generation of diasporic film directors of Indian origin, company that includes the aforementioned Gurinder Chadha and Deepa Mehta, but also Shekhar Kapur, Tarsem Singh, Jagmohan Mundhra, Ismail Merchant, Kiran Rao, Pratibha Parmar, M. Night Shyamalan, Prashant Bhargava, and a number of others. Nair has been nominated for an Academy Award, and she won the Caméra d'Or Prize at the Cannes Film Festival (for *Salaam Bombay!*) as well as the Golden Lion Award at the Venice Film Festival (for *Monsoon Wedding*); she is only the second woman director to ever win the latter prize. But Nair must also be seen in association with a group of avant-garde feminist filmmakers from an international background whose films began to emerge in the 1980s and '90s, including Julie Dash, Trinh T. Minh-ha, Jane Campion, Claire Denis, and Lizzie Borden; an earlier generation of feminist film critics included Nair as part of an emerging international women's art cinema (see Stuart 1994). Just as her awards indicate Nair's reception within the international community of film critics and scholars, several of Nair's films have been major commercial successes, challenging the divide between the art house and the mainstream. With her two signature crossover successes, *Salaam Bombay!* and *Monsoon Wedding*, Nair broke new ground for Indian art films in the international film market; these films also had a surprisingly large impact on the mass market within India itself, despite the gap between Nair's visual and narrative styles and the styles prevalent in the various commercial Indian cinemas.

Biographical Sketch of the Filmmaker

Nair's approach to filmmaking is clearly marked by a set of quite singular personal experiences—a family background that made her emigration from India in the 1970s possible, as well as continuing social and familial connections that have influenced her approach to India after the Indian government's move towards liberalization radically transformed urban Indian life in the 1990s. Nair was born in 1957 in the state of Orissa, in eastern India. Her ethno-linguistic background is Punjabi, and many of her family members are today among the large cosmopolitan Punjabi community that has established itself after 1947 in New Delhi. Nair herself was raised partly in eastern India, in Orissa, where her father, Amrit Nair, a member of the Indian Administrative Service, was stationed for several years. Nair's mother, Praveen Nair, is a social worker who worked with Orissa's Social Welfare Board, the Red Cross, and famine relief efforts before eventually signing on to administer Nair's own charity organization for street children in Delhi, the Salaam Baalak Trust, for several years (Bharadwaj 2007). Nair has at times described how her relationship with her parents, especially her father, impacted her career choices in the early stages (her father played a key role in enabling her to go abroad to study at Harvard University in 1976). However, in an interview from *Cineaste* in 2004, Nair also described how Amrit Nair's connection to the Indian bureaucracy inspired her—negatively—to aim for something different in her own career. As she puts it, "I don't think I got political awareness from him [Amrit Nair] because I viewed bureaucrats as having to ride the winds of the ministers that were in power.... Political awareness came almost as a result of questioning, rather than admiring, that" (Badt 2004: 12). Nair's comment here is part of a longer conversation about political awareness, but it is also valuable as part of a biographical account. So much of the trajectory of Nair's career from that point forward is connected to that early choice to follow a different path—to find a way to defy the prevailing social, political, and even aesthetic norms of middle-class Indian life in the 1970s.

Most of Nair's primary and secondary education occurred at Tara Hall, an Irish Catholic boarding school in Simla heavily oriented toward British colonial values (it was here that Nair says she first encountered Thackeray's *Vanity Fair*). Nair began her postsecondary education at Miranda House at the University of Delhi, where she intended to major in sociology but instead became heavily involved in the theater, acting in English-language plays like *Antony and Cleopatra*, as well as political and experimental theater associated with Barry John's Theatre Action Group. Nair played against friends and future collaborators in this period, including Khalid Tyabji (who would later perform under Nair's direction in *Kama Sutra*), and Lilette Dubey (one of the stars of *Monsoon Wedding* and a major figure in the Delhi theater world in her own right). In 1976, Nair transferred to Harvard University on scholarship, where she studied documentary film after finding that Harvard's theater department was too conservative for her interest (Redding and Brownworth 1997: 165). At Harvard, Nair made many connections that would be important to her future, professionally and personally. Perhaps most importantly, it was at Harvard that Nair met her future repeat collaborator and fellow Indian expatriate, Sooni Taraporevala. Nair also met her first husband and collaborator, the photographer Mitch Epstein, at a Harvard summer school course on photography. Epstein would be an important collaborator on Nair's early documentaries, including *So Far from India*, where he is credited as cinematographer; Epstein also did production design for *Salaam Bombay!* Nair graduated from Harvard in 1979, submitting as her senior thesis her short film *Jama Masjid Street Journal*, which would be screened at New York's Film Forum in 1986. Though not widely known today, a videotape version of Nair's *Jama Masjid Street Journal* has been preserved and is available at a handful of university libraries as well as through Icarus, an academic film distributor (this early short will be discussed at greater length in chapter 2).

After graduating from Harvard, Nair and Taraporevala both relocated to New York, though they did not immediately begin to work together. For her part, Nair sought out the cinéma vérité documentary filmmaker D. A. Pennebaker, who, as she's indicated, helped her secure the grant that would enable her to make her first feature-length documentary, *So Far from India* (see Muir 2006: 29). Nair continued to make documentaries, including *Children of a Desired Sex* (1987), for Canadian television (Cine-Com, Montreal), and *India Cabaret* (1985); the latter film won several awards including Best Documentary at the Global Village Film Festival in New York (Foster 1995:

277). But the path of Nair's career changed dramatically when the success of *Salaam Bombay!* in 1988 opened up Hollywood studio financing for her next feature films, *Mississippi Masala* and *The Perez Family*. Nair also used her personal proceeds from *Salaam Bombay!* to create a charity for slum children in Delhi, the Salaam Baalak Trust; that organization is still active.

Around 1989, Nair met the writer and historian Mahmood Mamdani while on a research trip to east Africa related to the project that would become *Mississippi Masala*. Mamdani, a member of the Indo-African community in Uganda exiled from the country by Idi Amin in the early 1970s, had, by 1989, returned from England and resumed teaching at Makerere University in Uganda. In an interview, Nair described the beginning of the relationship as follows: "I had heard of him [Mamdani]; he was a political writer and academic who had written a very moving piece on the Asian expulsion from the country. . . . I fell in love with the country and with him" (Stuart 1994: 215). Nair and Mamdani lived in South Africa for a time in the mid-1990s, while Mamdani was teaching at the University of Cape Town. Nair and Mamdani's son, Zohran, was born during this period of transition for the couple, in 1991. While in South Africa, Nair directed a short fiction film dealing with the end of the Apartheid era, *The Day the Mercedes Became a Hat* (1993); she also began working on the script that would become *Kama Sutra: A Tale of Love*. Since 1999, Nair and Mamdani have been largely based in New York (they also own a house in Kampala, Uganda), where Mamdani teaches history at Columbia University; Nair also occasionally teaches courses on filmmaking at Columbia. In 2000, Nair founded a filmmaking school for girls in East Africa called Maisha Film Lab, which she continues to work with during regular visits to Uganda. One of Maisha's most prominent alumni is Lupita Nyong'o, who won an Academy Award for her role in *12 Years a Slave* (2014), and who also starred in Nair's recent film *Queen of Katwe* (2016). Since the early 2000s, during the fall, winter, and spring seasons, Nair often appears as a speaker and honoree at cultural events in New York City, as well as at universities and film festivals across the United States. Nair has recently released two new major film adaptations, *The Reluctant Fundamentalist*, starring Riz Ahmed and Kate Hudson, and *Queen of Katwe*, starring Lupita Nyong'o and and David Oyelowo. While not without its flaws (see chapter 8 of the present study), *The Reluctant Fundamentalist* proved to be a compelling film, demonstrating that Nair's career as a filmmaker exploring and documenting South Asian diaspora life may be a book that has a few more chapters left to be written. Finally, in *Queen of Katwe*, Nair returned to her early cinéma vérité–influenced documentary realist technique, filming a group of slum children in the Katwe slums of Kampala as they learn chess from a devoted teacher. While box office returns were modest, this latter film has been a critical success, with many commentators celebrating its unique status as a Hollywood-financed film (*Queen of Katwe* was financed and distributed by Disney) set in Africa with an all-black primary cast.

Mira Nair's Hybridity: Contextualizing a Postcolonial Filmmaker

Early in the process of writing the present book, the author approached the editor of a monograph series dedicated to film directors at a university press that shall remain nameless. When the suggestion of a title on Nair was put to the editor, the response was, "Probably not—she's a little too Hollywood for us!" This response is understandable but mistaken. While Nair is certainly more mainstream than classic auteurs like Jean Luc-Godard or Francois Truffaut, a close viewing of her major films leads us to conclude that Mira Nair can and should be understood as a distinctive film author; her direction is visible in all of her films, including the early documentaries as well as her more recent work. That said, in this study I will not refer to Nair as typically an "auteur" in the manner of classic film criticism in the vein of Andrew Sarris and others. For one thing, while auteurist film criticism since the 1960s has tended to emphasize independence from commercial film studios (see Sellors 2010: 20), Nair has made some of her recent films commercially, where her directorial independence has sometimes been limited—though she has also continued to make smaller, independent films that bear the strong stamp of her creative signature. But there are a number of other good reasons to maintain a distance from auteurist theory for this particular study. First, a wave of feminist film theorists has since the 1970s been interrogating the male-centric and intensely exclusivist tendency of early auteur theory (see Mayne 1990: 95), though recent critics such as Geetha Ramanathan (2006) have nevertheless come to rework auteurism from a feminist perspective, positing a "feminist auteur." Another comprehensive critique of auteurist film studies comes from C. Paul Sellors, who, in *Film Authorship: Auteurs and Other Myths* (2010), demonstrates the many slippages in this model of film analysis, including the significant fact that even the canonical film auteurs made their films collaboratively and under constraints associated with film studios and distribution systems. In his study Sellors suggests that symptomatic analysis of the works of film auteurs might be insupportable.

Rather than using criticism of films to divine the mysterious motives of their authors (auteurs), Sellors suggests we might be better served thinking of film authors as the "causes" of the films they produce (Sellors 2010: 2); the task of the critic is, consequently, to interpret the films as visual and narrative *texts*. An engagement with directors is still relevant for Sellors as part of the critical process, but in a much more constrained and less absolute way than was the norm in the classic auteurist film criticism of the 1960s. As Roland Barthes might put it, we are not looking for the Author-God behind the curtain, but rather using a set of analytical tools by which to interpret (filmic) texts as fundamentally collaborative and intertextual. One the one hand, it is certainly the case that my interest in this study is in following the works of a single filmmaker whose directorial vision and aesthetic sensibilities evince a strong sense of unity and coherence. But my interest is in interpreting Nair's thematic interest in diasporic communities and her methodological investment in documentary realism ("diaspora vérité"), where her films are presented as texts to be read and analyzed in their own right, not as a means of glorifying the director as auteur.

Accordingly, throughout this study, we will be paying close attention when Nair's collaborators seem to play a critical role. Particularly important collaborators include Nair's frequent screenplay writer Sooni Taraporevala and cinematographers like Mitch Epstein and Declan Quinn; both have worked with Nair on many of her most memorable films. Another important collaborator is Lydia Dean Pilcher, an American film producer who has specialized in making films foregrounding non-Western cultures that are accessible to Western film audiences. Notably, the "diaspora vérité" method I am proposing serves as a powerful tool for analyzing quite a large number of Nair's films, but not quite all of them; two of Nair's feature films, *Amelia* and *Hysterical Blindness*, do not really fit the parameters of what I am calling diaspora vérité and will consequently not be discussed in any great detail here.

Centrally for this study, I see Mira Nair as a film author who is in dialogue with postcolonial theory, feminist theory, and theories of diasporization. Along those lines, the film historian and theorist Gwendolyn Audrey Foster contextualizes Nair aptly as follows:

> Mira Nair is a cineaste of uncompromising feminist postcolonial subjectivity in the making. Her work explores the nomadic space of postmodern feminism, displacing the essentialism of the idea of "First" and "Third" worlds. . . . Nair's nomadic identity . . . has had a liberating and formative effect on her creative choices. In interview,

Nair sums up her feelings towards the issues of home, displacement and Nomadism as a "brown person, between black and white, I could move between these worlds very comfortably because I was neither." (Foster 2002: 263)

Here, Foster's description of Nair's project as exploring "feminist postcolonial subjectivity in the making" is particularly helpful. Below we will explore in greater detail the implications of Nair's feminism as well as her status as a postcolonial artist; here it seems important to note that Nair's characters are very frequently attempting to chart out hybrid versions of social identity for which there are no straightforward precedents; they are very much what Foster describes as subjectivities "in the making." Hers are diasporic subjects with complex national affiliations, fluid cultural identities, and approaches to feminism that are intensely oriented to the aspiration to intersectionality and cross-cultural communication. Along the lines of cultural hybridity in particular, Nair herself has stated that "to be Masala, to be mixed, is the new world order" (Stuart 1994: 212). While Nair was, in making that claim, referring primarily to the ethnicities of the primary characters in her film *Mississippi Masala*, by "mixed" and "Masala" Nair may well have been referring to her own range of cultural influences. Nair's cultural hybridity, the influence of many cultural and national milieus on her work and point of view, is framed largely in the negative by Foster (as "displacing ... essentialism"). As I see it, Nair's "nomadism" can also be a powerful creative impulse enabling the filmmaker to confidently tackle different kinds of stories of migration and displacement, even though they might require familiarity with multiple cultural contexts.

Nair's films demonstrate a thoroughgoing hybridity that extends from production and behind-the-scenes elements (i.e., transnational cast and crew members), cross-generic hybridity in the content and style of the films themselves, and transnational distribution and marketing. Each of these aspects of Nair's hybridity needs further comment. Even an abbreviated and partial list of the subjects Nair has taken on in her career demonstrates that thematic diversity quite aptly: she has made films about cabaret dancers in Bombay, the Indo-African diaspora after the 1971 expulsion from Uganda, the struggles of Bombay slum children, Cuban refugees after the Mariel boatlift, India's laughing clubs, middle-class life in Delhi in an economic boom, the spread of AIDS in the Indian countryside, William Thackeray's *Vanity Fair*, Vatsayana's *Kama Sutra*, challenges faced by American Muslims after 9/11, the American aviator Amelia Earhart, Mohsin Hamid's *The*

Reluctant Fundamentalist, and a girl from the slums of Kampala who went on to become a chess prodigy. Despite the diversity of topics she's addressed in her work, Nair's films do seem to reflect certain recurring preoccupations and concerns—especially the diaspora theme, but also the challenges facing women desiring greater freedom from restrictive social frameworks—and a central goal of this project is to elucidate thematic links between and amongst Nair's various films that might not be superficially evident. Allusions have already been made to the centrality of women protagonists using migration and exile as opportunities to define themselves against social expectations; there are also pronounced threads in Nair's work encountering and facing down media censorship and the social suppression of taboo subjects (such as child abuse and AIDS), as well as powerful critiques of various forms of ethnic and racial exclusion.

A form of hybridity that poses an evident challenge for any analysis of Nair's work is her shift in format from documentary to fiction films in the later 1980s. According to the conventions of film studies, documentary films tend to be interpreted with different sets of analytical tools than fiction films. Here we will respect those conventions and aim to apply appropriate analytical tools, but an essential part of the larger argument of the present study is the idea that Nair's fictional films continue to deploy a form of documentary realism she developed in her early work, which suggests that some cross-format and cross-genre dialogue will be necessary. There are, for instance, powerful formal and thematic links between Nair's fiction film *Salaam Bombay!* and her documentary *India Cabaret*; Nair even indicated that the idea of focusing a fictional film on a brothel's "tea boy" occurred to her as a result of interactions she had with a real Bombay tea boy at the dance bar where she filmed *India Cabaret*. Thematically, both films seem committed to representing the lives of sex workers in Bombay without sentimentality or moralizing—even as the subjects of the films themselves are at times smitten by "Bollywood" glamor and illusions about their status. Similarly, there are numerous evident thematic links between *Monsoon Wedding* (2001) and Nair's documentary *The Laughing Club of India* (1999)—both films aim to document the post-liberalization middle-class culture that emerged in Indian cities in the 1990s. And there could be several other examples of such cross-format dialogue in Nair's body of work; the approach here will acknowledge and explore those links where such exploration appears productive.

Nair's body of work also evinces a form of geographic hybridity (or transnationalism) that might put an analysis of her work in tension with the national framing that has historically tended to dominate much of film studies. Geographically, some of Nair's best-known films have been set in India (i.e., *Salaam Bombay!* and *Monsoon Wedding*), but in fact most of her feature films have been filmed in other parts of the world, including the United States, the United Kingdom, and East Africa—and a number of her important films (including *Mississippi Masala*, *The Namesake*, *The Reluctant Fundamentalist*, and *Queen of Katwe*) are actually filmed on more than one continent. This geographical range is an essential part of Nair's diasporic sensibility, but it poses a methodological challenge, especially given that film studies has historically tended to focus around cinematic traditions in a single national language (Anglo-American cinema, French cinema, Russian cinema, and so on). Not only are Nair's films frequently transnational in setting, several of her major films use multiple languages, which poses problems for classification.

The idea that Nair's body of work makes straightforward national classification difficult is also apparent if we consider the production side of filmmaking. Nair has had links to numerous national film industries as well as film studios. She has worked at times with the commercial film industries in both the United States and India (in India, she has worked with "Bollywood" stars like Irrfan Khan, Tabu, and Naseeruddin Shah and received funding for some films from state agencies such as the Indian National Film Development Corporation [NFDC]), but she has also been eager to continue directing small and independent films, even after establishing herself in the commercial sphere. Since *Salaam Bombay!*, Nair has emphasized the funding and producing of her independent films through novel transnational partnerships, a pattern that has continued and even expanded in recent films like *The Namesake*, which was produced through a partnership between Fox Searchlight (the art house branch of a major Hollywood studio), UTV Motion Pictures (a new Indian company with its roots in the software industry), and Entertainment Farm (a Japanese company). More recently still, Nair turned to the Doha Film Institute, a new player on the international film scene, for the bulk of the financing for *The Reluctant Fundamentalist*. Nair's most influential films have broken new ground on aesthetic grounds, but she has also been influential for charting out a new trajectory as a film director who can work both transculturally and among different kinds of audiences (art cinema to popular cinema) *within* given national film communities. Other directors have made the move from avant-garde to commercial cinema, and some have had success in multiple national film industries (Ang Lee and Iñarritu come to mind), but very few have moved so fluidly through as many intellectual milieus and film worlds as has Mira Nair.

At times, one hears anecdotally of disdain within the Indian film studies community about diasporic filmmakers like Nair, Chadha, and Mehta; their hybridity and transnational context is sometimes thought to render them as something less than "authentically" Indian. This is a complex problem, but we can begin to address it with a look at the *titles* of some of Nair's most well-known films. These might be one kind of evidence of the hybridity I have been positing; the use of a combination of English and Hindustani (Hindi/Urdu) in these titles suggests an attempt to bridge national and linguistic communities. Take, for example, the following four titles:

India Cabaret
Salaam Bombay!
Mississippi Masala
Monsoon Wedding

Interestingly, all four titles use exactly two words, one indicating or referencing what might be clumsily described as a connection to India or Indianness, and the other perhaps pointing to something either more general or not spatially connected to India: "Cabaret," "Mississippi," "Wedding." Three of the titles might also be described as gently bilingual—the words "Salaam," "Masala," and "Monsoon" have origins in Indian and Middle Eastern languages but are nevertheless recognizable to a broad Anglo-American audience. This bilingualism is itself a way of announcing the cosmopolitanism of the films' intended audience and also indicating geographic and cultural specificity ("India," "Bombay," "Mississippi"). Perhaps the most powerful and memorable of the titles above, *Salaam Bombay!*, is, even as a title, intended as a form of address to the city—a greeting—underscored by the use of the exclamation mark. The person "salaaming," as it were, must logically be the transnational film audience—in fact, within the film itself there are very few foreign characters, and none of the Indian characters in the film ever uses this particular phrase. For some critics, this self-conscious hybridity may be alienating or off-putting; one can contrast the title *Salaam Bombay!*, for instance, to the title of Sudhir Mishra's 1991 film about Bombay slum life—*Dharavi*—referring to an area of the city that, at least at that time, would not have been known to many viewers outside India. A critic could presume (correctly) that Mishra's film (funded by the NFDC, which also funded part of Nair's film) was addressed to domestic Indian audiences who would know what and where Dharavi was, while Nair's aimed for a broader, international audience. However, it's not clear at least to this critic that Nair's approach to the subject of slum life in *Salaam Bombay!* is any less compelling or authoritative than Mishra's, despite their differential rhetorical positioning vis-à-vis their respective intended audiences. In this study I will presume that diasporic status, whether paratextual (i.e., in the title of a film or its marketing) or internal to the substance and form of the film, does not disqualify a film from also being understood as "authentically Indian," or as engaged in a serious dialogue with Indian institutions or discursive frameworks internal to Indian society.

I have already referred to Nair as a *postcolonial* filmmaker. While I have begun to describe some of the ways in which Nair might be seen as a new kind of hybrid, transnational filmmaker, the specific relevance and meaning of the term "postcolonial" might require further comment. The term "postcolonial" is both a chronological and spatial marker (i.e., it refers to cultural artifacts produced in formerly colonized areas of the world after 1945) and a reference to a more conceptual framework (i.e., the advent of new aesthetic sensibilities following the end of formal colonialism in South Asia, Africa, and the Caribbean). While British colonialism ended in India and Pakistan in 1947 and in most of sub-Saharan Africa and the Caribbean in the early 1960s, the legacy of colonialism continues to have an impact both within those independent societies and in the West. This is not surprising, given that the system of European colonialism lasted more than three hundred years and radically transformed much of the world—politically, socially, culturally, linguistically, and economically. To many postindependence writers and artists, the power alignments that followed the end of colonialism did not seem very different from those that held sway during the colonial era; it was with the emergence of the term "postcolonial," mainly in the 1980s, that critics (many of them in literary studies, and many of them from the Indian subcontinent) began to challenge the epistemological basis of colonial power relations through a concerted critique of the Orientalist and Eurocentric biases inherent in political and cultural discourses. Patrick Williams and Laura Chrisman hint at the symbolic and epistemological interests of the idea of the "postcolonial" in their introduction to *Colonial Discourse and Post-Colonial Theory*: "If colonialism is a way of maintaining an unequal international relation of economic and political power . . . then no doubt we have not fully transcended the colonial. Perhaps this amounts to saying that we are not yet post-imperialist" (Williams and Chrisman 1994: 4). Along these lines, the field of study often referred to as "postcolonial theory" takes it as a premise that the historical legacy of colonialism continues to shape relations of power in material as well as cultural realms, in both formerly colonized societies

(Asia, the Middle East, Central America, and South America) as well as the colonizers (Europe and the United States). It is especially in the latter, cultural sphere that Nair's films have reflected a postcolonial consciousness as she has considered the legacy of colonialism, from her revisionist, South Asia–centric adaptation of the Victorian novel *Vanity Fair*, to her exploration of the interaction between geopolitical upheavals and highly localized dynamics in a southern US town in *Mississippi Masala*. The latter is evidently postcolonial for its South Asian diaspora interest (the Ugandan Indian expulsion has been widely viewed as a postcolonial tragedy); it can also be seen as postcolonial for its engagement with African American life in the US South, which, with its legacy of plantation slavery, has itself been seen as a space undergoing "decolonization" in the era after the civil rights movement by some cultural critics and theorists (see Loomba 1998: 12).

As we situate Nair chronologically and thematically in the postcolonial era, it seems important to note how closely her personal biography resembles the model of a whole community of diasporic postcolonial writers, critics, and artists, who have made a major impact both in their respective countries of origin as well as in metropolitan cultural spaces in the UK and North America. Nair's secondary education in a colonial-era English-medium boarding school in Simla, India, is in part a reflection of the British legacy in the Indian subcontinent, as is the curriculum and cultural orientation of the university where she began her college education, the prestigious Miranda House at Delhi University. Nair is far from the only influential postcolonial figure from her generation to have come from this type of background. In her early experience and education, and in her subsequent exploration of the new world of transnational culture, migration, and dispersion in the wake of the British empire, Nair is a peer of a generation of writers and critics from the literary world that includes Salman Rushdie, Gayatri Chakravorty Spivak, Homi Bhabha, Wole Soyinka, Pankaj Mishra, Anita Desai, M. G. Vassanji, Amitav Ghosh, V. S. Naipaul, and Derek Walcott. Like these approximate postcolonial peers, Nair received a predominantly English-medium education in a society where British English was, at least in her youth, primarily an elite language, and—also like those peers—Nair received a significant component of her advanced education abroad. Her interest in diasporic issues overlaps with the theoretical interventions of Bhabha, Spivak, R. Radhakrishnan, and others, and her particular brand of Indian feminism resonates with that espoused by critics and theorists such as Chandra Talpade Mohanty (another Delhi University alumna), Kum Kum Sangari, Ania Loomba (Nair's classmate at Miranda House of Delhi

University in the late 1970s), and Rajeswari Sunder Rajan. Though this study will not explore the "social network" of the Delhi University intellectual diaspora in detail, suffice it to say that one goal of the present study is to posit Nair's films as worthy postcolonial texts alongside the predominantly literary materials that have in recent years dominated the interdisciplinary field of postcolonial studies—to suggest we view a film like *The Namesake* as a paradigmatic narrative of hybridity and diasporic life alongside novels like *The Satanic Verses* or *The In-Between World of Vikram Lall*.

Needless to say, South Asian film critics have been arguing a version of the above idea for years, though literary and cultural critics have tended to continue to favor analysis of written texts over other media. For example, in her study *The Cinematic ImagiNation: Indian Popular Films as Social History*, Jyotika Virdi questions why postcolonial theory "privileges the literary text" over more popular cultural artifacts (Virdi 2003: x). The present study shares the conviction about the value of filmic texts implied by Virdi's provocation and suggests that carefully interpreting and contextualizing the works of a filmmaker like Nair may be every bit as rewarding to close reading as that of written texts by the novelists named above; in that respect we are also aligned with the anthropologists Arjun Appadurai and Carol Breckenridge, who argued, referring to *India Cabaret*, that Nair "belongs to the world of novelists such as V.S. Naipaul and Salman Rushdie, artists of the exiled consciousness" (Appadurai and Breckenridge 1991). Having said that, as film studies has continued to develop in the past two decades, the primacy of literary texts over other modes of artistic expression has begun to be displaced, and the association of Nair with these other, "prestigious" postcolonial artists is no longer likely to be as much of a surprise.

From Postcolonial Studies to Diaspora Studies

One of the most important social phenomena of the postcolonial era has been the migration and resettlement of peoples around the world, which has led to the creation of new, specifically diasporic, cultural identities. These diasporic identities are complex formations wherein groups of expatriates and their descendants undergo cultural and sociopolitical transformations while adapting to new environments.

Since the early 1990s, a rapidly expanding body of scholarship has appeared that focuses on documenting and theorizing migration and the emergence of new transnational cultural formations. The theorist and social historian Avtar Brah was cited along these lines above; scholars associated with the journal *Diaspora: A Journal of Transnational Studies* have also covered this ground, and quite a number of independent book-length studies have also appeared in recent years. Theorists of diaspora such as Khachig Tololyan, William Safran, Avtar Brah, Vijay Mishra, and R. Radhakrishnan have theorized and catalogued a wide array of diasporic communities, both traditional and "new." This scholarship tends to take it as a given that diasporas can form for any number of reasons and that diasporic status might relate to a broad array of social issues. As Tololyan put it in the inaugural issue of *Diaspora*, "We use 'diaspora' provisionally to indicate our belief that the term once described as Jewish, Greek, and Armenian dispersion now shares meanings with a larger semantic domain that includes words like immigrant, expatriate, refugee, guest-worker, exile, community, overseas community, [and] ethnic community" (Tololyan 1991: 4–5). While there are obviously real differences between refugees and voluntary immigrant communities, their experiences may be seen to fall under a single umbrella. Notably, Tololyan's broad concept of diaspora might also help to enhance the thematic concerns of Mira Nair's films, bringing together the seemingly involuntary emigrants of *My Own Country* and *Mississippi Masala* with the voluntary expatriates of Nair's adaptations of *The Namesake* and *Vanity Fair*. All of these films can, in the newer theoretical idiom, be unproblematically understood as diasporic.

More recently, scholars such as Vijay Mishra have theorized the workings of the Indian diaspora in particular. Mishra draws an important distinction between what he calls the "old" diaspora of Indian indentured laborers in Fiji, Malaysia, East Africa, and the Caribbean (Trinidad, Guyana) and the "new" South Asian diaspora that has emerged with "late capital" (Mishra 1996: 421). Mishra describes the old Indian diaspora as "exclusive," as it tended to simply reproduce "little Indias"—islands of static cultural and linguistic homogeneity—while the new diaspora is much more likely to see hybridity, linguistic shifts, acculturation, and extensive interaction with host cultures. Signs of this dynamic new South Asian diaspora are visible in the United States (with more than three million South Asian immigrants, according to data from the 2010 US census), the United Kingdom, Canada, and Australia, among other sites. Not surprisingly, perhaps, Mira Nair's interest in Indian diaspora culture falls largely into the "new" diaspora, though this is more apparent in her later films (*Monsoon Wedding*, *Mississippi Masala*, and *The Namesake*) than in early films like *So Far from India*.

In addition to the old and new concepts of diaspora, an important idea in diasporic communities is the idea of *home*. As Avtar Brah has argued, diasporic communities retain a sense of association with a home country that may be for some migrants a distant memory ("'home' is a mythical place of desire in the diasporic imagination" Brah 1996: 192). For Brah herself (a Ugandan Indian who was educated in the United States before settling in the United Kingdom), as well as for the characters in Nair films like *Mississippi Masala* and *My Own Country*, ideas of home may be subject to further fracturing as a result of historical displacements. For a displaced Ugandan of Punjabi Indian origin, is home in Kampala or Ludhiana—or London? As Brah points out, the idea of home never really disappears in diasporic communities but rather remains present as a constitutive feature of the imagined communities that emerge amongst groups of migrants: "The concept of 'diaspora' places the discourse of 'home' and 'dispersion' in creative tension, *inscribing a homing desire while simultaneously critiquing discourses of fixed origins*" (Brah 1996: 192–193, emphasis in original). As Brah goes on to explain, the "homing desire" should not be taken as implying that diasporic communities are actively yearning for a lost homeland or thinking of returning home. Rather, narratives of home play a role in the construction of new narratives about identity and belonging. The final result is a "concept of identity that is always plural, and in process."

Brah's concept of diasporic identity as "always plural, and in process" might be a good descriptor for the ways in which the diasporic theme has dominated Nair's most successful and important films relating to South Asia; this concept of diaspora can also be seen in smaller ways even in films that are geographically quite rooted (or that feature "domestic" dislocation), as well as in those of Nair's films that do not relate primarily to South Asia. In this section, we will briefly describe the depth of Nair's engagement with the diasporic theme before briefly exploring some ideas from postcolonial theory related to diasporic studies—a body of scholarship that provides the present study with tools and a conceptual vocabulary that will be important in subsequent chapters. From Nair's oeuvre, the films *So Far from India* (1983), *Mississippi Masala* (1991), *The Perez Family* (1995), *My Own Country* (1998), *Monsoon Wedding* (2001), *The Namesake* (2006), *11'09"01* (2002), "How Can It Be?" (2008), and *The Reluctant Fundamentalist* (2013) chart out an impressive range of issues and problems in the constitution of diasporic community identity, for the most part with a focus on South Asians in the United States. As I'll describe below, Nair's approach to these issues has shifted considerably over time, from a preoccupation with the loss of home in early films like *So Far from India* to a more complex and multiform concept of diasporic experience as a space of both gains and losses in later films like *The Namesake*.

One exception to the South Asian focus in the above list is of course Nair's *The Perez Family* (1995), which centers on the experience of Cuban refugees who came to Florida as part of the Mariel boatlift of 1980. However, even if the ethnic community involved in that film differs, the theme of the film strongly overlaps with Nair's films more centered on South Asia, since both Nair's Cuban Americans and her South Asian Americans must contend with the loss of a homeland and then the struggle to adapt to a new way of life in the United States. Another outlier might be Nair's short film *The Day the Mercedes Became a Hat* (1993; henceforth *Mercedes*), about whites on the verge of expatriating from South Africa during the period of transition from Apartheid to African National Congress rule. *Mercedes* shares with *The Perez Family* and *Mississippi Masala* a concern for ambivalence in exile. In this short film of Nair's, there is great joy about South Africa's imminent democratization, but the film also registers the anxieties felt by even pro-reform white South Africans as their claim to Africanness comes under threat.

Technology enables an important shift in how diasporic communities have related to "home" in recent years. Shailja Sharma and Gita Rajan, in "New Cosmopolitanisms," argue that the newest (post-1990) era of diasporization needs to be seen as differing from earlier moments, as today's diasporas retain real-time digital links to their home cultural environments—via the internet, satellite television, and mobile phone technology (Sharma and Rajan 2006: 2–3). As a result, diasporization is increasingly seen not through the lens of permanent separation but as the imagining of parallel cultural frames. While the characters in Nair's early documentary film *So Far from India* do have the ability to talk on the phone occasionally while they are thousands of miles apart, the high cost of the call and the poor reception pose a barrier between the husband and wife in the film. Nair's decision to jump back and forth between Gujarat and New York in that early film works as a surprising, anomalous choice, highlighting the gaps rather than the links between her characters. The tone of Nair's approach to diaspora has changed as technology has evolved. In Nair's 2001 *Monsoon Wedding* (followed up closely by *The Namesake*), the filmmaker is able to fully meld different cultural and aesthetic worlds and create a visual sensibility embracing a nascent sense of connectedness. In the present digital era, we see that even while living abroad, home can be a continuing phenomenon in the lives of immigrants, rather than a territory of the past.

In the chapters that follow, I will explore how the diasporic focus of the films named immediately above can also be seen as impacting even those of Nair's films that are not as evidently diasporic, including films such as *India Cabaret*, *Salaam Bombay!*, *Kama Sutra: A Tale of Love*, *Vanity Fair*, and *Queen of Katwe*. In some cases, the connections are simply thematic—many of her protagonists in the films named above are internally displaced people who might have been forced to leave one part of their "home" country for another in search of economic opportunity. Others find that changing circumstances broaden their horizons, altering what Brah calls their "homing desires" in some profound ways.

Another outlier film that can be understood in connection with Nair's diaspora vérité thematic despite its lack of focus on a migrant community might be Nair's 2009 biopic *Amelia*. *Amelia* is ostensibly the story of a pioneering white American woman aviator that was produced on a sizeable budget by a Hollywood studio with a nearly all-white cast. However, the film does engage diasporic themes in that it figures Amelia Earhart as a feminist aviator motivated by a desire to "wander." Nair structures this film around the events leading up to Earhart's ill-fated 1937 solo flight around the world, featuring brief scenes in Africa, Papua New Guinea, Hawaii, Ireland, Wales, and Mali—an impressive degree of globalization for a traditionally "all-American" subject. As Earhart sets down in Mali, Nair inserts a voice-over in Amelia's voice that would not be out of place in any of her more explicitly postcolonial or diasporic films: "I am on my shining adventure. Flying the world. With no borders, just horizons, only freedom." Figuring Amelia Earhart as a feminist "vagabond of the air," motivated in large part to find freedom through airplane flight—the sky being a space where she can transgress terrestrial social and political boundaries—Nair finds a way to "globalize" this early twentieth-century American icon. Though we will not explore *Amelia* in depth in this study, thematically, at least, the film appears to fit Nair's continually expanding diasporic sensibility quite well.

Mira Nair and Transnational Feminism

Filmmaking is a creative field that has historically been male-dominated, especially in India, so Nair's emergence as a woman director is particularly noteworthy. Nair's feminism has been present in her choice of themes, beginning with her central focus on the experiences of seemingly marginal women in her early documentaries, *Jama Masjid Street Journal*, *Children of a Desired Sex*, and *India Cabaret*, and evolving over the course of her subsequent films. But feminism has also been evident in Nair's more mainstream fiction films, including some films that do not feature women as protagonists, such as *Salaam Bombay!* and *The Namesake*, where Nair's approach to gender relations evinces a special sensitivity to the condition of women not evident in the work of some of her male counterparts (one thinks, for example, of the care and attention paid to the everyday lives of prostitutes in *Salaam Bombay!*, which rhymes in some ways with American director Lizzie Borden's famous depiction in *Working Girls* [1986]). Nair's affirmative approach to representing female sexuality, in films like *Kama Sutra: A Tale of Love*, *Mississippi Masala*, *The Perez Family*, *Vanity Fair*, and *Amelia*, has sometimes provoked controversy and, in the case of *Kama Sutra*, censorship from the Indian censor board; details of that history will be explored in our discussion of that film below. However, it should also be said that Nair's feminism, shaped by her documentary realist background, is a little different from that seen in the work of other Indian diasporic women directors such as the aforementioned Deepa Mehta, Gurinder Chadha, and Pratibha Parmar. Even in Nair's most "transgressive" films, the filmmaker generally eschews overt moralizing and avoids plots centered on obviously villainous conventional patriarchs such as those seen in Mehta's *Fire* or Chadha's *Bhaji on the Beach*. In Nair's *Monsoon Wedding*, for instance, the largely traditionally Punjabi patriarch Lalit Varma (Naseeruddin Shah) makes a public stand against an abusive family member in support of his adopted daughter, whereas in *Fire*, nearly all of the men in the family are complicit in the oppression of women. Also, Nair's feminism has been transgressive from the start, with the filmmaker sympathetically portraying sex workers in films like *India Cabaret* and *Salaam Bombay!*, and it has continued to evolve in her recent work. Nair's films explore the complex conditions and possibilities of women's freedom in the context of patterns of global migration, and there is a subtlety in her approach to these issues that is sometimes lacking in the works of her peers.

Alongside some of the South Asian diasporic women filmmakers mentioned, Nair might be seen as part of a larger cohort of international independent women film directors who emerged in the 1980s and '90s including Jane Campion, Kathryn Bigelow, Lizzie Borden, Julie Dash, Aparna Sen, and Trinh T. Minh-ha. Nair's feminism may be aligned with the modalities that the feminist film theorist B. Ruby Rich, in an influential early essay, described as "validative" (as in, validating everyday experiences and unheard voices) and "reconstructive" (as in, adapting conventional narrative and filmic forms for feminist purposes) (Rich 1994: 37–39). Though Nair is an avowed feminist, it is probably not accurate to say that her films are comfortably part of what in the 1970s and '80s was referred to by film theorists as a "feminist aesthetic" or "women's cinema." Indeed, at an early point in her career, Nair distanced herself from some approaches to academic feminist theory, after she was criticized by some Indian feminist viewers of *India Cabaret* for focusing on women in the sex trade.[2] It may be that Nair's feminism aligns with Teresa de Lauretis's approach to women in cinema; it is derived from the fact that her films can be said to address "the spectator as a woman, regardless of the gender of the viewers" (De Lauretis 1994: 144); De Lauretis claims that presumed female *spectatorship* is the key criterion for filmic feminism, criticizing the idea of a separatist "women's cinema" that was widely discussed in feminist film theory after Mulvey (1975) and Bovenschen (1976). Also, Nair's woman-centric, sexually-explicit adaptation of the *Kama Sutra* represents a challenge to the antipornography line taken by Andrea Dworkin and Catherine MacKinnon (MacKinnon 2013), as well as by those Indian feminists who have embraced censorship as a means to combat exploitative images of women in the media. In *Kama Sutra*, women are both figures of desire of the male gaze and desiring subjects in their own right—clearly suggesting a different approach to representing women on screen than is seen in antipornography feminism. Nair's approach to representing women aligns her, instead, with the anticensorship school represented by activists and scholars like Madhu Kishwar and Ruth Vanita in India (Kishwar and Vanita [1986] 2006: 107–15) and Linda Williams in the United States. Nair's films, in short, are certainly in line with what might be seen as the mainstream of the contemporary feminist filmmaking project, and films like *India Cabaret*, *The Perez Family*, and *Kama Sutra* seem to suggest that Nair's interest as a feminist filmmaker lies in positing roles for women on screen that are at once transgressively embodied and ethically complex.

Specifically within the South Asian context, Nair's feminist concerns can be thought of as aligned with the works of a number of social historians and scholars interested in the same swath of issues her films have explored. Nair was considerably ahead of her peers in exploring the Indian practice of sex-selective abortion, which she engaged in the documentary *Children of a Desired Sex*. Scholars such as Rashmi Bhatnagar, Renu Dube, and Reena Dube

(2005) have explored this subject (as well as the associated practice of female infanticide) in considerable detail in recent years, but in the mid-1980s, few scholars had yet picked up on this issue. Similarly, scholars and journalists such as Flavia Agnes and Sonia Faleiro have explored the sociology of the "dance bar" women that are the subject of Nair's *India Cabaret* (Agnes 2008: 99–117; Faleiro 2012), though here again Nair's film was thematically well ahead of its time. Several other Nair films also make feminist statements specific to Indian society, sometimes as minor themes (one thinks of the critique of the treatment of women in Indian diasporic arranged marriage culture in *Mississippi Masala*), and sometimes more centrally, as seen in the focus on breaking the taboo on discussing sexual abuse within an Indian family in *Monsoon Wedding*.

In the years she has been active as a filmmaker, Nair's historically grounded postcolonial feminist ethos has given her audiences an array of powerful women-centered stories. We see this in studio-backed pictures like *Amelia*, *Vanity Fair*, and *The Perez Family* as much as in the independent films with South Asian themes. A number of Nair's most important films—including especially *Salaam Bombay!*, *India Cabaret*, *So Far from India*, *Mississippi Masala*, *Monsoon Wedding*, and *Queen of Katwe*—are not just feminist but espouse ideas from postcolonial feminism that might align them with critiques of first-world feminism made by theorists like Chandra Talpade Mohanty. Nair is able to do this, first of all, through her investment in historical and cultural specificity that comes out of her commitment to documentary realism; this aligns with Mohanty's resistance to the "assumption of women as an already constituted, coherent group with identical interests and desires, regardless of class, ethnic or racial location or contradictions" (Mohanty 1986: 336–337). Nair's protagonists might share certain experiences, but they differ in key ways depending on their circumstances and positioning; the path to empowerment for Mina from *Mississippi Masala* looks very different from the one for Phiona Mutesi in *Queen of Katwe*. Moreover, Nair's emphasis on themes of migration and diaspora frequently problematize the first-world/third-world binary that drives the analysis that writers like Mohanty aim to critique. For characters like Aditi Verma in *Monsoon Wedding*, leaving home is seen as a pathway to escape a repressive environment; by contrast, for the chess prodigy Mutesi, the aim is really to transform the social and material conditions that keep her family trapped in a cycle of poverty without leaving them behind.

Nair's Adaptations

Alongside the themes of diaspora and postcolonial feminism, this study will, where appropriate, interpret Nair's films in parallel with the literary texts that have inspired many of them. It is not an accident, and it is certainly a source of interest, that so many of Nair's films are adaptations of literary works. *The Perez Family*, for instance, is based on a novel by Christine Bell; *My Own Country* derives from Abraham Verghese's nonfiction memoir; and *Kama Sutra: A Tale of Love* is based on a modern Urdu short story by Wajida Tabassum called "Utaran" (Castoffs) as well as Richard Burton's translation of Vatsayana's classic Sanskrit text. One also shouldn't overlook Nair's provocative adaptation of *Vanity Fair*, a book with important connections to British colonial India, with a kind of diasporic theme in Becky Sharp's exile from England. Aesthetically, Nair's adaptation of *The Namesake* takes diasporic appropriation of nonfilmic texts to a new level, as Nair alludes not just to Jhumpa Lahiri's novel but to a whole host of Indian and American filmmakers, photographers, and design artists. Nair's recent film *The Reluctant Fundamentalist* productively enriched the rather spare narrative framework of Mohsin Hamid's 2007 novel, finding space for numerous other voices to enter into the story (including the voices of women) without straining the essential elements of Hamid's plot. Finally, Nair's 2009 biopic *Amelia* credits two different biographies as strong influences for the image of the aviator presented in the film, Susan Butler's *East to the Dawn* and Mary Lovell's *The Sound of Wings*. As I develop a reading of the efficacy of literary adaptation in Nair's films, I will refer to Nair's comments on these textual sources in interviews and director's DVD commentaries, paying close attention to Nair's occasional—but telling—divergences from the source material in her work.

Of course, Nair is only one in a long line of filmmakers to have engaged in adapting literary texts to cinema. Film historian Timothy Corrigan notes that adaptations of staged versions of literary texts were among the very earliest films made; examples include the films *Cinderella* (1900), *Robinson Crusoe* (1902), *Gulliver's Travels* (1902), and *Uncle Tom's Cabin* (1903) (Corrigan 1999: 19). Moreover, while the question of the "fidelity" of film adaptations is often stressed by popular reviewers, serious film critics and theorists such as Andre Bazin to Dudley Andrew have argued that fidelity may be at once impossible and besides the point, as the different material forms of film and literature have elements that are incommensurable. With Nair's own adaptations of well-known texts—*The Namesake* and *Vanity Fair* especially—I will use Dudley Andrew's classification of three forms of film adaptation, "borrowing, intersecting, and transforming" (Andrew 1984: 119), as a way of moving beyond the limitations entailed by reading Nair's film adaptations *only* for their fidelity to the source material.

In the present study, the three aforementioned aspects of Nair's filmmaking—diasporization, postcolonial feminism, and adaptation—are folded into chapters focused primarily on individual films, roughly following the chronological development of Nair's career. The most important films, *Salaam Bombay!*, *Monsoon Wedding*, and *The Namesake*, have their own dedicated chapters (chapters 3, 4, and 7), which aim to provide readers with a wide range of contextual material as well as primary arguments related to the diasporic and feminist qualities of the respective films. Nair's other films are grouped together in five other chapters, with documentaries in one group (chapter 2) and a series of films focused on the American immigrant experience in the 1990s in another (chapter 5). Nair's commitment to documentary realism from early in her career might seem to preclude her from approaching historical drama ("period pieces"), but with *Kama Sutra: A Tale of Love* and *Vanity Fair*, Nair has at times made films in that mode (as I will show, a version of her commitment to cinéma vérité is nevertheless evident even in these films). Though it may not be apparent on the surface, these two historical films in fact have a good deal in common with one another, as chapter 6 will show. Finally, the study concludes with a short chapter on Nair's most recent film, *Queen of Katwe*, where her investment in urban-oriented documentary realism, her feminism, and her investment in postcolonial societies all come back to the forefront.

A Note on Method

Why a book on Mira Nair? Why not, for instance, *Filmmakers of the South Asian Diaspora*? With its generally exclusive focus on the work of a single director, this study might appear to some readers to be a bit old-fashioned, and for that reason it might be helpful to reiterate briefly why we focus here exclusively on this particular filmmaker. To begin with, Nair's career has followed a trajectory that lends itself quite well to a long-form study: early documentaries like *So Far from India* seem to resonate richly with later films like *The Namesake*, and there are some surprising continuities between seemingly different films (*Salaam Bombay!* has, for instance, more than a little in common with *Monsoon Wedding*, as the analyses below will demonstrate). Moreover, some of the above-mentioned ideas and arguments, including especially Nair's interest in migration and diaspora and her particular form of transgressive feminism, have a strong through-line in Nair's work, from *India Cabaret* to *Kama Sutra* to *Vanity Fair*. The most important through-line for our purposes, however, is Nair's commitment to documentary realism, which has been felt in all of her best work (and indeed, the films that have been less successful in her oeuvre have generally suffered from the decision to deviate from that principle). A book-length project on this single filmmaker therefore allows us to trace the evolution of that documentary realist style from a mode of social realism oriented to the representation of poor and disenfranchised people (*India Cabaret* in the documentary format and *Salaam Bombay!* as a fictional film) to a broad social palette that includes both working-class and bourgeois subjects and settings (*The Laughing Club of India* is a documentary that does this; *Monsoon Wedding* is an example of a fiction film). A unified study of all of the filmmaker's major works also allows us to note some surprising links and connections—such as traces of documentary realism even in a period picture like *Vanity Fair*, or a shared theme of domestic displacement within India in *India Cabaret, Salaam Bombay!,* and *Kama Sutra: A Tale of Love.*

Nair has also made films with a level of consistency and quality that her diasporic peers do not quite match. Both Shekhar Kapur, an Indian filmmaker who lived and worked abroad for several years before returning to India, and the Indo-Canadian filmmaker Deepa Mehta (*Fire*), for instance, have made influential films with diasporic connections that might seem to resemble those behind *Salaam Bombay!* But both Kapur's *Bandit Queen* and Mehta's *Fire* are "crossover" successes that have also been marred by significant failures. Mehta, for instance, was widely criticized by Indian feminists as well as the gay and lesbian community for a rather stilted approach to the lesbian relationship depicted in *Fire*. Kapur's *Bandit Queen* had its own problems relating to the alienation of its still-living biographical subject, Phoolan Devi, which has considerably soured its reception, especially amongst feminist critics (for a more detailed account of this controversy, see the discussion of censorship in chapter 5 below). And while the British-Indian filmmaker Gurinder Chadha did make two excellent comedies in *Bhaji on the Beach* (1993) and *Bend It Like Beckham* (2002), several of her films since 2002 have been poorly received (*Bride and Prejudice*) or too facile to merit serious consideration (i.e., *It's a Wonderful Afterlife* [2010]). Nair, by contrast, has made a long array of ambitious, well-received films set in multiple national contexts with a great deal of care and precision—and without the blemishes that have marred many of her diasporic peers' films.

At least for this critic, even a comparative study of the most effective and accomplished South Asian diasporic filmmakers would likely end up rather centrally focused on Nair, even with intentions to the contrary.

As has already been indicated, the goal of this study is to figure Mira Nair as a transnational figure. As such, her work is not defined by any singular national cinema tradition or framework. While the present study does acknowledge and affirmatively engage recent scholarship on Indian cinema, the account of that body of work—exemplified by scholars such as Ashish Rajadhyaksha (2009), Ravi Vasudevan (2010), Sangita Gopal (2011), and Tejaswini Ganti (2012), to name just a few—is admittedly far from definitive. Care has been used with regards to contested terms such as, especially, "Bollywood," and also to the widely discussed particularities of commercial Hindi cinema's visual, aural, and narratological conventions. Nair's filmic critiques of the commercial Hindi cinema are explored in some depth (especially with reference to *Salaam Bombay!* and *Monsoon Wedding*), but, especially in recent years, it has become clear that the conventions of commercial Hindi cinema are themselves evolving and changing—so Nair's critiques should be seen in historical context. When Nair pays homage—while also asserting her aesthetic differences—to a film like *Biwi No. 1* in *Monsoon Wedding*, or *Mr. India* in *Salaam Bombay!*, the critique should be taken as narrowly applied. As scholars such as Gopal have pointed out in recent works, the "new Bollywood" has itself increasingly come to critique many "Bollywood" conventions in recent years.

One final qualification is in order. The author of the present study has primary training in literary and cultural studies rather than film studies, but hopefully this will not be seen as a disabling impediment in a work focused on this particular filmmaker. Visual analyses of mise-en-scène, shots and camera framing, and editing are used where relevant, but traditional filmic analysis is only one of the tools appropriate to reading Nair's films. Also relevant are the conceptual tools and terminology of postcolonial theory, ethnographic concepts related to diaspora studies, and of course, feminist theory. That said, interested readers will nevertheless find several instances of extended analysis of Nair's visual rhetoric in this study; I might particularly flag the analysis in chapter 4 where a song sequence in Nair's *Monsoon Wedding* is contrasted to a song and dance sequence using the same song ("Chunari Chunari") in David Dhawan's popular melodrama *Biwi No. 1*. In many instances, it is enough to use internal elements alone to show how Nair uses documentary realist style and an emphasis on diaspora thematics to develop her diaspora vérité aesthetic. As Nair herself has put it, "I always believed that movies have to be about life, not about other movies" (Badt 2004). However, in a study like this, some element of comparison will be inevitable; at times, I will underline Nair's commitment to realism by contrasting her filmic language to that of more commercial filmmakers in both the "Bollywood" and "Hollywood" traditions.

Chapter 2

"OUR HEARTS AND EYES ARE WIDE OPEN"

Mira Nair's Documentaries

As of the present writing, Mira Nair has directed five documentaries, of which only three are likely to be accessible to readers: *So Far from India* (1983), *India Cabaret* (1985), and *The Laughing Club of India* (1999).[3] A fourth, *Jama Masjid Street Journal* (1979), was Nair's undergraduate film thesis at Harvard; it is only available for viewing on VHS at a small number of university libraries in North America, but it is discussed here because it is especially important to our study both as Nair's first film and as an example of Nair's early experimental style and emerging feminist perspective. Nair's other documentary, *Children of a Desired Sex* (1987), a film on Indian sex-selective abortions made for Canadian television, remains virtually inaccessible through either commercial distribution or the university library system. It also appears to be a relatively minor work in the broader scheme of Nair's career and will therefore not be discussed here at any length.

It was through her early documentaries that Nair found her voice as a filmmaker, developing a distinctive formal style that reflects the profound influence of cinéma vérité documentary realism, even if her approach to making documentaries does not, on the whole, strictly follow the parameters of cinéma vérité. In her early documentaries, Nair also came to develop a pair of thematic concerns to which she has repeatedly returned in her subsequent filmmaking career: the psychic and social consequences of migration (the diaspora experience) and gender relations in Indian society. The diasporic theme is front and center in *So Far from India*, but it is also clearly part of the story in *Jama Masjid Street Journal*, which takes an experimental approach clearly associated with the American avant-garde documentary tradition of the 1970s and applies it to a predominantly Muslim neighborhood in old

Delhi (the area around the Jama Masjid—the largest Mosque in Delhi). The short film is literally and self-consciously the work of a diasporic college student returning "home" to Delhi; it also thematizes a sense of alienation from home as its subject, thus putting it squarely in line with other Nair films that adhere to what I have been describing as Nair's "diaspora vérité" method. The diasporic qualities of *India Cabaret*, a documentary about "dance bar" women (sex workers) in early 1980s Bombay are less obvious; it's never made clear within the film that the filmmaker is based abroad, though the funding for the film derived from American sources, and some of Nair's crew came with her from New York to Bombay. However, the sex workers interviewed in the film are themselves part of a community of women geographically displaced *within* India: their anonymity (and arguably, their freedom to pursue their chosen profession) is possible in part because their families and communities live in other parts of India. Thus *India Cabaret* may be thought of as domestically diasporic along the same lines as Nair's first fiction film, *Salaam Bombay!* (that film is the subject of the following chapter).

The subjects in Nair's early documentaries are primarily defined by a profound sense of loss that follows from displacement. The sense of loss is particularly powerful in the first two full-length documentaries as well as her first fiction feature film, *Salaam Bombay!* Indeed, one very good reason to look at Nair's early documentaries today—apart from their aesthetic and intellectual value—is the story regarding the meaning of displacement and migration that one can derive from them, including both her later documentary work as well as the fiction films she has made since the early 1990s. As Nair's career continued to progress through the 1990s and 2000s, new possibilities around the idea of emigration begin to emerge. In her later films, a new embrace of hybridity and the freedom that can come with departure comes to balance the sense of displacement associated with the loss of home—though that sense of loss never entirely disappears. The later films, in short, can be read as responses and elaborations on the themes of these early documentaries.

Steadily emerging over the course of Nair's career, we see the advent of new perspectives on the diasporic cultural experience. In her more recent films, Nair develops characters who experience migration as an opportunity to experience new cultural contexts and a chance to reconfigure social relations. These possibilities are central to several of Nair's later films, including *Mississippi Masala*, *The Perez Family*, *The Reluctant Fundamentalist*, and *The Namesake*. Nair's 1999 documentary, *The Laughing Club of India*, seems of a piece with these other more recent films in that it suggests a path to fulfillment through a reinvented form of yoga (laughing yoga), in which the gap between India and the broader world is highly porous. In short, the approach to the theme of diaspora we see in Nair's documentaries anticipates (and at times, mirrors) a shift in the image of migration evident from the path of her career as a fiction filmmaker.

A bit more should be said about Nair's relationship to the cinéma vérité school of filmmaking, which has played a key role in Nair's understanding of herself as both a documentary and a fiction filmmaker. Nair has explicitly cited her early experience making documentaries as a major influence on the aesthetic of her later fictional films, especially *Salaam Bombay!* and *Monsoon Wedding*, though the cinéma vérité aesthetic is also unmistakable in *Hysterical Blindness* and *Mississippi Masala*, as well as in some of Nair's issue-oriented shorts, including *Migration* and *11'09"01*. The aesthetic is less strongly in evidence in some of Nair's other films (especially her period pieces), though in many cases links can be identified—the emphasis on an observational mode, as well as the strong interest in social realism, pervades even Nair's period pieces.

Both *So Far from India* and *India Cabaret* circulated widely upon release and were critical successes, finding popularity on the film festival circuit and being broadcast on North American public television at the time. *So Far from India* was honored with a Cine Golden Eagle Award (1984), and *India Cabaret* won the Golden Athena Award at the Athens International Film Festival (1986), Best Documentary at the Global Village Film Festival (1986), and the Blue Ribbon Award at the American Film Festival (1986). More importantly, the complex reception of the two films, particularly the polarized reception of *India Cabaret* within India itself, clearly had a catalytic effect on Nair's imagining of her future projects (Nair and Taraporevala 1989: 58–71). Nair has acknowledged that she used a documentarian's emphasis on observation and an ethos of letting the subject dictate the story when she and Sooni Taraporevala researched Nair's first fictional film, *Salaam Bombay!*

> Our eyes and hearts are wide open, and we're simply observing and trying to grasp the enormity of the dimensions. . . . There is so much to be done in the way of research, that scripting will only follow later, once we have a lot of material. And the world of children on the streets here is idiosyncratic and varied, that is where the true richness of the film lies. If we simply construct it from our own ideas and not from the world as it really is for them, we would certainly resort to clichés and predictability—when in fact this subject is exactly op-

posite to that. Necessity truly is the mother of invention for these children—and we must see that firsthand. (Nair and Taraporevala 1989: 7)

Nair has often described how her fictional films based in India, especially *Salaam Bombay!* and *Monsoon Wedding*, are indebted to her background in documentary filmmaking, and in passages like this one, we can see that the two are grounded in the same impulse: to perceive the world as it really is and shape that perception into art. There is also here an admirable selflessness; as she was writing in 1986, Nair clearly believed that the film she wanted to make was not about "our own ideas"—that is to say, the ideas of partially Western-educated, English-speaking elites—but rather "the world as it really is" for her subjects.

Of course, Nair has also talked about her frustration with the documentary form at various points (see especially the interview with Karin Luisa Badt [Badt 2004]). Also, as Nair and Taraporevala were beginning to work with the street children whose stories would become the story of *Salaam Bombay!*, she made the following comment in a letter to Mitch Epstein: "I feel very liberated when I think that what I am seeing is not my material per se, that is, I am not tied to it faithfully as I would be in the case of a documentary" (Nair and Taraporevala 1989: 9). While documentary has been a crucial component of Nair's oeuvre, it proved not to be an end in itself. As Nair put it in an interview with Caryn James of the *New York Times* in 1988 about why she turned to fiction film-making, "I wanted to control light and gesture and drama.... But I never wanted to give up the documentary, the gift of it—the inexplicabilities and the contradictions and the way people are in life.... I still wanted that kind of edge" (James 1988). Even as Nair has moved, on the whole, to the format of the fiction film, many of her films have retained an emphasis on the "inexplicabilities and contradictions and the way people are in life."

As these interviews related to her education in documentary filmmaking show, Mira Nair has often referenced the cinéma vérité movement that emerged in the United States and France beginning in the 1960s. But her debt to cinéma vérité is complex, and a brief exploration of the history and formal attributes of the cinéma vérité movement is necessary to understand its role in Nair's development. Fundamentally, however, Nair's approach to documentary filmmaking has followed three principles: 1) to observe complex, and sometimes extreme, aspects of modern life in South Asia and the South Asian diaspora; 2) to use the documentary film to report on those aspects of modern life without sentimentalism or reductive politicization; and 3) to use her films to challenge Indian double standards on gender issues, as seen in *Jama Masjid Street Journal*, *Children of a Desired Sex*, and *India Cabaret*. It's worth noting that while her methods have changed as Nair has moved from the documentary format to fiction films, these three concerns have remained central in her filmmaking; we see the emphasis on realism, the observational quality, and the interest in gender issues at work in many later fiction films, including *Monsoon Wedding* and even her recent film *Queen of Katwe*.

Cinéma vérité has been an important movement in the evolution of the documentary film form, albeit one with a contested history. In recent film criticism, there have been vibrant debates about what the essential principles and methods of cinéma vérité actually were, as well as how exactly it relates to "direct cinema," a term used by some critics as a synonym for cinéma vérité, but which is understood by others to be something quite different. One of its initial advocates described cinéma vérité as attempting "to eliminate as much as possible the barriers between subject and audience. . . . [It] is a practical working method based upon a faith in unmanipulated reality, a refusal to tamper with life as it presents itself" (Mamber, quoted in Allen and Gomery 1985: 216). In effect, Stephen Mamber is describing an attempt to invent a new, unprecedented level of immediate realism in filmmaking, in which the mediation (or "manipulation") of the director is minimized. Among the attributes of cinéma vérité are: complete absence of staging scenes for the camera, minimum or nonexistent voice-over narration, minimum or nonexistent intertitling, the use of synchronous sound, and the use of handheld cameras. The strictest cinéma vérité documentaries are relatively small in number, and a rigorous definition like Mamber's would likely exclude Nair's early documentaries from the canon, despite her own avowed commitment to the cinéma vérité label. And yet many filmmakers, including Nair herself, have used the term to describe their method, sometimes creating terminological confusion.

I find that the term cinéma vérité is effective as shorthand, but rather than dwelling on it at length, I will use a somewhat narrower and more piecemeal terminology in the analyses of Nair's documentaries here derived from Bill Nichols's work. Nichols has articulated four modes of documentary production, "expository" (the most conventional), "observational" (the mode closest to the cinéma vérité ideal), "interactive" (i.e., interviews), and "self-reflexive" (Nichols 1991: 32–75). While Nichols uses the above classifiers to categorize whole films, in practice most documentary filmmakers use some elements of each of the four primary documentary elements. More recent critics have questioned Nichols's classificatory system (especially Stella Bruzzi [2006: 26]), but at least for my examination of Nair's work, these classifiers will be useful as analytic terms that are more precise than the generic label "cinéma vérité," helping us understand what the films do on a scene-by-scene level.

At a general level, it should be noted that Nair's own documentaries are largely structured around interviews with her subjects, making them "interactive" in Nichols's schema, though the observational method can also be quite important. Nair's films also contain some moments that might be described as "self-reflexive," especially *Jama Masjid Street Journal*, but there are also some self-reflexive moments in films like *So Far from India* and *The Laughing Club of India*. All of Nair's major documentary films do use synchronous sound (*Jama Masjid Street Journal*, a student film made while Nair was an undergraduate at Harvard, does not), though Nair also uses voice-over narration, mainly to provide literal translations—though there are also some isolated moments of "interpretive" voice-over narration in the early documentary films.

Jama Masjid Street Journal (1979)

Jama Masjid Street Journal, Nair's first film, is a complex meditation on the act of looking, where the ethnographic impulse of the documentarian is, from the start, in tension with the fact that the filmmaker herself is the object of the gaze of many of her subjects. That gaze is often a gendered gaze; there are several shots of men leering shamelessly at the filmmaker in a manner that will likely be familiar to women who have spent time in public places in Delhi. Foster describes the film as a "reversal of the traditional objectification of woman in film and photography as veiled object of gaze, thus claiming a site of an active and subjective female subaltern gaze" (Foster 2002: 264). Foster's point about the reversal of the gaze is well taken, though more could be said in this case. Nair's experimental first film is not exclusively or simply focused on how men look at women; many of the girls and women she films are equally prone to stare, sometimes quite boldly, and sometimes playfully, at the camera and the woman holding it. Quite a number of the shots reveal (and perhaps subvert) the supposed illusion of the observational documentary method. As the filmmaker disturbs, by her presence, the scene she is attempting to observe, the mode of the film becomes effectively interactive. In anthropological terms, one could argue that the documentary filmmaker is always in some sense a "participant observer," rather than a simple outsider.

Jama Masjid Street Journal opens with an image of a young girl on the street staring boldly at the camera Nair holds in her hands, accompanied by the following voice-over:

> There's apparently nothing more novel than a woman making a film in Old Delhi. I am not easily categorized. My looks and dress betray that I am not just any foreign tourist. [pause] What is a woman speaking Urdu doing walking the streets with a movie camera? (Nair, *Jama Masjid Street Journal*, 1979)[1]

In light of the career in film that has followed *Jama Masjid Street Journal*, this self-reflexive comment is remarkably prescient. Indeed, at the time Nair made the film, in 1979, there were virtually no women film directors working in India, so there might be reason for Delhiites to be astonished at the sight of an Indian woman with a film camera on the street. The same interlocutors might have been less astonished by a foreigner filming the streets of Delhi as a filmmaker-tourist—there is in fact a long tradition of this type of filmmaking in India. As Nair observes and is observed by Delhi, it is specifically her *non*-foreignness that turns out to be remarkable.

The statement at the opening might seem self-involved to some viewers, but even at this very early point in her career, Nair's instinct is in fact to look beyond herself rather than remain in the pose of navel-gazing or solipsism. After acknowledging the complex nature of her relationship to her subject, Nair's focus turns outward, to the conservative Islamic community that lives in the neighborhood, and she meditates on the women wearing burqas, who behave quite differently in front of the camera than do the girls and women she meets who are unveiled.

> I find the younger unveiled girls more openly curious and my reaction to the burqa was so strong because it served to both physically and mentally suppress this impulse of curiosity so natural to the younger unveiled girls. Is it possible that these women are happy with their veiled existence? Not to me. But then perhaps it is the most effective way of maintaining privacy in this extraordinarily public community. (Nair, *Jama Masjid Street Journal*, 1979)

From the theme of Islam, Nair moves to a more general meditation on privacy, introduced via voice-over: "There's no such thing as privacy in this community; I certainly did not have much while I was making the film." This in some ways again takes us to the relationship between filmmaker and filmed, viewer and viewed. Much of the film consists of Nair's street-level exploration of often shadowy and enclosed spaces in this part of Old Delhi, including small shops, alleys, and a marketplace for live chickens.

Jama Masjid Street Journal ends with a radical departure, with a long shot image of thousands of Muslim men engaging in the daily prayer ritual, filmed from high above the main area of the Jama Masjid mosque itself. Nair's camera is positioned above the men, presumably from the women's section, and her closing comment contains both an editorializing sting and a self-conscious acknowledgment of the limitations of her own perspective: "As thousands of men face Mecca and bow with what strikes me as an almost totalitarian discipline—this intensity is just too big for me to understand, leave alone question." Intriguingly, after this first documentary foray, Nair shied away from religious topics for many years. She did return to the representation of South Asian Islam more than twenty years later, in two short films produced for charity projects, as well as in her recent feature-length fiction film, *The Reluctant Fundamentalist*. These films have some important resonances with *Jama Masjid Street Journal* and will all be discussed in greater depth in the final chapter of the present study.

So Far from India (1983)

While *Jama Masjid Street Journal* is certainly an important starting point for Nair's career as a filmmaker, there is no denying that it is limited as a student film. Its explorations of issues related to gender, geographical displacement, and religion are all consistent with Nair's broader body of work, but it's also clear that later Nair films explore these themes more richly and therefore merit more substantial discussions. With that in mind, we move on to *So Far from India*, Nair's first full-length documentary. *So Far from India* opens up many of the social themes as well as the aesthetic ideas that have been important in Nair's career. The film is, for one thing, fundamentally diasporic, focusing as it does on how the emigration of a young man from Gujarat can have significant ramifications on the people he's left behind, especially his wife. While the narrative of the film remains narrowly focused on the Seths, a couple separated by emigration, there are certain moments in the film that suggest an awareness of the broader diasporic theme. Of particular interest for this study, *So Far from India* shows us Nair's understanding of the gendering of diaspora: we see men as the first to depart, leaving women behind. But the theme of displacement can also be seen with respect to women in the film, especially the married women like Hansa Seth who have left behind homes and families to live in extended-family patriarchal households. One way of reading *So Far from India* we will explore is as a film that suggests parallels between the internal (intranational) displacement of Indian women through marriage and the external (transnational) displacement of men in the first waves of diasporic migration. While there are real differences in these two forms of migration, in *So Far from India* we see that the sense of displacement, disorientation, and loss of social context experienced by domestic migrants (mainly women) and transnational migrants (who were, in the first wave of diasporization, disproportionately men) are common to both.

The theme of displacement can be seen in the very first shot of the film. Nair opens *So Far from India* with an unnamed traveling folk singer performing a traditional rendition of the *Ramayana*—the epic story of Rama, who himself was forced to cross an ocean in his war with the demon Ravana. Through a voice-over, Nair translates the folk-singer's lyrics as follows:

> I sing the story of Ram, who crossed the oceans to save his wife from the evil king Ravan. I sing of the story of the journey across the ocean, a journey of great distances, a journey filled with troubles and god's blessings. . . . I sing of these comings and goings, these comings and goings. (Nair, *So Far from India*, 1983)

If it weren't clear from the context that the "comings and goings" described in the song refer to the *Ramayana*, the song could very well be about the main subject of *So Far from India*, Ashok Seth. The overlap between the mythical theme and the present-day theme of economic emigration suggests that this narrative—in which a protagonist experiences leaving India as an epic struggle—runs very deep in the Indian imagination. (Incidentally, Nair uses traveling folk singers for symbolic effect again in *The Namesake*, which features the young Gogol Ganguli transfixed by a Baul singer on the street in Kolkata.)

A second abstract gesture towards a broader concept of diaspora can be found at the end of *So Far from India*, where Nair presents an image of an open country road from the point of view of a moving truck in a rural Indian

So Far from India. Traveling folk singer reciting stories from the *Ramayana.*

setting. While the opening image gestures backwards in cultural history (the deep-seated Hindu taboo against leaving home to cross the "black water"), the final image gestures forward, at the uncertainty of what lies ahead.

While the shot of the traveling folk singer at the beginning of the film suggests a clear point of departure and a grounded cultural context (in traditional Indian culture, grounded by Hindu mythology), the closing image in *So Far from India* is much more abstract and arguably deterritorialized. The image suggests that at the end of the film, Nair's characters do not have a clear sense of territorial grounding but are rather fated to remain in a state of displacement. Importantly, both images are situated within the Indian context, suggesting that at this early point in her career Nair sees the experience of diaspora as an internal facet of Indian life at the moment of modernization, rather than as an opportunity for the creation of hybrid cultural identities in which the idea of home may remain alive even in the diaspora through the possibility of connectedness through technology.

From these two rather abstract framing images, let us begin to look more closely at the main narrative of *So Far from India.* One surprise in a film that foregrounds Ashok Seth's emigration from India is that displacement is as much figured in the film as a domestic event within India as it is as a transnational phenomenon: several members of Ashok's family, as well as his wife, reference their own experience of domestic displacement within India. Ashok's family, as his eldest sister, Bhadraben describes it, was quite powerful

So Far from India. The road ahead (final shot of film).

before Indian independence; they were involved in the spice business with royal patronage from a local Indian prince. Since independence, however, they have had to abandon their ancestral mansion and are now a relatively ordinary, middle-class Gujarati family:

> Life there [in the old mansion] was beautiful. We couldn't come downstairs too often, because our tenants lived below, and if we came down, they wouldn't sit with us because they thought we were big people. That's what it was like in that generation. . . . Only once a day we could go in that room and get out. There was such happiness there. Living in this house I feel I am trapped. Life was better then. Even now when I go out to shop and my old tenants see me there, I can't come home carrying my own basket. They say, how can you work like this and I am still alive? (Nair, *So Far from India*, 1983)

Though several of Ashok's family members seem to miss the life they once had, all of them are relatively comfortable in their current relatively spacious and well-appointed new home. The only one who feels acutely displaced is Hansa, who, upon marrying into the family, had to leave behind her family and village to live with strangers. Unfortunately, her in-laws do not seem to like her much, and Nair often films Hansa doing endless household chores, utterly on her own. Here is Nair's voice-over along those lines: "When she

So Far from India. Hansa preparing to hand-wash laundry.

married Ashok, she left her father's house and moved to her father-in-law's house in Ahmedabad city. She says, 'At that moment, my own people became strangers, and strangers became my own people.'" At this moment Nair introduces an intriguing parallel between Hansa's and Ashok's respective experiences, though for various reasons neither wife nor husband can recognize the similarity. Both Ashok and Hansa, it appears, are displaced: both have left something precious behind and are, in effect, lost.

The story in *So Far from India* is relatively straightforward: Ashok Seth left his pregnant new wife, Hansa, behind in Ahmedabad, Gujarat, to start work in America. Nair films in both India and New York, including at Seth's gritty place of work (a newspaper stand in the New York City subway), at Seth's cramped apartment, and at various diners and restaurants. Seth dresses in a western style (at one point we see him buying sneakers at a shoe store), and lives in a modest rented room. Seth largely speaks Hindi with Nair, though he sometimes shifts to English. The theme Seth returns to again and again as Nair interviews him in these various settings is his desire to establish himself independently in the US ("Now I'm here, I need my own everything"), which entails making as much money as he can ("Where money is concerned, life is better here, because we are earning more"). While Ashok's life seems severely curtailed, pleasureless, and solitary, he himself seems unaware of the losses he has incurred (and is continually incurring), as he insists that "life is better here."

So Far from India. Ashok buying sneakers in New York City.

The opening scenes of *So Far from India* feature a series of jarring jump-cuts between Ashok's life in New York and his family in Ahmedabad, where Hansa and Ashok's family members speak about their experience of his absence. Except for Ashok's father, most of Nair's interviewees are women, and they openly wonder about the value of migrating to America. As one of Ashok's sisters asks, "What is there in America? Something to see, perhaps? Do they sit around like this, brothers and sisters? If not, what's the point?" Ashok's father doesn't make the same criticisms, and Nair suggests that he—as a man—has had greater access to cultural landscapes outside of India throughout his life. Unlike the women in Ashok's family, Ashok's father speaks English, and in the segment with him that Nair uses in the film, he recites a long list of classic western films he's seen.

The interview with Ashok's father is a remarkable departure from everything that precedes it and follows it, in part because it contains a moment of marked self-reflexivity. One of the films Ashok's father praises is a filmic adaptation of *Crime and Punishment*, which is filmed "naturally":

[Ashok's father, speaking to the camera] And then 22 February was *Crime and Punishment*. That is the best film I have ever seen. See this film again and again. It is pure. . . . You have seen *The Bicycle Thief*? [Yes] It's just like that. Simple story, without any arrangement, what you call it, by the filmmaker. (Nair, *So Far from India*, 1983)

In effect, what Ashok's father finds appealing about the version of *Crime and Punishment* he remembers from many years earlier (it's possible he's referring to the 1951 Mexican version of the film, directed by Fernando de Fuentes) is its ostensibly neorealist approach ("without any arrangement... by the filmmaker"). The comparison to *The Bicycle Thief* (1948) seems to underline Ashok's father's preference for this kind of filmmaking. Such a comment about film-making methodology, in a film which is itself very keen on presenting a largely observational (to again use Nichols' term) account of what dislocation does to a family, seems like an example of self-reflexivity that is hard to ignore. In effect, it is a mise-en-abyme moment, since the man being interviewed, though far from central to the action of Nair's film, refers to an idea of filmic naturalness that also expresses the ostensible goal of the cinéma vérité documentary filmmaker who is in fact filming him.

Separate from the self-reflexivity of the interview with Ashok's father, it is difficult to know exactly how to place his account of the many foreign films he reports having seen earlier in his life, including not just *Crime and Punishment* and *The Bicycle Thief*, but also *The Gay Divorcee* (1934) and *16 Fathoms Deep* (1948). Perhaps surprisingly, Ashok's father's experience with western cinema does not render him a figure for cosmopolitanism in the context of *So Far from India*; rather, it only underlines his marginal role in the family, as he seems to be completely disconnected from the struggle between Ashok and Hansa happening in the present tense in his own household. While Hansa worries about when (or whether) Ashok will ask her to join him in New York, and Ashok worries about the demands Hansa's family is putting on him, Ashok's father seems to mainly be interested in talking about experiences in his own, rather distant, past. No one else interviewed seems to have time for films; judging from her ignorance of western customs, it appears that Hansa has hardly had any exposure to this kind of entertainment at all.

At the midpoint of Nair's documentary, Ashok returns to Ahmedabad to spend two months with his family. Some of the footage here shows, startlingly, the growing disconnect between Ashok and his family. This is the first time he's seeing his son—who is a year and a half old—and as he walks off the tarmac at the Ahmedabad airport, he barely pauses to greet his wife. The suggestion is of the total failure of communication between wife and husband. Hansa has no idea when her husband will invite her to join him in New York, and it becomes clear over a period of days that she's intimidated even to ask him about it.

The disconnect between Ashok and Hansa reflects how profoundly the early diasporic experience is filtered through gender. To Nair and the camera (with Ashok's wife absent from the room), Ashok reveals that he's actually unsure whether he has any active intention of sending for his wife and child. He questions the marriage itself, insinuating that his wife's relatives agreed to the marriage mainly because they saw him as an "engine who will pull a whole train of cars to America." Most starkly, he states to Nair that "I think this marriage happened only because of America, not because of who I am." In effect, he feels trapped by the marriage—he has no personal feeling for Hansa—though he has no clear way to remove himself from what appears at this point to be a dysfunctional union. To Hansa's relatives, Ashok pleads that he'd like to send for Hansa, but at the moment he doesn't have the money to do so. Hansa is also unsuitable for America in some ways, as she herself admits—she doesn't speak English or have much knowledge of life in America. Nair suggests a clear gender divide regarding mobility—women are restricted to traditional Gujarati life, while the men are empowered to have other kinds of experiences, whether it is merely watching foreign films or actively traveling outside of Gujarat. (Incidentally, the diasporic gender divide is hinted at again, albeit more subtly, in some of Nair's later films, including the groom character, Hemant Rai, in *Monsoon Wedding*, who has returned to Delhi from Houston, where he works in the high-tech industry. By contrast, a film like *The Namesake* will show how women's experiences can be a central part of the diasporic story.)

To be clear, *So Far from India* is not simply a to and fro between a husband and wife in an uneasy, transitional point in their relationship. There is also a didactic argument about the loss entailed with the diasporic experience, which Nair inserts in an extended voice-over towards the end of the film. With footage of anonymous night-time street scenes in Ahmedabad, Nair in effect delivers the thesis of the film to the viewer:

> Ashok has become used to the anonymity and freedom of America. In Ahmedabad, his family goes back more than forty generations. Here he belongs to so many people. When Ashok came back to India he perhaps thought he was coming home. But when you leave to find your own way, it is hard to return and find comfort in what you left. (Nair, *So Far from India*, 1983)

The voice-over comment here is perhaps a heavy-handed gesture (and certainly one that would not have been employed by strict cinéma vérité practitioners like Pennebaker), but this scene (along with the opening and closing shots of the film) helps to broaden the frame from the narrow marriage-separation dilemma faced by Ashok and Hansa. In fact, what is at issue in *So Far from India* is the fundamental question of how to relinquish one's old world identity in favor of something new. In Ashok's case, the question remains unanswered—and the future of his relationship with both his family and with India more broadly is presented merely as an aporia.

So Far from India ends with Ashok tentatively committing to bringing Hansa with him to New York in subsequent months. But several of his earlier statements to the filmmaker regarding his relationship with Hansa are shown to be somewhat deceptive, either by his own statements to other interlocutors, or by Hansa herself. Because of these inconsistencies and the thinness of Ashok's final "realization," the viewer is left with room to doubt the likelihood that a reunion between husband and wife will transpire anytime soon. The overall account of diasporic life is doubly negative. Ashok's life in New York is shown to be squalid and unfulfilling, and the lives of the relatives he has left behind in Gujarat are largely shaped by his absence. In the middle of the film, we see him return to India, but even at that moment, the filmmaker underlines how uncomfortable he has become at "home." At this early point in Nair's career, the diasporic experience in her film is defined largely by loss and displacement; the individuals who think they are succeeding in New York are deluding themselves. By the time she makes *The Namesake* (2006), Nair's approach to this experience will be radically different in many different respects (the dialogue between these two films will be explored in chapter 7). But even with her next film, *India Cabaret*, the image of migration would be markedly different.

India Cabaret (1985)

India Cabaret was filmed primarily in Bombay in 1983, with some sequences filmed in southern India, in a village outside of Hyderabad, near the home of one of the interviewed dancers. Most of the filming occurs at the Meghraj nightclub in Ghatkopar (in what is today suburban Mumbai), where Nair interviews and observes dancers, patrons, and the club owner, though there is also one particularly surreal interview with a patron of the club and his wife at their home.

India Cabaret is remarkable, first and foremost, because of Nair's insistence on remaining editorially neutral with regards to the dancers' lifestyle and "morality." Nair is also neutral with regards to the owner of the club, Suresh, as well as the club's patrons, though the film is also generally less interested in the men than in observing the women and trying to elicit their stories. As critic Amit Shah wrote, approvingly, in *Cineaste* in 1987,

> *India Cabaret* is *cinéma vérité* at its most lucid and challenging. Mitch Epstein's camera prowls the tiny back rooms and gaudy nightclub stages, glides through kitchens, train compartments, and village verandas, while Alex Griswold's wireless mikes pick up glee, sorrow, rage, propositions, and insults. Barry Brown's editing is never static; he connects image, thought and language with versatility. [. . .] Nair's approach is not polemical; she remains true to her desire to *reveal* and not merely to *tell*. (Shah 1987: 23)

Shah's emphasis on the various technical components of the film—camerawork, sound, and editing—is appropriate (and indeed, as we have suggested above, the specific elements of camera and sound are all quite important to the idea of cinéma vérité). In an interview with her later collaborator Sooni Taraporevala, Nair herself supports Shah's final point about Nair's desire "to *reveal* and not merely to *tell*" when she says,

> Many of us come to see the film with preconceptions; we expect to see victims, we wish to help the fallen, we want to feel pity for them. What is unsettling perhaps about *India Cabaret* is that the women in it do not ask for our help, refuse to be viewed as victims, and do not need our pity. They struggle and survive with great humor, strength, and resilience. This is why the film exists and why their lives are a source of inspiration to me. (Nair 1986–87: 67)

The dilemma presented by the dancers in *India Cabaret*—the fact that they are neither straightforward moral victims of male oppression nor "fallen women"—leaves many viewers of the film, particularly men, in an uncomfortable position. In the same essay, Nair goes on to defend her film as a feminist work, though many Indian feminists did not receive it as such upon the film's release. She also gives an account of a controversy over the film in New York around this time: a local public television station decided not to broadcast the film after members of the local Indian community complained that it presented a negative image of life in contemporary India.

One of the issues affecting any film about sex workers is the question of perspective. Is Nair's camera itself going to exploit the women's bodies or adopt a point of view that identifies with the women themselves? From the

India Cabaret. Lovina before she enters the club.

beginning, Nair aims to align her camera with the perspective of the dancers. The film introduces three women with on-screen titles in the first few minutes—"Lovina," "Rekha," and "Rosy"—though there are several other women who also speak and dance on camera at various points in the film. Of the three, Rekha and Rosy are really the primary subjects of the film; Lovina appears in a more limited capacity at the beginning and the end of the film as a dancer but does not have any speaking lines. Nair's feminism is visually evident in the simple sense that the dancers are never filmed as eroticized objects, as if from the point of view of patrons of the club. That said, *India Cabaret* does render on screen—realistically and unglamorously—the women's exposed bodies, both in casual postures in the dressing room of the Meghraj, and also in their striptease dances on the floor of the club.

The cabaret dancers, when not in the dimmed lighting of the club's main floor, are shown as emphatically "normal," demystified. To wit, the first medium close-up shot of Lovina shows her just before she enters the main room of the club. The lighting is neutral, and Lovina is seen laughing and performing mock "diva" postures for the camera, as a seeming shared or inside joke between filmmaker and subject regarding the performance of femininity. As the camera follows her into the darker dance hall in the club, the point of view generally remains at her level, rather than at the seated level of the club's patrons. In a later scene, the camera accompanies her onto the

India Cabaret. Hand-held camera approximating point of view of the dancer herself.

dance floor, and as the dancer spins around the room, the cameraperson spins along with her, following her face as she dances in circles. That last image, more than any other, moves the perspective of the filmmaker close to the perspective of the women in the film itself—and here at least, that perspective is deliriously mobile and empowered. (In notes about *India Cabaret* made during the planning stages for her next film, *Salaam Bombay!*, Nair expressed regret that the film hadn't had more sequences like this.)

The dancer at the center of the film, Rekha, is also the first person to speak on camera, immediately after the introductory sequence showing transit to the club and then Lovina's dance. Rekha appears, as she generally does when not dancing, in a formal, light-colored sari, with her hair braided and a decorative *tilak* on her forehead. Though she does eventually explain the tragic backstory that led to her going into "the line," her opening words are completely unapologetic:

> Cabaret dancers, you know, not all are good, not all are bad. Some are good, some are bad. Among the bad, I'm number-one wicked! [Hindi: *Ek number badmashi.*] When I leave home, I'm a good woman, a virtuous virgin, no one would think I'm a cabaret dancer. If anyone goes by, I look like this, never look a man in the eye. But in the club, I'm number-one wicked. Nobody is worse than me. Any customer asks me, I screw him, rip him off. (Nair, *India Cabaret*, 1985)

India Cabaret. Nightclub clients in frank conversation with the filmmaker.

Here, Rekha is unashamed, bordering on boastful, of her "wickedness." And while the image of her that emerges as the film develops is somewhat different from this, this amoral introduction marks a clear choice by the filmmaker not to see the cabaret dancers as helpless, fallen women, or victims. That said, this introduction is shortly followed by Rekha's explication of her past, which featured an alcoholic, abusive husband who prostituted her out to other men against her will, prompting her to leave home and to work in the cabarets in Bombay.

While the focus in *India Cabaret* is on observing the dancers in the club, Nair does interview a few male patrons of the Cabaret at various points. After we meet Rekha and then briefly see her at work on the dance floor, the film cuts back to the roof of the club, where a group of men are drinking and smoking. Two men are the primary speakers, identified here as "Man #1" and "Man #2." The attitudes of the men are every bit as unashamed as is Rekha's attitude to her work. Rather than be embarrassed about being interviewed at a strip club, they express frustration with the hypocrisy of middle-class Indian society:

> MAN #1: Politicians are the first to say, "Shut this place down!" But they are the first to get here.
> MAN #2: They come to the cabaret and say, "Does this go on here, does that go on here?"

MAN #1: It's all hypocrisy, everyone loves it.
MAN #2: What does a man think? "I can do what the hell I like. But my woman, she must stay within the four walls of our home." He wants a virtuous virgin.
MAN #1: My woman should sleep with only one man. She should be a virtuous virgin [Hindi: *sati savitri*].
MIRA NAIR'S VOICE, OFF CAMERA: And the man?
MAN #1: He can sleep with as many women as he likes. Morally, it's not right.
[ROSY FLIRTING WITH MAN #2]
MIRA NAIR: Yes, yes, but what do you want?
MAN #1: The same, a virtuous virgin. (Nair, *India Cabaret*, 1985)

What is remarkable about this dialogue, initially, is just how aware the men are of the double standard that allows them to visit a strip club and, presumably, pay the dancers for sex, while "virtuous" women are forced to live restrictive lives. However, that openness and acknowledgment of a double standard ("Morally, it's not right") gives way somewhat at the end of the scene, as the same Man #1 admits that he nevertheless wants a respectable "virtuous virgin" ("sati savitri") for a wife—not a woman with a sexual history that resembles his own. If the men in this scene are somewhat admirable for their openness, as beneficiaries of a double standard, they are doing nothing to change the gender relations in their society.

Another remarkable aspect of *India Cabaret* can be seen in Nair's approach to making the film. Rather than simply meet her subjects in neutral locations, Nair chooses to spend three months living with the women in their shared flat. This proximity allows Nair to observe her subjects in settings at once more intimate and more mundane. After a series of introductory interviews with both Rekha and Rosy, the men mentioned above, and the club owner, Suresh (who improbably insists, in English, that he's never been the dancers' pimp), the film follows them home. We see one dancer waking up, reaching for a newspaper and a box of cigarettes—the women smoke surprisingly much—as well as cutting vegetables, cooking, shopping, and playing with their children. Appadurai and Breckenridge, in their 1991 essay, describe the method on display in both this film and *So Far from India* in terms borrowed from anthropology:

> These two films are remarkable and (at least for an ethnographer) enviable. They show that Mira Nair knew how to enter people's private

lives, and narrativize and normalize them in ways that ethnographers seek successfully to do. She knew how to talk to her subjects while they were on camera, how to put them at their ease. Even while they are clearly performing, there is an artlessness about them, a transparency that recalls the early Godard, who was able to make actors talk at the audience without losing the sense of narrative contingency. (Appadurai and Breckenridge 1991: 96)

Appadurai and Breckenridge go on to qualify this reading of the film, suggesting that there are limits to how much the line between ethnography and Nair's form of cinéma vérité documentary can actually be blurred: "She was too involved, too much part of an exchange with her characters to be just an ethnographer." But here Appadurai and Breckenridge do pinpoint what may be *India Cabaret*'s greatest strength, namely the extent of the access Nair is able to achieve with her subjects.

Appadurai expands upon his discussion of *India Cabaret* in his 1996 book, *Modernity At Large*. Here, Appadurai argues that one of the key contextual references in *India Cabaret* is commercial Hindi cinema:

> What is most important about this film is the way in which it shows that the cabaret club is not simply a marketplace for desire but also a place where imagined lives are negotiated: the dancers act out their precarious sense of themselves as dancers; the second-rate band tries to work up its musical passions, which are fed by the aspirations of the Catholic community in Goa (western India) to play European and American instrumental music well. The men who come as customers clearly see themselves as participants in something larger than life, and they behave exactly like the customers in cabaret scenes in many Hindi commercial films. In fact, the scenario that provides the meeting ground for all these characters is provided by the cabaret sequences from Hindi commercial cinema. (Appadurai 1996: 62)

The imputed connection to Hindi cinema is an important part of the context behind *India Cabaret*. Despite the evident sordidness of the club and the frequent degradation of the cabaret dancers, the patrons and the dancers all seem to want to continue the illusion—though the gap separating the posh and exciting illusion of film cabarets and the reality Nair's film explores is so large as to strain "cabaret" as a category. Appadurai's premise is that the "cabaret" culture seen in Nair's documentary is effectively an attempted simulacrum of cabarets as depicted in masala Hindi films.

Along these lines, scholars such as Ranjani Mazumdar, in *Bombay Cinema*, have explored the emergence of the "cabaret" space in commercial Hindi cinema beginning in the early 1970s as a particular "creation" of Bombay cinema (Mazumdar 2007: 85–87). Certainly, both the patrons and the dancers in the real cabaret of Nair's film seem to be in dialogue with the vamps and heroes of Bombay cinema—though instead of the glamorous Helen in the commercial films of the 1970s, we see uninspired dancing, a sense of stasis or paralysis among the club's clients, and thinly veiled prostitution. Dancers like Rekha are sometimes shown to be thoroughly disengaged from what they are doing and "out of it," either because of overdependence on alcohol or because other life issues such as raising children or the possibility of settling down and getting out of "the line" are bearing down on them. They do not, to put it quite simply, have romantic ideas about the work they are doing; their goal is simply to make as much money out of it as possible while they can. The symbolic power of the cabaret, described by Majumdar as a space of danger, temptation, and glamor in the masala Hindi films of the 1970s, falls apart utterly in the world of the Meghraj nightclub depicted by Nair only a few years later.

Another important point made by Appadurai is the theme of dislocation ("deterritorialization" is the word he generally uses) in *India Cabaret*. Not only is the music intriguingly dislocated—many of the songs played by the band in the cabaret are covers of western pop hits from the 1970s—but the dancers themselves are in some sense dislocated "guest workers in Bombay" (Appadurai 1996: 63). One of the key narrative sequences in *India Cabaret* demonstrates this when Nair follows Rosy to her village home in Hyderabad, only to find that her family resists capitalizing on Rosy's economic success as a cabaret dancer or prostitute because of the extreme dishonor associated with her profession. As a result of her loss of family and a sense of home, Rosy confesses that she can never really be happy, even if she is successful. This sequence is also important for our understanding of *India Cabaret* in Nair's broader body of work, as the image of domestic displacement one sees here finds an echo in the displacement of "Chaipau" and "Solasaal" in Nair's subsequent fiction film, *Salaam Bombay!*

Some degree of narrative closure in *India Cabaret* is offered by Rekha, who decides, over the course of filming, to get out of "the line." She agrees to marry one of the men who has been courting her (the man is not filmed). The theme of escape is introduced about midway through *India Cabaret* and recurs in various ways until the final scene of the film, where Rekha collects her pay from the club owner Suresh and then, shortly thereafter, goes to Juhu beach to celebrate her freedom from her old life by wading, seemingly relieved of a pressing burden, in the Arabian Sea. Some aspects of Rekha's resolution seem questionable, in part because we never meet the fiancé, though she is quite ready to describe his occupation when pressed about what he does. As with Ashok Seth at the end of *So Far from India*, it's left open as to whether Rekha has constructed yet another illusion for herself—a fantasy of a more grounded life and a new image of "home" that in fact has no hope of becoming a reality.

The Laughing Club of India (1999)

After a hiatus of nearly twelve years, Nair returned to the documentary genre in 1999 with the thirty-minute film *The Laughing Club of India*. Though documentary has given way to the fiction-film format in the main body of Nair's work since the mid-1980s, she clearly continues to feel that it has an appeal for her as a way of tackling certain subjects (and, moreover, as we will show in the subsequent sections, several of her fictional films use a style inflected by documentary realism). The continued interest in the form as a way of representing changes in contemporary Indian society also reflects how, even though she has long been based abroad, Nair has retained an interest in staying closely engaged with everyday Indian realities in her more recent work. The interweaving of documentary and fictional formats can be seen in some of the shots of city life in Mumbai in *Laughing Club*; those quick cuts of life on the street, filmed in passing or from the margins, resemble some of the shots of Delhi in Nair's 2002 *Monsoon Wedding*. Both that film and this short documentary take as their focus the new urban India, with advertisements for cell phones and internet services on billboards above, and a hustling, sometimes struggling, populace moving on the streets below.

Shot on digital video, *Laughing Club* was screened on the television channel Cinemax in August 2001 and generally well received. As with Nair's point of inspiration for several of her other films, she came across the subject of *Laughing Club* serendipitously, as she describes in a 2001 interview with the *Christian Science Monitor*:

> Indian film director Mira Nair . . . was stuck in a traffic jam in Bombay, steaming with impatience like everyone else in the cars around

her, until she looked up and saw about 2,000 women in white saris crossing the street and laughing in unison. The banners they carried said "World Laughter Day."

"My frustration at being stuck in a traffic jam just dissolved," said Ms. Nair in a recent interview. "So I mentioned it to a friend of mine, a photographer named Adam Bartos, and he thought it would make a great film. I wanted to make an absurdist film on the power of laughter. But then, when we got there, like life, you think it's for one thing and it turns out to be for another." (Mason 2001: 19)

Though the finished film is straightforward and appreciative rather than "absurdist," *Laughing Club* does contain some moments that border on absurdism. The opening sequence, for instance, dramatizes the potential strangeness of the first impression made by a laughter club in action, in this case a laughter club made up primarily of workers at a factory in Mumbai. Though much of the film is in what Nichols would call the "interactive" mode, featuring interviews with the founder of the laughter clubs, Dr. Madan Kataria, as well as practitioners from a wide array of backgrounds, Nair does at many points emphasize the "observational" mode. Numerous sequences in the film feature the laughter clubs in action, for the viewer to interpret as she wishes, without commentary or evaluation.

Nair's *Laughing Club* does differ from her first few documentaries in some important ways. Nair's chosen subject here, for one thing, is somewhat safer and more domesticated than the subject of *India Cabaret* or *So Far from India*. In contrast to the cabaret dancers figured in *India Cabaret* or the burqa-clad women in *Jama Masjid Street Journal*, many of the voices featured in *Laughing Club*, starting with Dr. Kataria himself, are well-adjusted, prosperous citizens of Mumbai. The practice of "laughter yoga" did start in the public parks of Malabar Hill, one of the wealthiest sectors of Mumbai—though it should be said that, as public parks, these parks are visited by an economically diverse constituency, and the membership of the laughing clubs has reflected that diversity from the beginning. At various points, Nair's film also explores laughter clubs in more decidedly lower-middle-class and working-class settings, in Dadar and Lokhandwala, and her subjects are both Hindi-speaking ordinary people and English-speaking elites.

In part, Nair uses the vehicle of the laughter clubs simply as a way of exploring the lives of a diverse group of modern Indian subjects in Mumbai. After opening on a light note, *The Laughing Club of India* begins to look behind the surface, exploring the lives of some practitioners, including,

The Laughing Club of India. Hand-held camera suggesting the filmmaker's participation in the event.

movingly, an interview with an older man who lives in a cramped room with fifteen people. That interview is followed by another speaker, a woman, describing how thirty to thirty-five people live in her apartment with her, of which twenty of the inhabitants are members of her immediate family. These interviews give an acute sense of the importance laughter yoga has for these Mumbai residents.

That said, much of Nair's 1999 documentary focuses on the beneficial and therapeutic qualities of the practice itself. For example, one interviewee in the film is an older lady in a pink sari who speaks from the rooftop of her apartment building in what appears to be a middle-class neighborhood. She describes how she came from a village in Gujarat and moved to Mumbai with her husband upon marriage at age sixteen. Since then she has remained in the same crowded flat. She took to the laughing club after her husband's death: "When my husband died, I didn't leave this house for six years. My husband was a great laugher. So I decided if I want to live, I should laugh." Other examples of Dr. Kataria's laughter as therapy for people include a young man named Sandeep, who was paralyzed in a road accident, and a vocational school for the blind.

As with *India Cabaret*, the filmmaker-interviewer in *The Laughing Club of India* often seems closer to her subject than one would expect from a conventional ethnographic documentary. Nair prefers filming the laughter yoga at eye level rather than from a bird's-eye view, and at several instances in the film the cameraperson (presumably Nair herself) appears to be actively participating in the practice along with the local laughing club members.

Nair makes the personal connection explicit as the closing credits roll at the end of *The Laughing Club of India*: the widow mentioned above is performing a kind of laughter dance on the same apartment-building roof where she had earlier given her interview. At the very end of her performance, Nair herself emerges from behind the camera and gives the woman a hug, and verbally thanks her for her contribution. We also see Nair laughing herself and looking at the camera as the film fades to black. Reading the self-reflexive moment in the broader context of Nair's struggles as a filmmaker in the 1990s (this film was made on the heels of her long struggle with the Indian censor board following *Kama Sutra*), one might speculate, reading between the lines, that the laughing clubs may appeal to the director personally as a way of dealing with the frustrations of working as a feminist filmmaker.

As a final note on *Laughing Club*, it seems important to mention the choice of music, which is highly suggestive. As with Nair's other India-based films, *Laughing Club* features some very intriguing musical choices. There is, to begin with, a classic song by Mohammed Rafi (a vocalist whose songs appear in several other Nair films, including *Monsoon Wedding* and *Mississippi Masala*), "Yeh hai Bombay Meri Jaan," a light-hearted song that thematizes the heartlessness of life in Bombay (in my own translation: "There are buildings, there are trams, there are motors, there are mills / But though you'll meet with everything, meet a heart you never will"). Another important inclusion on the soundtrack is Asian Underground musician Nitin Sawhney's ambience-laden track "Migration," which has a meditative (sometimes ominous) sound that helps to create the tone for Nair's shots of Mumbai city life in the interstitial sequences of *Laughing Club*. Nair would again use Asian Underground music (the Midival Punditz) for the interstitial sequences in *Monsoon Wedding*, suggesting yet another thread linking the two primary modes of filmmaking in Nair's body of work.

Chapter 3

THE AESTHETICS OF DISILLUSIONMENT

Salaam Bombay! (1988)

Salaam Bombay! is Mira Nair's first fictional feature film. While it does mark a career transition out of documentaries, the film retains a strong documentary inflection. Without a doubt, it is the emphasis on realism—without sentimentality or melodrama—in its depiction of the lives of street children, that gives *Salaam Bombay!* its continuing power. Though its setting is mainly domestic, the film can also be described as diasporic in some ways, as we will explore below. Also important are the transnational influences on Nair's filmmaking process, especially from the neorealist school; below we will briefly explore the parallels between *Salaam Bombay!* and Luis Buñuel's *Los Olvidados* (1950). All of this is en route to a close reading of *Salaam Bombay!* as a critique of the illusionist conventions of commercial Hindi cinema; in contrast to "Bollywood," it will be argued, the experience of internal displacement at the heart of *Salaam Bombay!* forces characters into disillusionment—into an engagement with unfiltered reality. Various mythical narratives and false modes of storytelling need to be interrogated and disavowed, Nair suggests; only a resolute engagement with the realities of the world around us will ensure a path to survival. While Nair's adaptation of cinéma vérité to the conventions and forms of a fiction film is the central theme we will be discussing with reference to *Salaam Bombay!*, a diasporic sensibility and a degree of transnationalism are important elements of the film. In short, despite its domestic setting, *Salaam Bombay!* is a compelling example of the diaspora vérité idea that is at the core of nearly all of Nair's major work.

Admittedly, the transition from documentary to fiction film raises some challenging questions regarding form and the relevance of a term ("cinéma vérité") that has traditionally been only applied to a narrow range of documentary films. Here, Nair has actually spoken of the change in form that occurred in this phase of her career several times. Here, for instance, is the filmmaker's comment from a 2004 interview in *Cineaste* about her thoughts as she was initially contemplating making *Salaam Bombay!*:

> CINEASTE: What was going on in your life that made you want to do *Salaam Bombay!*?
>
> MIRA NAIR: It was everything coming full circle—taking the tradition of protest theater into cinéma vérité, seeing how people really lived, getting passionate about truth being stranger than fiction—which led to seven years of making cinéma-vérité documentaries.
>
> Then I realized the irony that if I had made a fiction film, I would have been better able to convey the reality of street kids than with a hit-and-run documentary approach. I also got very impatient with struggling for an audience for documentary, and wanting to reach larger audiences through fiction. In India, we had no language, no means to understand a documentary. (Badt 2004: 13)

In effect, Nair believes that it is only through a fictional project that she can meaningfully capture and represent the reality of the lives of the children in *Salaam Bombay!* That is to say (and she is not the first to say it), fiction can at times be more "truthful" than documentary, owing to the inherent limits of the latter genre. In the second part of her comment to *Cineaste*, Nair also suggests a practical issue, that of audience size. Until recently, the audience for documentaries was minuscule, while fictional films, especially in India, are inherently more legible—and by extension, marketable. Nair's comment about the absence of an audience for documentary films in India in the 1980s might take us back to the issue of audience and address discussed in chapter 1. Arguably, Nair's choice to make a fiction film allowed her to address *Indian* audiences in a way that neither *India Cabaret* nor *So Far from India* could have done at the time. So besides the shift in form, Nair's turn to fiction could be read as a particular mode of 'returning' to India and Indian markets.

At the time it was made, in 1987, *Salaam Bombay!* was effectively unique in both the Indian art and commercial cinemas. Viewed today, the film retains considerable power both as a work of art and as a social statement, especially in comparison to other widely talked-about films engaging poverty in urban India such as Danny Boyle's *Slumdog Millionaire* and Kiran Rao's *Dhobi Ghat*. *Salaam Bombay!* was also a significant commercial and critical success, both within India and in the west. It grossed more than $2 million in the United States, which was unprecedented for an Indian film in 1988. The film also earned Nair a Caméra d'Or prize at the Cannes Film Festival in 1988, and the buzz from that award also helped launch the film around the world. Finally, *Salaam Bombay!* was nominated for an Academy Award for Best Foreign Film in 1988, only the second Indian film in history to be nominated for that award. A major chunk of the proceeds from the film were used by Nair to establish a foundation for street children, the Salaam Baalak Trust. The Salaam Baalak Trust was for many years administered by Mira Nair's own mother, Praveen Nair, where it came to take on a life of its own (indeed, some recent media coverage of the work of Salaam Baalak Trust does not even allude to its origins [Gentleman 2006]). The child actors in the film were paid for their work in stages, including through direct payment as well as the establishment of trusts. As Nair recounts in the director's commentary to the *Salaam Bombay!* DVD, released in 2003, most of the principal child actors in the film were able to rise out of poverty and be educated in the years following the film's release.

Salaam Bombay! as Transnational, Diasporic Film

It may be controversial to assert that Nair's *Salaam Bombay!* is in some sense "diasporic," because some readers might be disposed to use that descriptor to challenge the "authenticity" of Nair's film. Indeed, at least some scholars, including Jyotika Virdi and Poonam Arora, have criticized the film along exactly those lines (Arora 1994; Virdi 1992), and we will consider their criticisms briefly below. That said, it seems mistaken to ignore the several constituent elements of *Salaam Bombay!* that make it somewhat more than a purely Indian film, including Nair and Taraporevala's respective educations in the US, their exposure to avant-garde art and theater practices in New York (including especially avant-garde feminism and cinéma vérité documentary film), the transnational funding support for the film, and the international backgrounds of much of the crew. Of these four elements, the matter of education at a US university probably does not need further discussion, though the other three elements do merit a more detailed response.

While it is clearly a transnational production, *Salaam Bombay!*, like *India Cabaret*, might also be said to be diasporic in the sense that it centrally features characters who have been displaced *within* India. The protagonist of *Salaam Bombay!*, Chaipau (whose nickname translates as "Tea-Bread"), is from a village only identified as "Bijapur, near Bangalore," and it is painfully clear from the film's opening that he has lost any connection to a sense of local community or home; he moves to Bombay, like millions of other recent arrivants to the city, because he has no other option where he is. On the one hand, this domestic migration does not lead to the same level of cultural alienation he might have felt if he had ended up in New York or London. But in other respects, Chaipau's experience resembles that of a transnational migrant: he has no preexisting social network, and no family or kinship group that can offer him support upon initial arrival. As a result, he falls into a surrogate kinship with the first group of street children he encounters after leaving the train station in central Bombay. In this sense Chaipau is quite similar to several of the internally displaced sex workers in *India Cabaret*—and all of these characters have something in common with characters like Ashok from *So Far from India*, as well as a range of diasporic characters seen in Nair's later films.

In addition to the theme of displacement associated with the domestic migrations depicted in *Salaam Bombay!*, it's also important to be aware of the transnational elements that contributed to the production of Nair's film. First, the idea for the *method* of working with the street children in an actors' workshop setting derives from a model Nair and Taraporevala were exposed to through New York film and drama circles. In interviews with John Kenneth Muir, Nair and Taraporevala have described how they were inspired by New York playwright Elizabeth Swados's work with teenage runaways in an extended acting workshop setting (Muir 2006: 37). Swados's concept of a theater workshop with street children from New York City led Nair to approach Barry John of Delhi's Theatre Action Group, to oversee a three-month workshop with Bombay slum children during the summer of 1987. John, an English dramatist settled in India, might be seen as another example of a "foreign" influence on the film, though he would in fact better be described as an immigrant to India, with a long and vested interest in Indian culture and society (Barry John has lived in India for more than 30 years; today, he runs a professional acting studio in Mumbai). Alongside Barry John, several Americans involved in Nair's project made valuable aesthetic contributions, especially Mitch Epstein, a coproducer who had earlier worked with Nair as a cinematographer, and Sandi Sissel, a documentary cinematographer whom Nair recruited to be director of photography especially for *Salaam Bombay!* As Nair recounts in diary entries recorded during the making of the film, Epstein also offered Nair personal support in taking on numerous government bureaucracies and reluctant donors throughout the production process.

For her part, Sissel's documentary approach to cinematography (Sissel had worked on several documentaries prior to joining Nair's team here) clearly contributes to *Salaam Bombay!*'s visual style.

All of this is not to say that India did not have its own, relatively well-established art cinema scene in the mid-1980s, as Nair and Taraporevala began to work on *Salaam Bombay!* In fact, along with Satyajit Ray, who was still making films in the 1980s, a parallel cinema did certainly exist—supported by an established government agency charged with funding such films, the National Film Development Corporation (NFDC), earlier known as the Film Finance Corporation. Indeed, the NFDC directly supported Nair's film, though additional funds also came from foreign production companies and sponsors, including the BBC—again, suggesting an important transnational connection for this otherwise "domestic" film.

Even though she was based primarily in New York at the time she undertook this project, Nair was aware of the parallel cinema scene in India, and indeed, some of the figures associated with that scene were involved in *Salaam Bombay!* as well. That said, Nair intended her own project to mark an aesthetic departure from the Indian art cinema idiom prevalent at the time, as we shall see. One important predecessor for *Salaam Bombay!* is the 1985 art film *Massey Sahib*, which starred Raghubir Yadav (who plays Chillum in *Salaam Bombay!*), Barry John, and, somewhat coincidentally, a very young Arundhati Roy. Other peers of Nair might be women directors such as Aparna Sen and Vijaya Mehta. Sen's first films, *36 Chowringhee Lane* (1981) and *Parama* (1985) explored feminist issues with a cosmopolitan sensibility (see Gokulsing and Dissanayake 2004: 75–87). However, despite the presence of significant talent, budgetary and distribution problems limited the influence India's art filmmakers could have in the 1980s, both within India and internationally (Chaudhuri 2005: 144–48). Overall, despite the contributions of these peers and predecessors, Nair found the art cinema scene in Delhi in the 1980s to be stale and parochial by comparison to the world she had encountered in New York. Here, for example, is a comment she made in a published diary entry regarding a Delhi art film festival in 1987:

> The festival is as always—the same faces more or less, the same mild chaos, the same bad projection, and unfortunately, the same unbelievably low quality of so-called serious Indian films. One can be devoured here, it is such a small world with little that is challenging happening. (Nair and Taraporevala 1989: 11)

In addition to its being a departure from commercial Hindi cinema's song-and-dance format, Nair's *Salaam Bombay!* represented a significant departure from the world of Indian art cinema, which had exploded on the scene in the 1950s and '60s, with Ray, Ritwik Ghatak, Mrinal Sen, and Mani Kaul, but which, by the 1980s, had lost some of its initial steam as it had become institutionalized. The film critic Ashish Rajadhyaksha has described the seeming decline in the quality of the "New Indian Cinema" of the 1960s as associated with the emergence of an official art-house style, a "state realism" (Rajadhyaksha 2000: 153). Apart from a few crossover successes (such as the NFDC-funded *Jaane Bhi Do Yaaro* [1984]), most art films supported by the NFDC during this period remained largely undistributed and unwatched.

Salaam Bombay! opens with an establishing shot of dingy canvas circus tents being dismantled by scrambling, barefoot workers. Chaipau appears in the second shot, walking while carrying a heavy load on his back. He is presented, from the beginning, as a social and amicable character, as he stops to greet the caged bears and circus dogs. It's representative of the overall theme of the film that we are introduced to him in a work setting; indeed, like many of the children we meet, he seems to constantly be working for others. And the fact that he is abandoned rather heartlessly by his boss foreshadows subsequent events in *Salaam Bombay!* quite well: Chaipau's later bosses in the red-light district around Grant Road in Bombay will be no different in their disregard.

The first serious display of emotion in the film is the shot of the face Krishna (Chaipau) as he takes in, with horror, the reality that the circus trucks have driven off, leaving him completely behind. Krishna then goes to the train station with the surplus money from his boss for the paan in his pocket. He buys a ticket to "the nearest city" from the station clerk, and only after the ticket is in his hand does he ask where it can take him. The clerk responds: "It goes to Bombay. Go—and become a star."

In effect, the focus on displaced people encourages parallels between *Salaam Bombay!* and the later, more obviously diasporic films, *Mississippi Masala*, *The Perez Family*, and *The Namesake*. Like the protagonists of those later films, Krishna has no established community to fall back upon; he has to go to a distant place to try and succeed there by his wits. His economic circumstances are considerably more extreme than are those faced by the relatively stable Indian immigrants we will meet in *Mississippi Masala*, but his cultural and contextual losses may be somewhat comparable. A more precise parallel to Chaipau's displacement can be found in *India Cabaret*, which explores the huge gaps between the cabaret dancers' lives in Bombay

The Aesthetics of Disillusionment: *Salaam Bombay!* 63

Salaam Bombay! Opening shot of film—closing of the circus.

and their distant, generally village-based family backgrounds. Finally, we might briefly mention Nair's return to the idea of internal displacement in *Migration*, a short educational film she made for the Gates Foundation in 2007. As in *Salaam Bombay!*, *Migration* features a character from an Indian village who is forced by economic circumstances to leave the countryside to go and work in Bombay, only to find unexpected hardship. The protagonist of *Migration* contracts HIV from a casual sexual encounter and later transmits the disease to his pregnant wife after returning to the village.

Contexts: Social Themes and Influences

Perhaps the most central social issue raised by *Salaam Bombay!* relates to the prevalence of poverty in the streets of Bombay (now Mumbai), a fact that has been known for years but that became significantly more visible internationally after the release of Nair's film; some of the same conversations about slum life were brought back into general conversation in Western media more recently with the release of a much more commercial film by Danny Boyle, *Slumdog Millionaire* (2008). A second social issue important in the film is prostitution; Bombay is undeniably India's prostitution capital, and the plight of the Nepali girl "Solasaal" (whose name translates as "Sixteen years"), might be emblematic of a second serious social problem alluded to in Nair's film. This is a theme that of course overlaps strongly with the theme of *India Cabaret*; Nair's 1985 documentary and 1988 fiction film are in fact

Salaam Bombay! "Solasaal" as she is first experiencing a brothel in Bombay.

quite directly complementary and even at times visually similar. As with the earlier *India Cabaret*, Nair's engagement with prostitution seems to suggest a dialogue with earlier Indian cinema. Several Indian film scholars have, in recent years, commented on the representation of prostitution in films like Guru Dutt's *Pyaasa*; Mazumdar, for instance, has noted that Dutt "evokes the metaphor of the prostitute to present a critique of the times" (Mazumdar 2006: 84). However, in contrast to what might be seen as melodramatic and metaphoric depictions of prostitution in classic Hindi cinema, Nair's approach in *Salaam Bombay!* seems matter-of-fact. Her prostitutes are not so much tragic metaphors as nontragic characters in a complex slum community—they are sex workers, not "fallen women."

Chaipau, an immigrant to Bombay, is emblematic of much of the city's population living either in substandard housing ("chawls"), illegal shantytowns, or on the streets. The rapidity of growth in the city is fueled in large part by poverty in the Indian countryside, a phenomenon described by a long series of scholars and writers from Jeremy Seabrook (1987) to Suketu Mehta (2004). For Seabrook, Mumbai is a "natural destination for those migrants of hope by the landless and dispossessed, not only from the state of Maharashtra . . . but from all over the country" (Seabrook 1987: 1). The issue of rural-to-urban mass migration has only worsened since Nair's film was made; the slum and pavement-dwelling population of Mumbai is, at the present writing, the world's largest (Davis 2006: 23), and the majority of slum dwellers continue to be internal migrants from India's economically devastated countryside. Such large-scale displacement of rural populations is also seen in many other large cities globally, both in the developing world and the West. But cities like Mumbai, Mexico City, and Shanghai have seen influx on a scale that exceeds that of New York, Paris, or London. The exploding "megacities" of the developing world have become so vast in terms of their raw demographics that they are impossible to know in any conventional way. Unfortunately, in Mumbai's case, the city's explosion into megacity status has been accompanied by an exponential growth in "megaslums," which continue to persist despite the most aggressive efforts by city planners to try and dislodge them. Though the characters in *Salaam Bombay!* are ignorant of all of this demographic and economic unrest, they are undeniably part of one of the most critical displacements of large masses of people happening anywhere in the world in the past thirty years. And though it predates the most recent wave of transformations of the face of Mumbai, *Salaam Bombay!* remains a salient starting point for any discussion of poverty in one of India's most stratified cities.

Alongside poverty and overlapping with it in some ways, Nair's film invokes the theme of prostitution in Bombay's red-light district, Kamathipura. Kamathipura is in fact a very old red-light district, dating back to the British Raj, when it was intentionally established by the British to service soldiers (Menen 2001). In more recent years, prostitution in India has received significant media attention, particularly with the spread of HIV/AIDS, but at the time of the filming of *Salaam Bombay!*, the red-light district was not a very widely discussed topic either in Indian or in international media representations of urban life in Bombay.[4] According to a recent study by Siddharth Kara, of the estimated one hundred thousand prostitutes working in Mumbai at the present moment, a disproportionate number are "trafficked" Nepali women, popular with Indian clients in large part because of their fair complexion and demure personalities (Kara 2009: 45–70). (Kara also raises an issue that was not quite on the surface at the time Nair made her film: approximately 70 percent of the Nepali prostitutes in Mumbai as of 2006 were found to be HIV positive.) Another study, by Jennifer Aengst, distinguishes between different modes of trafficking: "hard trafficking," which involves a family selling off a daughter into effective slavery, and "soft trafficking," where Nepali girls are lured to India of their own free will, with promises of legitimate work, only to be subsequently duped into prostitution (Aengst 2001). Though Nair does not develop the character's backstory, the plight of Solasaal in Nair's film is thus an image of a distressingly widespread species of human suffering occurring on a continuing basis in Mumbai.

An Important Predecessor: Luis Buñuel's *Los Olvidados*

One must be somewhat cautious about tracing influences and intertextual elements in Nair's films. As a kind of credo, Nair has insisted on fidelity to life before the discourse of cinema: "I always believed that movies have to be about life, not about other movies" (Badt 2004). That said, in terms of film history, it's important to be aware that *Salaam Bombay!* was not made in a vacuum. Nair and Taraporevala have both acknowledged a number of key influences and points of inspiration for *Salaam Bombay!*, including especially Luis Buñuel's *Los Olvidados* (1950), a film about street children in Mexico City. Here is what Nair wrote about *Los Olvidados* in 1986, before starting to film *Salaam Bombay!*:

> I have been reading Buñuel's script of *Los Olvidados* and I couldn't agree more with what Andre Bazin has to say about the depiction of the children in the film: "The greatness of this film can be grasped immediately when one has sensed that it never refers to moral categories. These children are beautiful not because they do good or evil, but because they are children even in crime and even in death. [. . .]" Although I do understand that in India—where injustice is so blatantly perpetrated, where disparities abound and the exploitative hierarchy prevails—it is difficult to reveal that the exploited are also human and also contain in them the seeds of evil and cruelty as the upper-class do—because the scales of society are so tipped against them—yet in my own heart I feel it difficult to shy away from this complexity of life and give in to the simplistic categories of good and evil. (Nair and Taraporevala 1989: 5–6)

These comments are prescient with regard to the complex moral universe that is as important in Nair's film as it is in Buñuel's. In both films, there is an innate sympathy with the street children—but they are certainly not depicted as saints. (That said, both films do have clear, identifiable villains, as well as accomplices who support the villains when they are on top, but not when they fall.) But perhaps even more important than Nair's meditation on morality here is the thematic choice of focus on children, who are, in Bazin's words, "beautiful not because they do good or evil, but because they are children even in crime and even in death."

Like the Italian neorealist classics *The Bicycle Thief* (1948) and *Roma, Open City* (1945), which were filmed entirely on location, *Los Olvidados* is shot in Mexico City, using mainly a nonprofessional cast. The location and the amateur appearance of the cast lends the film a degree of authenticity, which is heightened by Buñuel's merciless depictions of acts of violence, often against defenseless people on the fringes of Mexico City's society. Nair's *Salaam Bombay!* uses the same framework of a gang of boys, identified by various nicknames, and one girl. The girl in both films is sometimes with the boys and sometimes separate from them. Also, Nair and Buñuel's films share the theme of displacement with "Ojitos" (Little Eyes), an innocent child who has come from the countryside to Mexico City and who now has to find his own way amongst jaded and cynical peers, most of whom are already deeply involved in criminal activities. In Buñuel's film, Ojitos is a minor character, while in Nair's film, it is the protagonist, Chaipau, who is displaced, making the theme of internal displacement loom much larger on the whole. In both films, the innocent naïf from the countryside comes into contact with an older boy, who at times acts as a mentor but at other times simply terrorizes the younger boy.

While there are some clear similarities between Buñuel and Nair, the differences cannot be overlooked. For one thing, Buñuel's film has some moments of cinematic surrealism that seem somewhat idiosyncratic from a contemporary vantage point. Secondly, though Nair also uses nonprofessional actors, her film depicts their emotional lives much more intimately than Buñuel's does; perhaps Barry John's workshop enables the children to be more natural and vulnerable on camera than Buñuel's children are able to be. Third, Buñuel's film is, by a considerable degree, more violent than Nair's film is. Buñuel's children fight and indeed die on screen, sometimes with shocking violence. In *Salaam Bombay!* by contrast, there are some limited violent incidents in the early part of the film: Solasaal being slapped by the Nepali courier; and Chaipau first kicking the older boy in the chiller room, and then being scalded in return. But there is only one incident of irreversible violence in Nair's film, Chaipau's stabbing of Baba in the stairwell at the very end of *Salaam Bombay!* Buñuel's film, by contrast, features three visceral, brutal deaths, a rape, the stoning of a blind man, the terrorizing of a disabled beggar, a nonfatal street fight between two boys, and several scenes involving humans beating or killing animals.

The final difference between *Los Olvidados* and Nair's *Salaam Bombay!* is a formal one. At several points in his film, Buñuel uses voice-over "commentary" that has a didactic quality to it, linking it to classic, pre–cinéma vérité documentary films and news reels. By contrast, Nair's film eschews didactic voice-over in favor of complete immersion in the fictional world of the characters of her film, a reflection of cinéma vérité influence. With voice-over addressed directly to the viewer, Buñuel's film contains its own exterior, and this both orders the viewer's interpretation of the events depicted in the film and delimits those events within a moral framework dictated by the filmmaker. By contrast, a film without voice-over commentary is framed only by the film's beginning and ending and gives much more room to the viewer to interpret the film for himself or herself, along moral and other lines. Nair prefers the open-ended aesthetic of cinéma vérité (here transplanted to a fictional film). Thus, even controversial events in the film, such as Chaipau's stabbing of Baba at the film's climax as well as the final, ambiguous shot of Chaipau holding his spinning top, are not prejudged for the viewer.

Salaam Bombay! and the Critique of Commercial Hindi Cinema

Thus far we have been treating *Salaam Bombay!* in accordance with Nair's particular viewpoint, as a diasporic, cosmopolitan art film, having more in common with Italian neorealism or the French New Wave than with the Hindi "masala" films of the 1970s and '80s (sometimes referred to as "Bollywood"). But it is important to note that Nair's film is also deeply engaged in an active critical dialogue with commercial Hindi cinema. Indeed, both *Salaam Bombay!* and the film that is the subject of the next chapter, *Monsoon Wedding*, engage in a form of intimate critique of Bollywood—citing its influence but also subtly pushing back against its clichés. The Bollywood theme is prevalent both through direct citations and through sometimes minor and marginal allusions. For example, the first shot of Bombay itself that Nair presents to the viewer is of a busy street scene (near Victoria Terminus) lined by film posters.

Also, scattered throughout the film, there are at least half a dozen Hindi film songs that are quoted or bowdlerized in *Salaam Bombay!* Music plays from radios, and there is at least one scene that might be seen as analogous to the song-and-dance sequences that are so central to Bollywood films. This is where Chaipau delivers chai to Rekha's room during a heavy monsoon downpour, and he's then invited to spend time with Rekha and her young daughter Manju and sing and dance to "Mera Naam Chin Chin Chu," a classic Hindi song from the 1950s (first used in the film *Howrah Bridge*, where it was used as a kind of "item number" featuring Helen as a Chinese-origin dancer in Calcutta). Unlike the other direct Bollywood citation to *Mr. India*,

The Aesthetics of Disillusionment: *Salaam Bombay!*

Salaam Bombay! Film poster in Bombay.

a song-and-dance sequence to "Mera Naam Chin Chin Chu" plays out in *Salaam Bombay!* in its entirety. However, in contrast to the way this is done in commercial Hindi films, in Nair's film the scene is woven into the main diegesis of the film. Moreover, in contrast to the erotic nightclub setting that was the scene of the original song-and-dance sequence in *Howrah Bridge* in 1958, in Nair's appropriation of a Hindi song-and-dance number, the song features a mother, her daughter, and another young child; it is de-eroticized and if anything suggests the possibility of a new kinship group forming for the lost boy Chaipau (with Rekha emerging as a kind of mother figure and Manju as akin to a younger sister).

There are also two visually framed filmic citations within *Salaam Bombay!* from contemporary Bollywood films, one on a television screen showing a Hindi film playing on video in the Victoria Terminus train station in Bombay. The second citation is in an actual theater in Bombay, where the children go to see Shekhar Kapur's *Mr. India* during the very weeks that Nair was filming *Salaam Bombay!* (and in fact *Mr. India* did play widely at commercial Indian cinemas in the summer of 1987). Third, there are numerous references to commercial Hindi films and songs throughout the dialogue of *Salaam Bombay!*, suggesting that the characters in the film are almost constantly thinking about their life experience in terms of commercial film narratives and iconography. But *Salaam Bombay*'s engagement with "filmi" culture is deeply ambivalent, as the Bollywood image factory is sharply at odds with the gritty realities and limited opportunities for Bombay's street children. That Nair's street children know and enjoy Hindi films and films

Salaam Bombay! Unknown film on a monitor in Victoria Terminus, Bombay.

songs is realistic, but with the exception of the apparently joyful embrace of "Mera Naam Chin Chin Chu" described above, it is also clear that they are somewhat cynical about the iconic images that dominate their imaginations.

The very smallness of the opening of *Salaam Bombay!*, already briefly described, is Nair's first challenge to the conventions of the Hindi film industry. The choice of a circus closing down is clearly a gesture that might be analogous to Nair's directorial intentions: Nair shows us the circus not in the midst of its high illusionism and spectacle, but as its entertainments are being dismantled and put away (as arguably she will attempt to do filmically), to be tried in another town. Among the images Nair gives us of gaudy posters being rolled up and tents being dismantled, we see what appears to be a transgendered circus performer without her makeup on, folding clothes and placing them in a trunk in an undramatic, straightforward manner. This, then, is the first of the key anti-Bollywood themes in Nair's *Salaam Bombay!*—disillusionment. The realist aesthetic of *Salaam Bombay!* gives us an image of everyday life after the colorful and exotic performers have put away the tools of artifice and are instead grappling with their circumstances in the unfiltered light of day.

Some characters in Nair's film are better at handling the harshness of their reality than others. Krishna (Chaipau) turns out to be particularly good at handling his repeated disillusionments. The station clerk, handing him a ticket to Bombay, tells him to "go and become a movie star," but Krishna has no such dreams for himself. He has no hope of wealth, glamour, or power; he only clings to one remaining dream, namely the hope that he might return home to his mother. Meanwhile, the other characters around Chaipau all seem to be in the thrall of certain disabling illusions. Solasaal, the abducted Nepali girl, seems to believe Baba's promise that he will take her away from the brothel and protect her from the degradations faced by other sex workers. Chillum, for his own part, is caught up in another kind of illusion created by his growing addiction to heroin. Both ultimately will come to terms with "reality"—Chillum, when he dies, and Solasaal, when she is seen leaving the brothel in a client's car near the end of the film—on the verge of being inducted into the life of prostitution. Other characters are similarly in thrall to various illusions about their status and expectations and are similarly disillusioned over the course of the film. Rekha, Baba's girlfriend, hopes against hope that Baba will enable her and their daughter Manju to escape a life of prostitution and is continually disappointed. While she is protective of Manju, because of the nature of her work she must repeatedly expose Manju to age-inappropriate situations; she also lets her daughter roam the streets on her own for hours at a time. It's when she is on her own (with the boys—Chaipau and his friends) that Manju is picked up by the police and taken into custody. When Rekha loses her daughter to state custody in the second half of the film, she is no longer able to hold on to any illusion that her family can escape its situation.

Alongside the critique of Bollywood evidenced in the style and unsentimental approach to poverty in the thematic of Nair's film, there are more general issues relating to Bollywood in the background as well, including issues of the representation of sexuality, and the question of acting style. As will be discussed in our treatment of *Kama Sutra: A Tale of Love* in chapter 6, Nair has throughout her career fought against the censorship of her films in India and abroad. But her interest in challenging the representation of female sexuality on films goes back to her earliest documentaries, especially the film that immediately preceded *Salaam Bombay!* and inspired it in some ways, *India Cabaret*.

Salaam Bombay! continues the emphasis on the sex trade with its overall setting in the brothels of Kamathipura, Bombay. However, in contrast to *India Cabaret*, the overt sexuality in *Salaam Bombay!* is restrained; the focus is instead on the children who struggle to maintain innocence in the midst of a world of rampant exploitation. Outside of one provocative kiss between two consenting adults, *Salaam Bombay*'s sexuality is not particularly graphic, considering that much of it is filmed on location in a working brothel. The lives of prostitutes and madams are shown demystified and rather unglamorous; the occasional outlier is the life of Baba, the pimp. By contrast, commercial

Hindi films over the years have tended to feature courtesans and nautch girls, who are melodramatically posed as outside of the limits of bourgeois respectability without necessarily being prostitutes. Along these lines, one thinks of classic Hindi films like *Devdas* and *Pakeezah*, which depict their *tawaif* (courtesan) protagonists in beautiful, spacious settings constructed in the studio. Admittedly, commercial Hindi films have also depicted actual prostitutes (as in *Chetna* [1970]), but almost always with a strong dose of melodrama.

Though it does not depict any explicit sex acts on screen, *Salaam Bombay!* is nevertheless notable for featuring an involved lip-to-lip kiss between adults, Baba (Nana Patekar) and Rekha (Anita Kanwar). In the director's commentary on the *Salaam Bombay!* DVD, Nair describes how even this scene was controversial; the day after it was shot, the Bombay tabloids were abuzz with the news about the "racy" scene. Of course, it was not the first time a proper kiss had been shot in an Indian film; indeed, Indian film historians have indicated that the first lip-to-lip kiss in a commercial Hindi film was in 1933 between Devika Rani and Himanshu Rai (a real-life married couple, notably) in *Karma*. But particularly after independence, commercial Hindi cinema had become increasingly conservative. By the 1970s and '80s, on-screen kisses had completely disappeared from commercial Indian cinema, and Nair's film clearly crosses a line, not just with the on-screen kiss, but with the realistic and unsentimental depiction of the lives of prostitutes in a brothel.

The critique of Bollywood in Nair's film extends to acting style. Both in 1988 and again with the release of *Slumdog Millionaire* in 2008, there has been considerable discussion regarding why Bollywood refuses to confront the reality of Indian poverty. An earlier generation of "social" films from the 1950s, including Bimal Roy's classic *Do Bigha Zameen* (1953) and Raj Kapoor's *Shree 420* (1955), did reflect a serious interest in rural poverty, with relatively naturalistic acting styles. But just as often, and especially in the commercial films of the 1970s and '80s, the poverty figured in commercial Hindi cinema was generally unconvincing—the dirt is clearly painted on the star's face, and the handsome and well-built actor's skin tone and body type seem to suggest the poverty is just for show. The staging of poverty is nowhere more evident than in the aforementioned *Mr. India*, where Anil Kapoor plays a man who takes care of a group of implausibly well-fed and fair-skinned orphans in an implausibly spacious house.

Nair's decision to use actual street children as her main actors in *Salaam Bombay!* makes her depiction of poverty much more convincing.

Interestingly, while the young children cast in the film were all real street children, most of the older actors were professionals, though some were just starting out in their careers at the time they were cast for *Salaam Bombay!* There does not appear to have been much doubt about the need to do this with Raghubir Yadav (Chillum), Nana Patekar (Baba), and Anita Kanwar (Rekha)—nor has Nair ever expressed any ambivalence about dividing the cast between professionals and the nonprofessional street children. However, at least one of the characters, the Nepali prostitute Solasaal (Chandra Sharma) was at one point going to be played by an actual prostitute, as Nair recounted in an interview in 1988:

> In the red-light district, she found the appropriate brothel to use in her film, cast real prostitutes as prostitute extras, and auditioned a young Nepalese prostitute for the role of Solassal, the haunting teenage virgin who is forced into prostitution in the film. The real prostitute lost out to a neophyte actress. "The problem with the prostitute was that she looked like somebody who had seen the world," says Nair. "You just can't change people's eyes." (Hall 1988: B1)

The younger children cast in *Salaam Bombay!* also cannot hide their background from the camera. As Nair put it in another interview, "their faces and bodies were a kind of map of the journey that they had traveled" (Steritt 1988: 19).

But unlike the young woman who had actually worked as a prostitute in Kamathipura before auditioning for the film, the children demonstrate visually what might have been great suffering, but without appearing jaded. They are still children—and retain the beauty Bazin spoke of and Nair echoed in the passage quoted above. That said, in terms of performance, it would be a mistake to say that the choice to cast street children, the authenticity of the settings, and the workshop-created dialogue mean that the children aren't "acting." In fact, they are clearly operating from a script, and the realistic quality of their performances and the gritty quality of the locations do not lessen their effectiveness.

One of the key devices for deflating the potential to veer into melodrama is humor and play, and it's no accident that the children in Nair's film continue to play and joke around, even in the midst of immense suffering. We see this with Chaipau from the opening scenes, first in his amicable chatter with the caged bears, and then again as he waits in the paan walla shop. While he waits, he pulls out his spinning top and has a quick go-round. This small

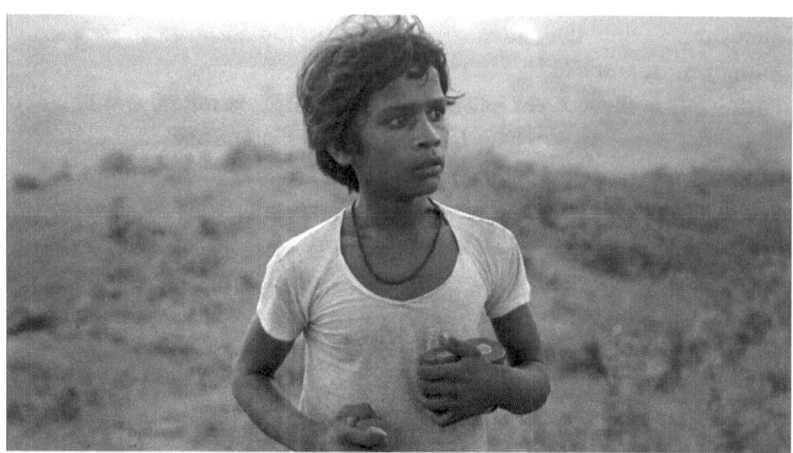

Salaam Bombay! Chaipau abandoned.

toy will stay with him as a talisman of his childhood and become Chaipau's main source of continuity with his past; he will retrieve the same top at the end of the film, holding it in his hands and slowly winding it up once again in the film's heartbreaking final scene.

Nair addresses the issue of acting style several times in her published diaries from the filming of *Salaam Bombay!* This is one of the most unusual aspects in the filming of *Salaam Bombay!*, so it seems appropriate to quote at length from some of the documents surrounding the acting workshop with Barry John and the street children. Here, for instance, is a description of the basic approach, written by Nilita Vachani:

> We spent two weeks recruiting boys in the age group of eight to seventeen from the pavements, slums and railway stations. On the first few days of the workshop, we had no less than 130 boys on our hands—eager, curious, restless, bored, self-conscious, even disruptive. From the chaos of the early days until the present time when the workshop has entered its fourth week, the progress made with the children has been very encouraging. We now work with nineteen spirited and expressive actors in an environment that is certainly unparalleled in the Indian cultural context, one based on affection and trust, that crosses boundaries of class, community, age and sex, and involves a mutual growth and development. (Nair and Taraporevala 1989: 35)

In her essay on the workshop, with which she was also involved, Vachani describes how the workshop, over a period of weeks, helped the children develop the basic tools of acting. They began with basic physical exercises and then moved on to introducing ideas of character and motivation, often using improvised mimed performances to help the children pay attention to physical gestures and body language. But soon, the workshop directors were encouraging the children to improvise scenes based on both their own life experiences and the plot and characters of the first working draft of the film script developed by Sooni Taraporevala:

> By the third week of the workshop, we felt that the children were ready for directed performances more closely related to the filmscript. . . . With the younger kids, we began doing improvisations loosely based on Chaipau's character. With the older kids we started doing loose improvisations based on the gang and its activities. . . . On the day of the screen-test, the success of the workshop was self-evident. The professional actors present on the day were overwhelmed by the children's performances. Shafiq, a ten-year old boy (who was selected as the protagonist) gave a powerful performance in a scene where Chaipau hands Solasaal a cup of tea, and she, enraged and helpless in her captivity, kicks the glass. Shafiq's awe-struck surrender to her beauty, the manner in which he implored her to drink tea, his shock at the kick, followed by irritation, childish petulance then quick forgiveness, were remarkable to witness. (Nair and Taraporevala 1989: 38–39)

Needless to say, many of the scenes rehearsed, often improvisationally, by the actors' workshop, would become some of the most memorable scenes in Nair's finished film. The scene involving Chaipau, Solasaal, and the spilled chai is one of the most powerful early hints in *Salaam Bombay!* of the selflessness and resilience of Chaipau's character.

Here is an example of Nair's own thoughts from early in the process, regarding her goals for the workshop. Though the children were in effect ignorant of acting methods, they were certainly not illiterate when it came to films or film acting in general. Indeed, their broad exposure to the acting style characteristic of Bollywood films was in some ways part of the problem:

> So slowly, "acting" has become a bad word with our children. For all of us in India, and especially for the children, going to Indian movies

is the only cheap form of entertainment available. Our "actors" have been bred on at least two to three-hour-long Indian movies daily; they know dialogues and songs of Indian movies backwards, always incorporating the latest star's mannerisms and speech into their own behaviour. I know that *this film* is going to be a total departure from this formula, knowing that no matter who I cast, I will be working completely against the stereotype of what is commonly known as "acting" in Indian cinema. (Nair and Taraporevala 1989: 42)

True to Nair's characterization, the children in *Salaam Bombay!* are constantly singing verses from Hindi film songs, often bowdlerizing them somewhat in the process. The most memorable is Chillum's twist on the famous song from the classic film *Aradhana*, "Mere sapno ki rani, kab ayegi tu?" (Queen of my dreams, when will you come?), which in Chillum's rendition becomes, "Mere sapno ki *randi*, kab ayegi tu?" (Whore of my dreams, when will you come?). Chillum's tweak of one of the best-loved songs from Hindi films reflects quite directly Nair's irreverent ethos with regard to commercial Hindi film culture. Her characters love and appreciate the raw material of "*filmi*" culture, but they render it in terms that are appropriate to their own, sometimes debased circumstances.

Perhaps the most direct and extensive citation of commercial Hindi cinema in *Salaam Bombay!* is to the film mentioned above, *Mr. India*, directed by Shekhar Kapur. First, the star actress of the film, Sridevi, is briefly mentioned in the card-playing scene by one of the boys; Salim kisses a card with her image on the back and calls out to her image, "Are meri Sridevi, sapno ki rani . . ." A few minutes later, the boys are seen in a cinema hall itself, watching *Mr. India*—an insufferably silly (but popular) song, "Hawa Hawaii," which features Sridevi again, in an absurd series of outfits, with backup dancers in nonsensical blackface. The boys, led by Koyla, are thoroughly entertained; Koyla in particular emulates Sridevi's dance mannerisms and *tumka*s with gusto, much to the annoyance of other more middle-class patrons sitting nearby.

There is an irony in this homage to a contemporary Bollywood film that might not be evident from this brief scene. In fact, *Mr. India* contains a plot that initially resembles that of *Salaam Bombay!*—a former orphan (Anil Kapoor) dedicates his life to looking after orphaned children and is hunted by an international criminal. The story diverges significantly, of course, as a supernatural element is introduced (an invisibility machine), as well as an element of naked jingoism designed to emulate Hollywood superhero movies like *Superman* (the protagonist, acting under invisibility, calls himself "Mr. India"). The two films share a concern for underprivileged children, but while Kapur's representation of them entails a clearly polarized world—and especially, a heroic "savior" who uses a supernatural device to enable him to defend the children—Nair's street children do not appear to have any adults consistently looking after them. They suffer indignity after indignity. In *Salaam Bombay!* the boys run the risk of ending up like Chillum, addicted to drugs; for girls, there are few options other than prostitution. There is no virtuous appearance from "Mr. India"; if the children are ever going to find a way to improve their circumstances, they have to take charge of their own destinies—as Chaipau does in the final scene when he stabs Baba, the closest thing he has to a father figure at that point in his life.

At the very end of the film, after killing Baba, Chaipau escapes the brothel area with Rekha. But they are immediately thrown into the chaos and tumult of the Ganapati Festival, with tens of thousands of devotees thronging the streets of Bombay parading massive icons of the Hindu God Ganesh. They are then separated in the crowd with no obvious way to find one another again. In the final shot of the film, we see Chaipau again sitting on the side of a road. The spinning top that we had seen him holding earlier in the film—his apparent sole child's toy also his only symbolic link to his past. While Nair's film by and large eschews overt symbolism in favor of documentary realism, it's hard to escape the conclusion that the spinning top and Chaipau's final long gaze at the camera are not in some way symbolic. The spinning top might be seen as representing his childhood, to which he is still attached despite the very adult situations he has been in since coming to Bombay (not the least of which being his just having murdered an adult man by stabbing him to death). The top also has what might be seen as ontological significance: it could be interpreted as representing human energy and capacity for action. Chaipau has just expended significant energy and performed a meaningful action and seems thoroughly spent by the ordeal he has just been through. And yet, at the very end we see him slowly and methodically rewinding the string around the top as he stares at the camera.

The meaning of Chaipau's final, long gaze at the camera might also merit a brief word. This final stare is highly ambiguous, with some viewers interpreting Chaipau as defeated (one student in a class where I taught the film interpreted Chaipau's look as almost suicidal), while others have seen him as defiant: he's survived, and he'll survive the next challenge as well. Either way, there might be an additional dimension to this final gaze—it's a gaze not just at the camera, but, in a metatheatrical shattering of the fourth wall, at the viewer herself. Whether defeated or defiant, it seems fair to interpret that final gaze as an address to the viewer (presumably middle-class or above) to respond to the moral challenge posed by the extremity of the suffering in the slums of cities like Bombay. It may be that the final disposition of Chaipau is less important than the final disposition of the viewer, who may be inclined to act on what she's learned through viewing the film—or not.

Audience and Reception: What Is an "Indian" Film?

While *Salaam Bombay!* was critically very well received by Western critics, it was the source of some controversy amongst Indian critics at the time of its release. The dynamic is perhaps familiar by now, as we've seen versions of this controversy with numerous other films since. What responsibility does an Indian filmmaker have in depicting Indian life to Western audiences? Should the seamier sides of Indian life be downplayed in favor of foregrounding middle-class Indians, or can the risk be taken of reinforcing stereotypes of India as first and foremost a site of poverty, disease, and misery? To explore that debate, it might be helpful to start with Mira Nair's defense of *Salaam Bombay!* from attacks from other Indian viewers, including the actor Amitabh Bachchan:

> Of course there are the usual vociferous attacks, some that I've read myself, others that I hear of, all based on the popular NRI [non-resident Indian] theme—how can you live where you live and have empathy with Bombay's street-folk—or that I've made a Western package, selling India's greatest wealth—poverty—to the international scene. These I should be used to, these notions that used to keep me up at nights in mental frustration throughout the exhibition of *India Cabaret* in 1986, and here they are again, rearing their predictable, myopic, envy-filled anything-to-tear-a-success-down heads under the guise of a mediocre thoroughbred, so-called nationalism. This is not a forum where I need to defend myself, my address and my passions—I have done enough in person—but finally, as far as *Salaam Bombay!* is concerned, the Indian box-office numbers are enough defence. Sooni and I conceived it primarily for an Indian audience, and here we have them in droves ... There is no more for me to say. With due respect to Amitabh Bachchan, who I think is a fine actor, the children and actors of *SB!* are outdoing his latest *Ganga Jamuna*

Saraswati and the Indian audience is proving itself to be hungry for films of quality, films whose skin they get under, films which make them feel and see a situation, usually described as so ordinary and boring, filled with so much life and *musti* and struggle. (Nair and Taraporevala 1989: 80–81)

Nair's defense of the film using box-office numbers might seem too simple, but in fact it is effective evidence on this point. Critics, film distributors and government censor-board bureaucrats might make any manner of presumptions about what Indian film viewers want to see (or should be allowed to see), but virtually no one traditionally involved in judging the average Indian film viewer could actually be described himself as an "average" viewer. The "average viewer" tends to be interpolated out of the discussion; it might not be inaccurate to say that, like Gayatri Spivak's "subaltern," she cannot speak, at least not directly (one should keep in mind that this was before the advent of social media). The one way in which, at least during the 1980s, we could see evidence of the viability of a certain film could then be through its popular, commercial reception.

Besides Amitabh Bachchan, *Salaam Bombay!* has admittedly been criticized by serious scholars of Indian cinema, including Jyotika Virdi and Poonam Arora. Let us here respond specifically to Jyotika Virdi, whose 1992 essay in *Jump Cut*, "*Salaam Bombay!* (Mis)representing Child Labor," raises several important issues, including 1) what Virdi sees as a lack of "analytical" rigor, particularly along the lines of class relations and the exploitation of labor by capital, 2) what Virdi perceives as a lack of cultural or historical specificity, and 3) Nair's positioning as a diasporic Indian from an elite background, "exploiting" her subjects in order to earn praise and cultural capital abroad. On the third point, Virdi argues as follows: "Had Nair situated herself, her own relation to the children, the factors that made her relation and intervention possible and the areas where her access to their lives and situation was impossible due to her specific subject position, the film would have been built on a much more honest and open account" (Virdi 1992). This at least seems fair; neither Nair nor Taraporevala come from the same class background as the children who are the subjects of their film, though most Western viewers of *Salaam Bombay!* did not recognize the implications of India's class division. Still, arguably if one reads Nair's film, as we have done, alongside the published diaries that describe the production process, the positioning becomes more transparent, as do the strategies by which Nair and Taraporevala attempted to circumvent the limits of their own respective backgrounds. One's response to the first two points depends to a great extent on one's ideological orientation. Arguably, the historical and cultural specificity are quite strong in Nair's film, and based on empirical realities: the "chai boy" who became Chaipau was based on an actual boy whom Nair met while making *India Cabaret*; the kidnapped Nepali teen forced into prostitution is based on a widespread phenomenon of trafficked Nepali women in the sex industry in India; and "Mere Sapno ki Randi" and other Bollywood reference points are quite specific to the Indian context (and likely to be totally unintelligible to viewers unfamiliar with Hindi film songs). Finally, Virdi is critical of Nair for capitalizing on the success of the film to propel her own career forward in the American film industry. While Nair has indeed achieved success as an international director, I differ with Virdi as to its implications. Nair's success as a diasporic filmmaker whose career began with a focus on poverty and injustice within India aligns her fairly closely with a tradition of diasporic postcolonial writers and intellectuals mentioned in the introductory chapter above—from Gayatri Spivak to Salman Rushdie (and yes, such a career trajectory has been criticized by theorists like Arif Dirlik—who has criticized the fetishizing of the "postcolonial aura" around certain South Asian literary stars). But "successful diasporic intellectual" is also a label that, Virdi admits at the end of her essay, might well fit Virdi herself ("We [Nair and Virdi] have a common class background and cultural apparatus that enable us to arrive on the shores of this country to pursue academic and artistic interests"). If authenticity is measured by the filmmaker's postal address or tenure status in a North American university, we may all be permanently condemned to a Mobius strip of circular disparagement and disqualification. In this chapter on *Salaam Bombay!*, I hope I have shown that Nair's film, both textually and paratextually, has strengths that supersede such a critique. The audience *Salaam Bombay!* aims to address is truly international—with Nair paying especially close attention to its Indian reception. The film is "diasporic" for the reasons outlined above, but for Nair the transnational status is enabling rather than disqualifying. Her film aimed to change the way Indian cinema was thought of internationally, while also changing the way poverty might be represented *within* Indian cinema.

Chapter 4

A TALE OF TWO "CHUNARIS"

The Critique of Bollywood in *Monsoon Wedding* (2001)

While *Monsoon Wedding* is filmed entirely on location in India, I interpret it as a film that thematizes diaspora and aligns quite closely with the diaspora vérité concept I described in the first chapter—it is, in essence, a film that explores, in a documentary realist style, the influence of the Indian diaspora on the rapidly transforming "home" culture of urban India. The frame for the plot is a wedding within a Punjabi family with members who are currently based in the United States, Australia, and the United Arab Emirates (UAE). Hemant, the groom, has flown in from Houston, where he works in IT, and soon intends to go back there with his new bride, Aditi. Indeed, while many viewers have understood *Monsoon Wedding* as primarily focused on the cosmopolitan, globalizing culture of urban India, we will argue below that a key part of that new Indian cosmopolitanism is an internalization of values brought back from abroad by diasporic Indians. Part of the internalization of the diaspora is financial—the money represented by Hemant's American software job as well as the wealth displayed by the abusive US-based uncle Tej Puri—give them outsized influence over their Indian relatives. But another sign of diasporic influence is in the interplay of "domestic" and "Western" values that are at play in connection with the debates about gender relations that are the real core of *Monsoon Wedding*; some of these debates are connected to characters who have been abroad, while others are framed as purely domestic. However, before we unpack these themes in *Monsoon Wedding* in greater depth, it seems important to introduce the film with a brief description of its similarities and differences to *Salaam Bombay!*

From *Salaam Bombay!* to *Monsoon Wedding*

Between *Salaam Bombay!* (1988) and *Monsoon Wedding* (2001) is a very consequential period in Nair's filmmaking career, a time during which the filmmaker undergoes substantial changes. Some of those changes will become clearer as we explore some of the intermediary films in subsequent chapters. However, these two particular films—which are also probably Nair's two most influential works to date—do have a surprising number of commonalities that might be worth briefly enumerating. For one thing, they are both set in India itself (many of Nair's films from the 1990s were set in the US or transnational settings). And while *Monsoon Wedding* revolves around the stories of comfortable middle-class people—in contrast to the street children of *Salaam Bombay!*—Nair's later film does have working-class characters in some key roles. One also sees marked similarities in the production of the two films: both *Monsoon Wedding* and *Salaam Bombay!* were made quickly, with small budgets, and with considerable reliance on nonprofessional actors. After making *Salaam Bombay!*, Nair credited the cinéma vérité movement for paving the way for this method; with *Monsoon Wedding*, she credited the more recent Dogme 95 movement associated with Lars von Trier (Nair 2002a: 14). Admittedly, Nair does use some professional actors in *Monsoon Wedding*, but most of even the professional actors in the cast (outside of veteran Bollywood stars like Naseeruddin Shah and Roshan Seth) were likely to be unfamiliar to mainstream viewers.

Yet another key similarity in the production of the two films is in their acting processes: Nair decided to use actors' workshops held before filming began to create a sense of naturalism amongst her actors. The workshop for *Salaam Bombay!* took place over nearly two months and was used by Nair as a way of turning poor street children into compelling film actors. The workshop Nair organized for *Monsoon Wedding* was much shorter, only two weeks in duration, but in her DVD commentary for the film, Nair credits the work the various actors did together in rehearsals off camera (as well as other bonding experiences, such as group yoga) for creating a sense of intimacy and spontaneity amongst the cast.

Admittedly, despite the many similarities in the construction of the two films, *Monsoon Wedding* is a different kind of film than *Salaam Bombay!*, with many of the main characters members of an evidently well-fed and comfortably bourgeois milieu in Delhi, while some are diasporic Indians returning home for Aditi and Hemant's "monsoon wedding" (this

NRI-returnee group includes the groom, Hemant, himself). While *Salaam Bombay!* unsentimentally depicts and humanizes India's poverty, *Monsoon Wedding* has been described by Nair as a more "personal" film about the multilingual middle-class Punjabi community in which she herself was raised. Nair's thematic shift towards a bourgeois milieu in her more recent films is undeniable, though as we shall see, her film is in fact socially and politically engaged. At its center are arguments related to changing class relations, changing gender and sexual norms in Indian society, and the collapse of the traditional censorship regime in the Indian media.

Finally, it should be noted that both films enjoyed strong critical reception as well as broad commercial success both within India and abroad. In terms of film awards, Nair did not repeat her 1988 success at Cannes with *Monsoon Wedding*, nor was the film nominated for an Academy Award—but *Monsoon Wedding* did win Nair the prestigious Golden Lion Award at the Venice Film Festival, the first Indian film since Satyajit Ray's *The Unvanquished* to win the prize; Nair was also only the second woman in history to win that prize. Commercially, *Monsoon Wedding* brought in $14 million at the US box office after being filmed for $1 million. *Monsoon Wedding* was also a major commercial and critical success throughout Europe, the Middle East, and Latin America, as well as in India itself.

Most importantly for our purposes in this study, *Monsoon Wedding* evinces a powerful feminist sensibility that is also deeply connected to its stylistic critique of the aesthetic values of commercial Hindi cinema (Bollywood). This feminist critique of Bollywood can be seen in the design of *Monsoon Wedding*'s various plot arcs as well as in the way the filmmaker approaches the defining feature of Bollywood cinema, namely the song-and-dance sequence. Though *Monsoon Wedding* has been cited by recent film critics as a "crossover" film associated with Bollywood family musicals (and Nair's own comments and approach to marketing the film have admittedly contributed to this perception; see Nair 2002c), through a comparative visual analysis of a prominent musical sequence in the film against the commercial Hindi film it cites (*Biwi No. 1*), I will argue that in fact Nair retains important critical distance from the conventions and style of commercial Hindi cinema. In part, her critique of Bollywood can be seen as an artifact of her feminism, but in many ways, it is also inflected by her status as a diasporic filmmaker.

Monsoon Wedding as a Diaspora Film

Though it is, like *Salaam Bombay!*, physically set in India, Nair's *Monsoon Wedding* is explicitly and consistently preoccupied with the theme of diaspora, with several key characters in the extended family unit at the center of the film living abroad, some in the United States and others in Australia or Dubai. Even the film's central romantic plot involves a young man, Hemant, who lives in Houston and a woman, Aditi, who lives in Delhi—and the major consequence of their marriage, if successfully executed, will be Aditi's emigration. Interestingly, the diasporic characters in the film have access to wealth and dynamism that some of the film's India-based characters seem to lack, though in the end this diasporic advantage in *Monsoon Wedding* seems to be offset by a "centered" (though not stationary) vision of Indian culture, structured largely around family life. The film also suggests that cultural identity and family relationships can continue to remain strong despite geographic distance, even if the relations within diasporic communities and across generational divides are not always harmonious; geographical dispersal, in other words, does not necessarily lead to social fragmentation.

The diasporic framing I am proposing is particularly suggestive with respect to *Monsoon Wedding* because of the opportunity it gives us as viewers—and Nair as a filmmaker—to explore the intense dialogue between ideas of home and abroad that has been occurring in postliberalization India. The "homing desire" of South Asian diasporic culture that theorist Avtar Brah mentions (see chapter 1) is in full evidence in *Monsoon Wedding*; indeed, as the product of a diasporic filmmaker, the film as a whole might be taken as evidence of Nair's own "homing desire."

In *Monsoon Wedding* the diasporic "homing desire" leads us to a consideration of the ways in which the diaspora has changed Indian society internally. Since the early 1990s, the growing consciousness of the diaspora—and a broader, general turn towards cosmopolitanism and transnational engagement, has led to some significant transformations of "home" culture. Large numbers of Indian families, especially in southern India, have family members who are working and living abroad. Commercial films are often made with a concern for diaspora consumers. More broadly, globalization and liberalization have led to an increased engagement with transnational capital, imported goods, and the transnational market in ideas (what Arjun Appadurai might call the "ideascape"); these are also very much in evidence in *Monsoon Wedding*.

A brief historical overview may be in order for readers unfamiliar with developments in contemporary India. After facing a grave economic crisis in 1990, India's leadership embarked on a program of economic liberalization, opening the largely state-controlled Indian economy to foreign investment, and privatizing some government ventures (Kamdar 2007: 54). Though liberalization was controversial at the time—it represented a departure from the essentially socialist economic model that was introduced in India after independence by Jawarhalal Nehru—it quickly bore results. By the mid-1990s, India's gross domestic product was growing at close to 10 percent a year (Kamdar 2007: 43), after limping along for decades at much slower rates. Though poverty remains real and quite widespread (as Mira Kamdar points out, 40 percent of the world's population living below the poverty line are in India, and six hundred million Indians live on two dollars a day or less), since the 1990s, the segment of the Indian middle class has expanded by a considerable margin, bringing millions of formerly poor people into the global economy. Journalists and economists have charted the emergence of a new entrepreneurial spirit, encouraging people who might have earlier simply accepted poverty as their lot in life to start small businesses and chart a path of upward mobility through education.

In the DVD commentary to *Monsoon Wedding* and in several interviews, Nair mentions the new wealth being created by the economic growth in the Indian middle classes in Delhi as an influence on her film. This new wealth had the greatest benefit for the highly educated upper middle class, but new opportunities also appeared for the lower middle class, represented in the film by Nair's character, P. K. Dubey (Vijay Raaz). Dubey's obsessive use of his mobile phone emblematizes the cultural and economic shift that had begun to transform Indian society in the late 1990s. Though he comes from a modest background, the successful business he has started as a wedding organizer changes fundamentally how Dubey relates to his ostensible superiors in the Verma family. Where an earlier generation of wedding planners might have been deferential to an established, English-speaking family like the Vermas, in Nair's new India, Dubey drives a hard bargain—a scenario that is somewhat unsettling to his client, Lalit Verma (Naseeruddin Shah).

The rapid emergence of a new moneyed class, and the shift in relations between classes, does not mean that everybody is necessarily moving up at the same rate. The Vermas, who are in the textile export business, are still well-off by Indian standards, with an impressive home. On the other hand,

Monsoon Wedding. Dubey on the scaffolding.

Lalit Verma remains a rather traditional kind of businessman, who at one point has an argument with his wife regarding his continued resistance to using a computer; meanwhile, his wedding organizer Dubey, despite his working-class background, is an avid mobile phone user who is experimenting with email and the internet. In an early scene played for comedy, we see Dubey climbing scaffolding outside the Verma house to improve his cellular reception. As he climbs, he continues to loudly converse with a business colleague, never missing a beat. Lalit Verma, meanwhile, is struggling to pay the rapidly escalating bills for his daughter's wedding and has to borrow a significant amount of money from a close friend to pay for waterproof covering for the outdoor tents at his daughter's wedding reception. He also cannot afford to pay for his adopted daughter's potential education in the US at a prestigious university and accepts with only very minor resistance his brother Tej's offer to cover her expenses. The Vermas, in short, may be part of a highly privileged urban class in New Delhi, but that does not necessarily mean they are comfortable with the rising costs of their cosmopolitan lifestyle.

Alongside the liberalization of the economy, urban India has seen a marked liberalization in cultural values, especially with regard to sexuality, and these changes have been reflected in the exploding entertainment sector. With the film industry, the biggest change occurred in 1998 when the Indian government granted the film industry official "industry" status, an important step on the road to regularizing the economic underpinnings of the business (through the 1990s, commercial Hindi cinema is thought to have been largely funded by untaxed "black money" [Ganti 2004: 50–51]). The changes also affected television quite directly; until 1991 India had only one television channel, the state-owned and managed Doordarshan (Kamdar 2007: 52). Largely through satellite companies (StarTV) and cable networks, dozens—indeed, hundreds—of new private channels have emerged since then, completely revolutionizing the television landscape (Rajagopal 2009: 4). With the changes came a growing interest on Indian television for handling controversial or taboo topics, marking a sharp contrast to the more staid topics and themes characteristic of preliberalization, government-run television programming.

The diversity of television content is partly reflected in *Monsoon Wedding* in Ishaan's fascination with daytime cooking shows, a relatively new phenomenon on Indian television as of the late 1990s (now of course these shows are much more commonplace). The changing culture of Indian television is also thematized in the early scene where Aditi witnesses her lover interviewing a series of guests regarding the issue of censorship in the media for a television talk show.

The focus on censorship on television in Nair's film is probably no accident. Given her censorship battles over *Kama Sutra* just prior to this film (a subject that will be examined in chapter 6), it seems hard to avoid reading the scene as a pointed critique of the Indian film censor board's approach to handling adult material. The dialogue in the scene relating to censorship might be worth reproducing, at least in part, here. The scene is a fictional television talk show called *Delhi.com*:

> COMMENTATOR 1: Just because India has gone global, should we embrace everything? What about our ancient culture? Our tradition? Our values? You are saying censorship is unnecessary, absolutely unnecessary.
> MODERATOR: What is your response, Mr. Bhatt?
> COMMENTATOR 2: Let's take the example of America—
> COMMENTATOR 1: This is not America! This is India.
> COMMENTATOR 3: [In Hindi]: Look, these are our laws. First change the constitution, then change censorship.
> COMMENTATOR 2: [In Hindi]: What, do you think, because you wear handloom cloth and speak in Hindi, that you represent the common man? (Nair, *Monsoon Wedding*, 2001)

Monsoon Wedding. Delhi.com panelists.

It's highly revealing that the debate over censorship here is framed as a debate between a "domestic" (conservative) idea of representation and a "foreign" (liberal) model where censorship is not considered necessary. While Indian political discourse has a venerable tradition of rejecting foreign influence (note the allusion to Gandhian homespun clothing in the passage above), here commentator 2 is pushing back against that kind of nativist conservatism. In a postliberalization culture and in light of growing transnationalism (again, reflected in the increased movement of both people and ideas), the turn to Indian tradition is no longer a sufficient defense of a censorship regime that seems increasingly out of step with middle-class urban Indian values.

After this interchange, the moderator asks a professional "dubbist" to come in and recite dialogue from a recent television program. The dialogue is obviously pornographic as performed, though without mention of specific sexual acts and without profanity. Some panelists are embarrassed by the dialogue and performance, while commentator 2 shrugs his shoulders: "What's the big deal?" The audience in the studio laughs, at least partly at the spectacle of a middle-aged, conservatively dressed woman (who would typically be figured as asexual on Indian television and in Hindi films) performing such clearly sexualized dialogue.

The double standard around sexuality comes up again later in the film, when Aditi and her lover, Vikram, the moderator of this same television program, are harassed by the police in the middle of night, as they are "parked." Nair has this to say about this scene:

Monsoon Wedding. Dubber flouting censorship frameworks.

Almost everybody growing up in Delhi has had this nasty humiliation at the hands of the cops. The nasty pleasure that the police take in observing public affection, and then trying to take you to jail for it. It's a terrible perversity in Indian life. (Nair, *Monsoon Wedding*, 2001, DVD director's commentary)

The harassment of artists at the hands of the censor board in television and film and the harassment of everyday people at hands of the police are analogous to one another. Neither succeeds in preventing supposedly "forbidden" acts from occurring, but the police remain empowered all the same to make life extremely unpleasant for couples expressing any degree of public affection. And this "perversity" has not improved very much, even in the "new" India.

The diasporic and global influence is also felt quite powerfully in *Monsoon Wedding* at the level of language. Just as globalization has put pressure on questions of the censorship of sexuality in the Indian media, it has also impacted the way urban middle-class Indians speak—what languages they use and the contexts in which they use them. This aspect of globalization too is richly and sensitively explored in *Monsoon Wedding* as Nair's characters fluidly shift between several languages in various scenes. As educated, well-off Punjabis, the Vermas know several languages and seamlessly move between Hindi, Punjabi, and English. The language spoken at a given instant depends on who the listeners are, the level of intimacy, and what is to be expressed. English and Hindi are "public" languages, which the main characters use easily to communicate with one another as well as with strangers and business associates. So Lalit Verma speaks Hindi when negotiating prices with P. K. Dubey. Family members also generally use Hindi when speaking with Alice, the servant and cook in the household (she is identified at one point as coming from the Hindi-speaking state of Bihar in north-central India). Most of the dialogue amongst the Vermas themselves is in English. Some family members reside abroad, in the Middle East (the United Arab Emirates), the United States, and Australia, and for the diasporic members of the extended family English has become a comfortable medium. However, since the family is ethnolinguistically Punjabi, they continue to reserve the language for intimate conversation amongst family, especially on matters relating to emotional life; it is also the language spoken most comfortably by the oldest generation (the grandmother) of the Vermas. When Pimmi Verma chastises her son, Varun (Ishaan Nair), about his tardiness in getting ready, she teases him with affectionate words in Punjabi. Analogously, when Tej Puri, Lalit Verma's brother-in-law, offers to pay Ria Verma's educational expenses so she can go to the US to study creative writing, Lalit expresses his gratitude in Punjabi. And Lalit again uses Punjabi when speaking to his wife at a moment of crisis, trying to sort out how to respond to the revelation that his brother-in-law sexually molested Ria when she was a young girl and has now begun to do the same with Aliya, the youngest child in the family.

A Tale of Two "Chunaris": The Question of Bollywood, and Nair versus Dhawan

As the above discussions indicate, urban India became increasingly globalized and cosmopolitan beginning in the 1990s, and many aspects of these changes are explored in Nair's *Monsoon Wedding*. Commercial Hindi cinema—popularly known as "Bollywood"—has also been globalizing, albeit unevenly. Bollywood movies had long filmed song sequences in international locations (often without specifying the exact setting); beginning in the 1990s and 2000s, however, this pattern was intensified. A growing number of commercial Hindi films began to be filmed abroad, in their entirety, with the intent of reaching a combination of domestic Indian and South Asian diaspora audiences (a recent example might be *Dhoom 3*, which was filmed entirely in Chicago). And film critics who study Bollywood cinema have certainly taken notice; an important recent anthology has explored this topic (see Gopal and Moorti 2008).

That said, while settings and audiences have gone global, in terms of their formal and narrative structures (i.e., the continued prevalence of extradiegetic song-and-dance sequences and the intense reliance on melodrama), and especially their representation of gender and sexuality, Bollywood movies have been a bit slower to change. As of 2001, when *Monsoon Wedding* was made, the globalization of locales was well underway, but formally Bollywood film culture had remained relatively intact. (Since then, formal changes too have entered into mainstream Bollywood movies like *Queen* [2014] and *Piku* [2015]; and the "multiplex" niche market which has nurtured offbeat and nontraditional films has become even more vibrant.) In comments she made since the release of *Monsoon Wedding*, Mira Nair has been quite vocal in expressing a degree of admiration for commercial Indian cinema—an enthusiasm she did not evince earlier in her career (see chapter 3 on *Salaam Bombay!*). That said, Nair also continues to assert, insistently, the difference in her own approach:

> I love Bollywood films, I love commercial Indian films, which have these great song sequences. I wanted to do my own kind of song sequence in Monsoon Wedding. I come from a documentary tradition, and the great thing about that is that authenticity and real life become my treasure, become my inspiration. (Nair, *Monsoon Wedding*, 2001, DVD director's commentary)

With its emphasis on musical soundtrack, romantic theme, and a climactic song-and-dance sequence, *Monsoon Wedding* is without a doubt Nair's most Bollywood-friendly film, but it is all the same carefully designed to subvert Bollywood conventions in numerous ways. As her comments above illustrate, Nair recognizes and even embraces the role commercial Indian films play in everyday life, including especially the song sequences. But she continues to emphasize "authenticity and real life" over commercial Hindi film's stylization and melodrama. In various interviews conducted after the film, Nair repeats versions of this distinction: she acknowledges the permeation of Bollywood film culture in the everyday lives of middle-class Indians, and incorporates that into the film. But her aim is to capture that as "what is happening in our daily lives"—to make what she calls "homemade Bollywood" (Nair 2002b), and this in itself is a kind of subversion.

As *Monsoon Wedding* seems, superficially, to take an affectionate attitude toward commercial Hindi cinema, it has not been uncommon for reviewers or film critics and theorists to interpret it as itself a *part* of commercial Indian cinema, especially in light of the transformative impact of wedding-oriented romantic dramas in the 1990s, such as *Huma Aapke Hain Kaun* (1994) and *Dilwale Dulhania Le Jayenge* (1995). Some, such as Ravi Vasudevan, have suggested that contextualizing *Monsoon Wedding* this way might be, at least in part, a question of marketing, as when he refers to her appropriation of the "format of the brand" of the family multistarrer (Vasudevan 2010: 338). And Sangita Gopal, for her part, includes a discussion of *Monsoon Wedding* in a chapter on the changing role of music in the "New Bollywood." Gopal argues that the song and dance sequences, considered staples in classic Hindi cinema, have declined in number in recent films favor of showstopping "item numbers," and music that is used more diegetically in many recent Hindi films. Gopal is aware of the challenge of linking *Monsoon Wedding* to Bollywood, despite Nair's own apparent eagerness to allow the term:

> Mira Nair refers to *Monsoon Wedding* as a "Bollywood musical in my own terms." How does this film without a single proper song-and-dance sequence and with music composed by Mychael Danna . . . qualify as a "Bollywood musical?" Indeed, what can this film, a global arthouse hit, tell us about the fate of film music in New Bollywood cinema. *Monsoon Wedding*'s music, an eclectic brew of Punjabi folk songs set to a *bhangra* beat, Urdu *ghazals* remixed by a Delhi garage band called Medieval Pandits [sic], Bollywood samplings, and *filmi sangeet* (film-song) classics, provides an interesting instance of the mutations in form and function that film song is undergoing in the present. (Gopal 2011: 47)

There is no doubt that these critics are correct that Nair, in *Monsoon Wedding*, aims to affirmatively engage the Bollywood musical as a form. It is also likely that her turning in this direction in the marketing of the film helped the film find audiences—both internationally and within India itself, where, as Gopal notes, echoing Vasudevan, the film "clearly references the wedding extravaganzas that are a staple of the NRI genre in New Bollywood." Both Gopal and Vasudevan seem to suggest that Nair is having her cake—her art house and Euro-American credibility—and eating it too, by creating a highly commercial film product for a broad range of international audiences, including Indian audiences accustomed to marriage-oriented musicals.

However, just as one shouldn't judge a book by its cover, it might be best not to judge *Monsoon Wedding* by its trailer. Formally and aesthetically, it could be argued that it's really the film's *difference* from the narrative and aesthetic sensibilities of commercial Hindi cinema that is *Monsoon Wedding*'s defining feature. For while there is little doubt in this critic's mind that the New Bollywood is a significant and growing phenomenon (albeit one that has largely emerged *after* the release of *Monsoon Wedding*), the changes in commercial Hindi cinema have come slowly and the sense of newness that periodically emerges may be all too often interrupted by the continuation of very conventional filmic styles. In that sense, *Monsoon Wedding*'s critique of mainstream Hindi cinema's stylized fantasy worlds, the Bollywood star system, and the conservative gender politics of Bollywood romantic song-and-dance can be seen as a continuation of critiques we have seen in Nair's earlier works, including especially *Salaam Bombay!* and *India Cabaret*. Here we will look closely at Nair's direct citation of a Bollywood song-and-dance number, the performance of "Chunari Chunari" near the end of a *sangeet* (the traditional Punjabi prewedding celebration). Nair's use of the song for her own song-and-dance sequence is an example of a direct citation and appropriation of Hindi film music. While this usage helps position Nair closer to commercial Hindi cinema, her critique of Bollywood song-and-dance conventions, including some specific choices made by David Dhawan in a hit film released just two years earlier, suggest that Nair's documentary realist roots remain active and relevant even in *Monsoon Wedding*. Finally, a comparison between the deployment of the song in Dhawan's highly conventional family melodrama and Nair's rather unconventional (and avowedly feminist) story has implications for our broader interest in Nair's diaspora vérité filmic project.

Before working through the two versions of "Chunari Chunari" in an extended analysis below, it might be helpful to briefly discuss another citation of *filmi* music earlier in *Monsoon Wedding*. This is the scene where Nair uses Mohammed Rafi's "Aaj Mausam Bada Beimaan Hai" (Today's weather is very uncertain) while wedding planner Dubey and housemaid Alice first encounter each other. Nair's use of this particular track (from the 1973 film *Loafer*) is clearly a nostalgic allusion, and in many ways it corresponds to the Bollywood method of using music extradiegetically much more than does her use of "Chunari Chunari." In the "Chunari Chunari" sequence in the film, the viewer understands the song to be playing in the background, while here there's no indication that the Mohammed Rafi song is playing in the narrative frame of the story. This is about as "Bollywood" as Nair gets.

That said, Nair's depiction of "Aaj Mausam Bada Beimaan Hai," which shows us the first encounter of two working-class people, couldn't be more visually different from the song as it appears in *Loafer*. There, the hero and heroine are in a conventional romantic setting—a picturesque forest—and are dressed in fashionable, Western clothes. In Nair's version, Alice and Dubey are at work and are wearing their everyday clothes (he wears simple khaki shirt and pants, while she wears a plain sari befitting a housemaid). Nair's insertion of a working-class couple for the film's most conventional song sequence is an extremely pointed commentary on commercial Hindi cinema's class biases (couples seen as worthy of romantic songs in most commercial films are typically well-off, if not actually rich). Moreover, this commentary is part of an ongoing conversation about changing class and status norms in the emerging "new India." At times, Nair's depiction of how class relations are changing in contemporary India is impossible to miss; early in the film, for instance, Dubey tells his coworkers that "the one-rupee era is over!" (where the "one-rupee era" refers to a time when servants could be paid tiny, essentially nominal fees for extremely demanding labor). At other times, the critique is subtler; at one point Alice offers Dubey a glass of water but decides to ask him whether he would prefer "fridge water" or "tap water." Fridge water, of course, is distilled water typically reserved for guests, not "staff." In asking Dubey which water he drinks, Alice is acknowledging that Dubey's status is in fact somewhat in flux; she is giving him the opportunity to name his class status for himself. And fittingly for an upwardly mobile entrepreneur (even one with working-class origins), he chooses the "fridge water."

At this point, we'll turn to a visual comparison of Mira Nair and David Dhawan's respective approaches to the filming the song "Chunari Chunari," which plays an important role in resolving one of the major plot arcs of *Monsoon Wedding*. "Chunari Chunari" was first featured in David Dhawan's *Biwi No. 1*, a "superhit" from 1999 whose music was still very much current in 2001, when Nair filmed *Monsoon Wedding*. Thus, Nair's use of the song falls under the category of a current citation—in a different category from her allusions to more classical Hindi film songs or Punjabi folk songs elsewhere in *Monsoon Wedding*. Both Dhawan and Nair approach the song sequence by focusing on dancing women—which is only appropriate given the fact that most of the lyrics in the song are voiced by women. However, Nair's narrative frames Ayesha (Neha Dubey) as the character around whose agency the narrative turns, while in Dhawan's film the context is Salman Khan's sense of liberation from his traditional marriage and unglamorous wife. In Dhawan's film, the song represents the union of Salman Khan's character with Sushmita Sen. The song appears in the plot after Salman Khan has had a confrontation with his wife, Pooja (Karisma Kapoor), that's led him to temporarily walk away from his marriage. The song is technically a duet, though as mentioned, Anu Malik's lyrics give far more weight to the woman's voice attempting to seduce her lover—"Aa jaa na chu le meri chunari sanam / kuch na mein bolu tujhe meri kasam" (Come touch my *chunari* [scarf, a symbol of modesty], my dear / I promise I won't tell anyone about it), than in the male lover's voice.

It should be noted that the settings for Dhawan's "Chunari Chunari" all appear to be in San Francisco, which has no relationship to the plot of the film (otherwise consistently set in India); other song sequences in the film use Miami as well as Switzerland as backdrops. These narratively irrelevant and remarkably far-flung settings are consistent with commercial Hindi films' construction of fantasy, a phenomenon discussed by numerous scholars of Indian cinema, including, for instance, Ranjani Mazumdar (see the discussion of the Australian song sequences in *Hindustani* in her book *Bombay Cinema* [Mazumdar 2006: 105–7]). Also consistent with the fantastic presentation of commercial Hindi cinema are the several costume changes over the course of the song.

Dhawan introduces his stars using frontal mid-range shots in clear lighting, often posing in front of geographic landmarks with a large visual sweep—designed to produce a sense of awe in the viewer. Sushmita Sen, for instance, appears in the song before a large man-made pond at the visually imposing Palace of Fine Arts in San Francisco (she later appears on a hilltop overlooking the Golden Gate Bridge). She is wearing a red *chunari* (i.e., a *dupatta*, or scarf), and a black, somewhat modernized *lehnga* (a long skirt, often heavily embroidered). (Elsewhere in the film Sen wears "Western" clothes such as minidresses and athletic wear; here her lehngas suggests her new status as a potential second wife for Prem [Salman Khan], but still stand in contrast to the traditional saris worn by Prem's actual wife Pooja [Karisma Kapoor]). Unlike some "modern" women in earlier Hindi cinema, here Dhawan is interested in posing Sushmita Sen as a viable potential partner for Salman Khan's character; she is not to be thought of as a "vamp" or temptress. Again, Mazumdar's reading of the changes in the depiction of female sexuality in Hindi cinema are relevant here. Sushmita Sen in *Biwi No. 1* might have some superficial similarities to the Westernized vamps from 1970s masala films, but in fact in Dhawan's film she is a representative of the new "female youth culture": "The symbolic association of the commodity with fashion, globalization, and spectacular travel gestures to an image of a sexualized middle-class female consumer" (Mazumdar 2006: 108).

After an opening solo sequence at mid-range and close-up, Salman Khan's character enters as well in mid-range. As the vocals start, Sushmita Sen is

Biwi No. 1. Sushmita Sen (*front center*).

Biwi No 1. Salman Khan's character holds the chunari and "ropes" in Sushmita Sen.

shown in partial close-up. Between the first and second verses, Salman Khan appears with the chunari around his neck but then draws Sushmita Sen close and then places the chunari around her neck in a face-to-face, close-up profile shot—indicating romantic union.

After the first verses, the red chunari largely disappears from the song—though it reappears at the end to suggest consummation of Salman Khan and Sushmita's extramarital relationship. With the third verse, the song moves into a more classic romantic-duet visual framing, often with directly complementary and even synchronized dance moves. The New Bollywood this is not; indeed, it is hard to imagine anything more essentially conservative and typical of the genre than Dhawan's "Chunari Chunari" song sequence.

Mira Nair's version of "Chunari Chunari," by contrast, is all shot on location below ground in Delhi, inside a uniquely decorated emptied swimming

Biwi No 1. Synchronized dance signifying romantic union.

pool—with very little of the sense of background verticality emphasized by Dhawan. The choreography, credited to the established Bollywood choreographer Farah Khan, is not markedly different from the style of choreography used by Dhawan, though Neha Dubey's hip thrusts are appropriately a little less pronounced or finished than Sushmita Sen's highly exaggerated *tumka* movements in *Biwi No. 1*. First, Neha Dubey's figure is initially introduced in the dance with a long shot, partially obscured by an architectural feature of the pool, an approach very different to that taken by Dhawan. Second, as she moves through the space of the dance floor at a run, the camera follows her from behind, apparently via a handheld camera using Steadicam. Again, the visual dynamism, especially the use of obscured framing and the nonfrontal positioning of the actors, is in sharp contrast to the static shots preferred by Dhawan.

While Dhawan uses in effect three fixed camera positions—mid-range, close-up, and long range, with the two stars most generally frontally facing the camera, Nair uses a dizzying number of camera angles, often partial shots, extreme close-ups, and shots split between the observing crowd at the premarriage celebration and the dancer. Nearly all shots are at eye level or hip level, contrasting with Dhawan's frequent use of frontal shots and bird's-eye views. The multitude of camera angles and disordered visual framing often suggests a kind of "home movie" quality to Nair's "Chunari Chunari," though the final product is carefully orchestrated by Nair and Allyson Johnson (her editor on this film) so that nearly every shot advances plot points relevant to the cluster of main characters in the film.

Another marked difference in the style of the two song sequences can be seen in Nair's use of interstitial audio from the crowd. These include audio of

Monsoon Wedding. The dancer is partially obscured.

the crowd's reaction to Neha Dubey's dance moves (alongside visual crowd reaction shots) and the occasional background commentary of the evening's MC (described as a "clown" by another character). In the second half of the song sequence, after the entire party has entered the empty pool area to join the dance, Nair even occasionally cuts the audio of the song entirely to make it easier to follow brief snippets of dialogue important to the plot. This is in sharp contrast to Dhawan's approach to "Chunari Chunari," in which no audio is mixed in at all outside of the music for the song (adding to the sense of artificiality), and all lyrics to the song are shown to be directly lip-synced by the two stars. In Nair's version, Neha Dubey does occasionally mouth the song's lyrics, but large sections of the song are simply performed in the background, without any lip-syncing at all. One might not want to make too much of the lip-syncing issue, but her approach does suggest Nair's emphasis on a realistic scenario—as against the persistent illusion (now fading somewhat with the rise of the New Bollywood) entailed by commercial Hindi cinema's dependence on playback singers and lip-syncing stars.

The key feature of Nair's "Chunari Chunari" from a feminist point of view might be her choice to give primary possession of the chunari to Neha Dubey rather than to her competing male love interests. While in Dhawan's film Salman Khan must choose between two women, in Nair's film, Neha Dubey's character is choosing between two men. When Neha Dubey's Ayesha places the symbolic chunari around Rahul's unnamed rival's neck, it's figured as a kind of reward for his participation—and suggests the possibility of ownership (*her* ownership *of him*). Ironically, Nair's interpretation of the

Monsoon Wedding. The dancer faces away from the camera as she runs.

chunari's function may be closer to the meaning of Anu Malik's actual lyrics than Dhawan's version, where the agency (and the chunari) is put into Salman Khan's hands.

Yet another difference between the two stagings of "Chunari Chunari" is in the narrative context that surrounds the song. In *Biwi No. 1*, the song is introduced as one of the climactic moments in a developing melodramatic romantic plot involving a traditional Indian wife (Karisma Kapoor) and an eroticized, "modern" mistress (Sushmita Sen). The presence of the song straightforwardly signifies a romantic union that has been made possible by Salman Khan's decision to reject his wife in favor of Sushmita Sen. By contrast, in *Monsoon Wedding*, Ayesha's performance of "Chunari Chunari" is initially meant to be a duet between brother and sister, not as the centerpiece of the various developing romantic plots, but as a largely de-eroticized secondary event. (The lip-synced performance of popular Bollywood hits by children is commonplace in Indian social gatherings. In the diaspora, such performances are one of the key ways in which "Indianness" is performed for public consumption.) The competition between the two young men over Ayesha (where, as described above, Ayesha uses her "chunari" to choose her preferred suitor) occurs essentially by accident after Ishaan decides at the last minute not to do the planned dance duet with his older sister.

The sheer number of significant differences between Dhawan's version of "Chunari Chunari" in *Biwi No. 1* and Nair's in *Monsoon Wedding* suggest that the gap between Nair and the commercial Hindi film industry remains substantial and important. Nair's "Chunari Chunari" is far more visually

Monsoon Wedding. Here it is Neha Dubey's character who holds—and uses—the chunari.

and aurally complex—crowded, one might say—but her approach to the song also has feminist implications. Admittedly, the differences between the two "Chunari Chunaris" are not absolute: both Nair's Neha Dubey and Dhawan's Sushmita Sen wear modified lehngas, and both represent the two directors' visions of what a modern Indian woman might look like. And, as with *India Cabaret* (or for that matter Nair's *Kama Sutra*), Nair's approach to representing women's bodies on screen is not a prudish or censorious one; in her depiction here, Neha Dubey appears every bit as "glamorous" as Sushmita Sen in Dhawan's film. But the significance her performance of this dance in the film more broadly gives Nair's version a feminist dimension.

Finally, towards the second half of the song, the crowd enters the dance floor, and Nair's fixation on the romantic couple dissolves away entirely. Portly middle-aged couples, grandmothers, and children come to participate, and the visual focus on the two romantic leads (of the moment) essentially vanishes. Rather than isolate the romantic leads in a kind of iconic bubble (the norm in romantic duets in commercial Hindi films), Nair refocuses to suggest that a broad, one might say, democratizing kind of inclusive celebration: in her appropriation, "Chunari Chunari" becomes *everybody's song*. This and other choices Nair makes for her version of "Chunari Chunari" suggest her goal is to portray the lived experience of film music for ordinary middle-class people in contemporary India; it's a species of documentary realism melded with a feminist and democratizing ideological

Critique of Bollywood in *Monsoon Wedding*

Monsoon Wedding. Shift away from romantic couple to crowd dance.

perspective expressed visually in the scene. Interestingly, it might even be argued that Nair's citation of Dhawan in "Chunari Chunari" expresses an ironic form of prodiasporic Indian nationalism, through its self-conscious setting in New Delhi (rather than, say, San Francisco). Though Nair's film figures itself as intentionally diasporic (the Australia-returned Rahul's joining Ayesha on the dance floor reflects his willingness to publicly perform his Indianness as a diasporic subject, not just his masculinity), it is ironically Dhawan's film that uses non-Indian locales without reference to the geographical setting of *Biwi No. 1*. In Dhawan's film, like so many other Bollywood films of the 1990s and 2000s, globalization does not imply a serious engagement with diaspora culture; both his hero and his heroine are never shown to be anything other than comfortably and traditionally "Indian." Dhawan uses "foreignness" to connote glamor and visual sublimity without considering the cultural implications of his settings, while Nair suggests that even "bloody firangis" like the diasporic Rahul can claim ownership of a hybridized version of Indian identity through dance. As we have seen with other films in Nair's body of work (and as will be seen again in subsequent examples), her diasporic thematic focus appears to be deeply intertwined with a feminist and documentary realist method, so this song sequence encapsulates quite well the method we have been calling diaspora vérité. And Nair's provisional embrace of the commercial Hindi film industry (or, following Gopal, the "New Bollywood") is not without its strong points of critique.

Monsoon Wedding in the Context of Other Indian Diaspora Films

Monsoon Wedding was not produced in a vacuum. Indeed, Nair's film was released as part of a sizeable raft of art films made by directors of South Asian origin in the 1990s and early 2000s, which together might be seen as a kind of "Indian invasion" of the commercial art house segment of the Anglo-American cinema houses. The three best known directors—the "Bhenji Brigade," as it has sometimes been called—are Mira Nair herself, Deepa Mehta (*Fire* [1996], *Earth* [1998], *Bollywood/Hollywood* [2002]), and Gurinder Chadha (*Bhaji on the Beach* [1993], *Bend It Like Beckham* [2002], *Bride and Prejudice* [2004]). Interestingly, all three of these leading directors are women—which is an anomaly for both commercial Anglo-American and commercial Indian cinemas (both of which are, needless to say, heavily male-dominated industries). By another coincidence, all three of these women directors are from Punjabi backgrounds. Several other South Asian diasporic directors have also been active in this period, including Ismail Merchant (*The Mystic Masseur* [2001]), Shekhar Kapur (*Bandit Queen* [1994]), Nisha Ganatra (*Chutney Popcorn* [1999]), Anurag Mehta (*American Chai* [2001]), Krutin Patel (*ABCD* [1999]), and Udayan Prasad (*My Son the Fanatic* [1999]). Many of these more recent diasporic films are clearly indebted to pioneering earlier films based on screenplays by Hanif Kureishi, including *The Buddha of Suburbia* (1993), and *My Beautiful Launderette* (1985).

From the long list above, the films most immediately relevant to *Monsoon Wedding* are those that also enjoyed significant cross-over success, especially *Fire* and *Bend It Like Beckham*. *Bend It Like Beckham* is entirely a diasporic story, and thus it might be better compared to Nair's earlier *Mississippi Masala* (to be discussed in a subsequent chapter in the present study). But *Fire* at least shares with *Monsoon Wedding* a similarity in that they are both feminist films, set in contemporary urban India, shot by diasporic directors. However, the similarities effectively end there. *Fire* is fairly heavy-handed in its political message, vilifying the men in the family and glorifying the female protagonists, whose ensuing homoerotic relationship seems (problematically) to be the result of sexual desperation and neglect by men rather than organic same-sex desire. By contrast, *Monsoon Wedding*, which does engage a serious issue in child abuse, seems to take a less programmatic approach with regards to its possible political or feminist implications. Also reflecting the complexity of Nair's feminist vision is the fact that, while the film's best approximation of a "villain," Tej Puri, is male, the person who ultimately takes a stand in deciding to disown him from the family (admittedly under pressure from Ria) is also male, his younger brother-in-law, Lalit Verma.

One of the truly unique features of Nair's approach to the Indian diaspora in *Monsoon Wedding* is her interest in showing a highly dispersed family at a moment of provisional reunification. The gathering dramatized in the film is surely temporary, but some of the key conflicts in the film relate to an idea of Indian culture and values that are apparently shared by all family members, irrespective of where they live. Nair expresses the play between cultural centeredness and diasporic fragmentation in her director's commentary as follows: "And that was the idea—to celebrate being from India, rather than look upon the West as anything close to happiness in any way. The idea was, whoever came from abroad would become an Indian" (from the director's commentary on the *Monsoon Wedding* DVD). The idea of there being a grounding effect in the experience of returning from abroad is visible in the stories of several of Nair's characters, including the Australian Rahul, the US-based Tej Puri, and the Houston-based Hemant. Equally importantly, the prospect of emigration, for characters like Aditi or Ria, is not necessarily tied to deracination or cultural loss.

One concept of diaspora that informs my reading of *Monsoon Wedding* is from Arjun Appadurai, whose "Disjuncture and Difference in the Global Cultural Economy" (see Appadurai 1996) is widely considered a classic conceptualization of the "disjunctive" cultural dynamics of globalization. In the Appadurai idiom, Nair's films reflect the South Asian diaspora "ethnoscape," a shifting and fluid body of people—and a cultural imaginary—that extends from east Africa to the United States and in some ways specifically *includes* South Asians who remain within South Asia who have been impacted by the dispersal of their family and friends across the globe. Other facets of diasporic culture have been theorized by scholars like Vijay Mishra, who has described the distinction between old and new Indian diasporas (discussed briefly in chapter 1), and Shailja Sharma and Gita Rajan, who have emphasized the way today's diasporas retain real-time digital links to their home cultural environments—via the internet, satellite television, and mobile phone technology (see chapter 1). As a result, diasporization is increasingly seen not through the lens of permanent separation but as the emergence of parallel cultural experiences occurring in different places. There are some hints that emigration may prove to be freeing in Nair's early documentary film *So Far from India*, but it is really in *Monsoon Wedding* (followed up closely by *The Namesake*) that Nair is able to fully meld different cultural (and aesthetic) worlds and create a visual sensibility that embraces this nascent hybridity. In effect, by looking at Nair's directorial work as a whole, one can see the evolution of her diaspora vérité aesthetic as it develops and grows steadily more complex.

In films like Nair's *The Namesake, Mississippi Masala*, and her early documentary *So Far from India*, the pressure to move is figured as a *centrifugal* force, driving Indians to various sites in the diaspora (with a special focus, for Nair, on New York, the US South, and East Africa), and the urge to travel initiated by one generation is echoed and repeated in the next—as the children of migrants are frequently seen to migrate away from their parents. By contrast, *Monsoon Wedding* superficially appears to figure New Delhi as at least temporarily a *centripetal* site of return for families divided by diasporic fragmentation, though the idea of cultural fixity represented by such a return turns out to be more complex than might initially appear. Even domestically, what it means to be "Indian" appears to be in flux in *Monsoon Wedding*; Nair suggests that India's internal culture is in a state of transition regarding cultural identity, partly due to the intense permeation of western cultural values. Nair's description of her film as a celebration of "being from India" seems particularly apt, as her film reinvents the traditional Indian patriarch for a modern context while also supporting the concept of family associated with the tradition of arranged marriage—albeit with a progressive, feminist twist. That said, the centripetal representation of family life in *Monsoon Wedding* has a definite diasporic tilt.

The key line regarding the diasporic theme comes during the "Chunari Chunari" dance sequence described in detail above. "We've made you into a real Indian now," Ayesha says to Australia-returned Rahul after he takes the initiative and publicly competes for Ayesha's attention during her dance performance on the night of the wedding. His willingness to pursue the young woman he fancies reflects confidence in his masculinity, the film suggests, but more than that, it reflects a level of *cultural* assurance, both with the performative expectations of a large Indian family and with the conventions of Bollywood dance. But being (or "becoming") a "real Indian" is not, for Nair, contingent on whether one lives in India or abroad. After the wedding, the characters who have come from abroad will be returning to their diasporic lives, suggesting that for Nair, a continuous cultural sense of Indianness may be more important than geographic place of residence. This too suggests how dramatically the concept of diasporic life in Nair's films has evolved from its earlier instantiation in *So Far from India*. We will explore variants of the diaspora theme in the following chapter, with discussions of three of Nair's major films from the 1990s, *Mississippi Masala, The Perez Family*, and *My Own Country*.

Chapter 5

INTO THE DIASPORIC MIXING BOWL

Mississippi Masala (1991), *The Perez Family* (1995), and *My Own Country* (1998)

We now move back to an earlier point in Mira Nair's career—the early and mid-1990s. During this period, Nair's focus begins to shift from an intensive concern with social realities in India to the realities of the immigrant life she and others were experiencing at the time in the United States. Nearly all of the feature films Nair made in the 1990s fit the diaspora vérité concept we have been exploring quite well, in that they directly explore the tensions of diasporic life with a documentary realist sensibility. *My Own Country* (1998), *The Perez Family* (1995), and *Mississippi Masala* (1991) all depict people who were forced to leave home because of political conflict; the protagonists of the films are shown leaving Ethiopia, Cuba, and Uganda, respectively. Both *My Own Country* and *Mississippi Masala* have in common Indian families displaced from Africa who attempt to settle in the US South in the 1980s, a moment when the culture of the region was being transformed. *My Own Country*, filmed for cable television, is a close adaptation of Abraham Verghese's memoir of his experience working with AIDS patients in Johnson City, Tennessee, in the early and mid-1980s. Though it departs from its source text in some important ways, the film is effectively a "biopic"—and may be seen in connection to Nair's earlier documentary work. *Mississippi Masala* is based on Sooni Taraporevala's script, with a limited number of elements overlapping with Mahmood Mamdani's memoir of leaving Uganda, *From Citizen to Refugee* [1973]. *The Perez Family* is also an adaptation of a novel by Christine Bell, chronicling the chaos of Cuban immigration during the Mariel boatlift of 1980.

The three films make parallel arguments, namely that all members of a society, whether immigrant or indigenous, and irrespective of race, gender, or sexual orientation, have the right to pursue their own destinies—and thus all three films can be said to have an orientation to social justice. *My Own Country*, which explores the spread of AIDS in the 1980s, is perhaps most recognizable as a film singularly focused on a social issue. By contrast, *The Perez Family* and *Mississippi Masala* are films that have a slightly broader, more generalized scope and that seem to posit desire, especially female desire, as a central, and yet somehow disruptive, force in immigrant communities. All three films are also, of course, explicitly engaged with the themes and problems of the diasporic experience—specifically the questions of how and whether it is possible to be free in a state of exile, and how and whether exiled individuals can ever come to feel at home in the United States. Interestingly, these three films, set in the United States, seem to be less motivated to assert their *realist* credentials as against a commercial cinema. Classic Hindi cinema is cited here and there in these films, but largely as a figure of nostalgia, rather than as a current influence (one thinks of the brief reference to "Mera Joota Hai Japani" in *Mississippi Masala*, as well as the presence of the Bengali and Hindi cinema actress Sharmila Tagore in the film). Though all three of these films were financed by major Hollywood studios and at times reflect the aesthetic constraints of Hollywood studio films (especially *The Perez Family*), they nevertheless can be seen as engaging a version of the diaspora vérité concept we have discussed in earlier chapters. If Nair challenges the conservatism of Bollywood melodrama in films like *Salaam Bombay!* and *Monsoon Wedding*, in this trio of films, Nair begins to address and critique the American film industry's own forms of illusionism and artificiality.

Mississippi Masala (1991)

The most important background element for *Mississippi Masala* is clearly identified in the film itself—namely, the expulsion of Indians from Uganda in 1972. Because some readers may not be familiar with the history of the Indian diaspora population in East Africa, here we will briefly provide some background on that history. Though Nair's film is not usually read as an adaptation, the screenplay of *Mississippi Masala* bears similarities to a memoir by Mahmood Mamdani, *From Citizen to Refugee: Uganda Asians Come to Britain*. The similarities are enough to justify thinking of *Mississippi Masala* as a kind of adaptation alongside Nair's other adaptations; it is also, of course, a diasporic film as well as a feminist film.

Trade and migration between East Africa and India goes back thousands of years; there have even been hints that Vasco de Gama, who "discovered" the sea route to India in 1468, was shown the way by an Indian trader he encountered in southern Africa. However, it was during the peak years of the British Empire that large numbers of Indians came to East Africa, mainly brought by the British as indentured laborers. One example of the work these early laborers were involved with is the East African Railway, built in the late nineteenth century (Bizeck 2005: 112–13). Beginning in the early twentieth century, however, a growing number of Indians came to East Africa of their own accord as traders, where they became somewhat prosperous in relation to the indigenous population, leading to growing resentment. After East African nations such as Uganda, Kenya, and Zimbabwe became independent in the early 1960s, their new leadership initiated "Africanization" programs designed to improve the situations of indigenous black Africans and marginalize remaining European settlers as well as the prosperous Indian community. Arguably, the Indian community did not help its own cause in this era, as many Indians who had settled in Africa avoided mingling socially with local Africans and held themselves socially above the local population. After African independence, some of the eighty thousand Indians who had settled in Uganda elected not to become citizens of the new nation, preferring to remain "British" subjects.[5] As he ramped up his anti-Indian rhetoric in the months leading up to his expulsion order, President Idi Amin capitalized on these aspects of the Indian community settled in Uganda, reserving special ire for a community that he characterized as refusing to call itself Ugandan (for more on this, see Desai 2013: 206–7). However, at the time he issued his expulsion order in 1972, the twenty-three thousand people of Indian descent in Uganda who were certified citizens of Uganda were not exempted from the order—all Indians were required to leave the country immediately, taking no more than fifty British pounds with them in currency.

The Asian expulsion order, though shocking to the world at the time, is in hindsight somewhat understandable given the history of racial segregation in East Africa under the British. In 1971, Idi Amin Dada, an officer in the Ugandan army prior to the coup d'état, led a military coup against his former ally, Milton Obote, who had himself come to power in a coup just a few years earlier. Amin had, during the final years of the British Empire in Africa, been a career army officer, rising through the ranks and becoming one of two commissioned African officers in the "King's African Rifles." After

Mississippi Masala. Newspapers announcing the Asian expulsion order.

coming to power, Amin conducted a brutal campaign against his political rivals in other ethnic groups, leading to deaths on a massive scale—virtually a genocide according to some accounts (see Jorgensen 1981: 267–330). After concluding the civil war in 1971, he began an "economic war" directed primarily against Indo-Africans and Europeans, who continued to dominate the Ugandan economy. By September 1972, he had ordered all of Uganda's Indians to leave the country, and he oversaw the expropriation of their property for himself and his allies.

After expulsion, most Indo-Ugandans went, for at least a brief period, to "refugee" camps in England, and Mamdani's account in *From Citizen to Refugee* vividly depicts the confusion and desperation they experienced in those camps in 1972 and 1973. Others went back to India, and a fair number went to places like New Zealand and Australia. A small number came to the United States, where they quickly blended into the rapidly expanding Indian diaspora community settling all around the US after the immigration reforms of 1965. *Mississippi Masala* tells the story of a fictional family that found its way to the Deep South of the United States, where it became involved in the hotel business.

Though there is no reason to think that Mamdani's book is a *direct* source for Nair and Taraporevala's story, through a close look at the memoir, one finds a number of close parallels between Mamdani's version of the Indian expulsion from Uganda and its depiction in Nair's *Mississippi Masala*. Mamdani is not credited as a writer or contributor on the film, though Nair has openly discussed how she met him while filming the Uganda-based scenes of

Mississippi Masala. "Mera Joota Hai Japani" (My shoes are Japanese), a metaphor for diasporic identity.

the film; as is well-known, she also later married Mamdani, who now teaches at Columbia University in New York. The relevance of Mamdani's account to Nair's film is evident from some of his personal accounts, including the following account of violence at the hands of Ugandan soldiers during the expulsion:

> The first group of Asians to leave Uganda were those that went to India. From Kampala they took a train to the Kenyan port of Mombasa where a ship was to take them to Bombay. Letters from them told of being stopped on the way by bands of Ugandan soldiers, of all their belongings taken, of the men made to lie down on the ground while the women were raped. From the countryside news gradually filtered into the city telling of individual Asians who had been kidnapped by soldiers, of families who paid fortunes for the return of the male members and of other families who lost their father or brothers because they had no money to pay a ransom. (Mamdani 1973: 25)

In Nair's film, the violence involved in the expulsion is represented by a single tense bus ride where Jay's wife Kinnu (Sharmila Tagore) is singled out and harassed by soldiers. They make her demonstrate that the audio tapes she's carrying contain only music (the song that is played, momentarily, is a famous Kishore Kumar number particularly apposite to the diasporic context: "Mera Joota Hai Japani" [My shoes are Japanese]). Rather than subject her to violence, the soldier finally lets her go, while demonstrating unmistakably that he *could* act with impunity if he chose.

What is perhaps the strongest parallel between Nair and Taraporevala's Jay and Mamdani's account relates to an individual named Jagdish, who has a story that is strikingly similar to Jay's:

> Jagdish was one of the few people I knew who was not trapped by the social conditions he was born into; who had successfully risen above his social environment to be able to see its limitations. He revolted against the perverse nature of the society around him, especially the affluent Asian society, with its almost totally privatized existence and increasingly conspicuous consumption. . . .
>
> In the late sixties, [Jagdish started] a school for the children of farmers. Now he could realize his dreams and have his own school. Its staff and students would be multi-racial, its subject matter would be stripped of colonial content.
>
> When Jagdish found out he had to leave, his immediate concern was to make certain the school would not collapse on his departure. . . . He set about training one of the African teachers, Mugoba, in the mechanics of running the school. Every morning students would ask Jagdish whether he was leaving. He would remain quiet. One day he did not go to school. Instead he queued outside the British High Commission to get his passport stamped. Mugoba took charge. The students demanded Jadgish's presence, when that failed they took it out on Mugoba, beat him up and refused either to leave or behave. A few days later, Jagdish left for London. He told me not to go back to the school, for he did not ever want to talk about it. (Mamdani 1973: 42–43)

Jagdish's relationship to Mugoba is somewhat reminiscent of Jay's relationship to Okelo in Nair's film, though the incident where Mugoba is beaten after he fails to hand Jagdish over to the rebelling students is not present in the film. In both cases, a Ugandan Indian educator who is working to fulfil his idealistic vision of a racially integrated society is forced to grapple with historical forces that make that vision an impossibility, at least in 1972.

One final anecdote from Mamdani's book seems relevant as a way of setting the stage for a closer look at Nair's film. It involves one of Mamdani's colleagues at the university in Kampala where he has been teaching as a historian:

> A few days later I left. My English and American friends came to Airways House to see me off. In those days, for an African to be seen with an Asian was to risk both lives. It was sufficient evidence of intended sabotage. Even two months earlier, when I had gone to see Maria, a friend at the university, she had pleaded:
> "Please, Mahmood, we can't go out together. Don't you know how things have changed? It's not me, it's the times, I'm sorry."
> As I boarded the bus for the airport and looked out of the window to wave goodbye, John made one last attempt to make light of the situation.
> "Make sure this is the last time you are kicked out of a country on charges of being a bourgeois!"
> I tried to laugh. But I felt as if someone dear to me had died. (Mamdani 1973: 67)

This passage gives an unmistakable sense of an incommensurable gap between those on the receiving end of the expulsion order and those who benefit, either as members of the indigenous population (Maria, above), or as whites who are effectively immune to the kind of persecution to which Mamdani's community is being subjected (John). That incommensurability is also present in the opening scene of *Mississippi Masala*, where Jay and Okelo find their friendship affected by the changing dynamics of the political situation.

Mississippi Masala opens, like Mamdani's *From Citizen to Refugee*, at the dramatic moment of the expulsion of the Asians from Uganda. The opening shots are of Kampala in 1972, with Jay (Roshan Seth), driving with his friend Okelo, stopped at a police checkpoint. A radio voice-over establishes the historical context:

> This is Radio Uganda. Today the people of Uganda are witnessing the end of one chapter of the history of this country and the beginning of another. Today the last of the Asians who have been forced to leave the country will have done so in order for the indigenous people of Uganda to take control of the economy. (Nair, *Mississippi Masala*, 1991)

Jay and Okelo are having an argument about Jay's recent statements about Idi Amin to the BBC. Their dialogue resembles, in some ways, the kinds of arguments Mahmood Mamdani had with his friends and colleagues in the months before Idi Amin's expulsion order was issued:

> OKELO: You give an interview on BBC, saying that Amin was evil. Are you mad? What about Kinnu? What about Meena?
> JAY: What should I have done? Remained silent? That is the coward's way.
> OKELO: Don't talk to me about cowards. That's what you are. You're not leaving because you're scared to leave? You are scared of leaving Uganda.
> JAY: Why should I go? Why should I go? Okelo, this is my home.
> OKELO: Not any more, Jay. Africa is for Africans. Black Africans. (Nair, *Mississippi Masala*, 1991)

Like the real-life Mahmood Mamdani, Jay is a progressive intellectual—he simply refuses to keep his mouth shut in the face of what he perceives to be injustice. In this case, his statements in the media are seen by Okelo as dangerous for himself and his family, especially given Idi Amin's propensity to summarily destroy his enemies and their families at the slightest whim.

The dialogue establishes Jay and his family as unfairly targeted by the expulsion order—they are citizens of Uganda and also full participants in an emerging multiracial society with their black African neighbors. Jay has come to fully identify as a Ugandan; he tells Okelo that he's "always been Ugandan first and Indian second," and his friendship with Okelo runs deep enough that his daughter Meena calls him "Okelo Chachu" (Uncle Okelo). At one point in the film, one of his friends suggests that, in his law practice in Uganda, he had been especially committed to representing black Africans ("Meet our Jay Bhai [brother Jay]. In Uganda he was the champion defender of blacks. But the same blacks kicked him out.").

Despite the emphasis on the political situation and the darkness of the opening shots, Nair's visual approach to representing Uganda is actually quite affirmative. The countryside outside of Kampala is also shown in daylight sweeping pans, with lush jungle hillsides and stunning views of Lake Victoria in the background. The overall effect is of an idyllic, garden-like environment.

Despite his nostalgia for his earlier life in Uganda, Jay's experience of exile from the country, followed by an unspecified experience in England, has hardened and embittered him. And while he doesn't seem to harbor explicitly racialized hostility against black Africans (or against African Americans in the Mississippi town where he and his family now live), it's clear that he's most comfortable around other Indians. Okelo's comment that Africa is for "black Africans" only has apparently continued to haunt Jay in subsequent years, making it impossible for him to trust anyone outside of his ethnic

Mississippi Masala. The lush gardens in the suburbs of Kampala.

community. It is not Idi Amin who has most wounded Jay, but Okelo. The sense of loss has impacted Jay on other levels as well. Though they are no longer simple "refugees," the family has continued to be in some sense homeless. Jay and his family have had to move so often that they remain unsettled in their new environment—they're actually living, permanently, in the hotel where Meena works.

In addition to its foregrounding of the Asian expulsion from Uganda, *Mississippi Masala* is also notable for its exploration of race relations in the US South beyond the black-white axis. This is developed in Nair's film as a theme in its own right, though at the moment of dramatic crisis, the American racial problematic intersects with the lingering legacy of the Asian expulsion. Several scholars, including Jigna Desai (2004), Bakirathi Mani (1996), and Binita Mehta (1996), have commented on Nair and Taraporevala's provocative approach to American race relations in *Mississippi Masala*, and here I will try not to replicate their conclusions. Rather, with regard to the American race dynamics, my focus is on how race works, not so much between the various communities represented in Nair's film, but within those communities. Nair's film explores the problem of antiblack racism within the Indian immigrant community, as well as the phenomenon known as "colorism," the prejudice for lighter skin within minority communities themselves.[6]

The complex intersection of race and ethnicity in *Mississippi Masala* is evident in the Indian wedding scene early in the film. Here, a character played by Mira Nair herself introduces the well-known dynamic of colorism internal to the Indian community, which seems to have implicit and unconscious

Mississippi Masala. Colorism and classism. Cameo by the director.

ramifications for the incipient romance between Meena and Demetrius: "You think this one [Meena] has a chance. Aré, you can be dark and have money, or you can be fair and have no money. But you can't be dark and have no money and expect to get Harry Patel." From context, one gathers that Harry Patel is considered quite the catch for Meena, who described herself to her mother in the immediately preceding scene as a "darkie" ("Face it, Ma, you got a darkie daughter").

While some observers might wonder whether the preference expressed here for lighter skin is a form of internalized colonialism, many Indians understand it in the framework of colorism— where the preference for light skin is generally not a signal of preference for "whiteness" associated with individuals of European descent (Parameswaran and Cordoza 2009). All the same, because of the racial and complexional prejudices within the Indian community in *Mississippi Masala*, a dark-skinned African American as a love-object for an Indian American woman clearly places her outside of the norms of her community. The fact that the film's romantic plot does in fact develop along these lines is consistent with Nair's interest in transgressive romantic narratives (especially in *Salaam Bombay!*, *Kama Sutra*, and *Vanity Fair*).

While sociopolitical and historical factors can put people in the same geographic place, ultimately what leads individuals in different ethnic groups to become truly connected—or personally intimate—is who they are as individuals. In Meena's case, the young woman we are reintroduced to after a gap of eighteen years is shown in Nair's film as a rebellious, strong-willed

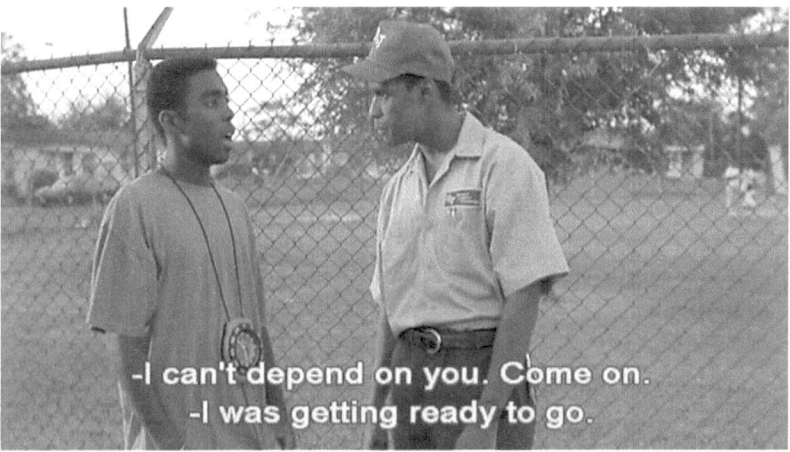

Mississippi Masala. Two brothers with differing approaches to inhabiting blackness.

person, rather at odds with the heavily Gujarati Indian community in the small Mississippi town where she and her family live. Her relatives and family friends are counting every penny, with little awareness of the way of life characteristic of the mainstream southern society that surrounds them. Meena, who has now spent most of her life in that society, has been toughened by her encounters and is frequently frustrated with the diasporic Indian community's self-absorption and conservatism. Her father, Jay, has remained somewhat aloof from Meena's struggles to define herself; when he is first reintroduced in 1990, he is seen writing a letter to the Ugandan government outlining his losses following the expulsion order of 1972. The implication is that his heart and soul remain in his home country of Uganda, not in the new world of the multiracial US South.

As should already be apparent, *Mississippi Masala* dramatizes, first and foremost, a split within the Indian diasporic community in Greenwood between conservative, money-obsessed motel owners, on the one hand, and the comparatively more relaxed and open-minded Jay, Kinnu, and Meena, on the other. At the same time, Nair and Taraporevala are also sensitive to schisms within the African American community. Meena's later love interest Demetrius owns a small carpet-cleaning business, and he struggles to hold his entire family on his back, as his father makes little money as a waiter, and his brother Dexter is unemployed. The relationship between the two brothers reflects a division within the African American community at the time over how to navigate identity in a racially polarized society. While Demetrius works hard and feels little race consciousness, Dexter speaks openly of "crackers" amongst his friends and wears a large plastic clock in the manner of the black nationalist rap group Public Enemy.

However, Dexter's attitude prevents him from connecting with anyone outside of the small group of friends (derisively described as "crackheads" by Demetrius) he hangs out with on the street corner. Similarly, there is a gap between Demetrius's approach to his career and the stylish—but shallow—approach taken by his ex-girlfriend Alicia LeShay, who has left Greenwood for the comparatively larger Jackson, Mississippi, to try her hand at a music career. While Meena is an outlier in her family and community in one way, Demetrius is in an analogous but opposite position within his community (he appears to be the only one in his family working hard to get ahead).

Meena is not damaged by the experience of the expulsion from Uganda in the same way as her father. Unlike the whites in Mississippi, she has no entrenched feelings about African Americans or black Africans (if anything, she has a positive memory of her "Chachu" Okelo, back in Uganda), and unlike her father, she has no cynicism about the possibility of being close to members of other ethnoracial groups. The possibility of a romance with an African American is, therefore, an event that is effectively unscripted in the narratives of both her family and her community. Demetrius also offers Meena the opportunity to transgressively rebuke the local Indian community, which is shown in the film to be faintly ridiculous, and which at any rate doesn't value someone like herself (i.e., a young woman who is "both dark and has no money") very highly. Outside of the Indian immigrant community, Meena seems much better acculturated; she is, for example, perfectly comfortable in African American social environments such as the Leopard Lounge nightclub she goes to with Harry Patel after the Indian wedding they both attend in Greenwood.

As minorities in a white-dominated society, Indians and African Americans have certain things in common, though Nair notes that the tensions and mutual mistrust between the respective ethnoracial groups far outweigh any provisional sense of unity that might be felt amongst these "people of color." In a scene that perfectly exemplifies the awkwardness of the connection between the Indian American and African American communities in Greenwood, the Indian motel owner known as Pontiac (Mohan Gokhale) approaches Demetrius and Tyrone, who are contracted to clean carpets at his motel, about Meena's accident.

> PONTIAC: I want you to try something special. [Carrying two glasses of Indian tea.] Relax. Sit down. Your people are very good at sports.

Kareem Abdul-Jabbar. Freddy Brown from Downtown. Hector "Macho Man" Camacho. (Nair, *Mississippi Masala*, 1991)

While Pontiac is performing his spiel enthusiastically, Demetrius and Tyrone laugh politely. He is trying to "make friends," and he apparently has no idea that many African Americans might find this approach flat-footed at best and patronizing at worst. Rather than object to Pontiac's stereotyping, however, Demetrius objects to the inclusion of Hector Camacho in the list:

DEMETRIUS: Macho ain't black though, he's what, Mexican?
TYRONE: Puerto Rican
DEMETRIUS: Puerto Rican.
PONTIAC: Black, brown, yellow, Mexican, Puerto Rican, all the same. As long as you are not white, it means you are colored. Isn't that so?
DEMETRIUS: Yeah, I guess.
PONTIAC: A girl had an accident with your van. But no damage was done to your person or your van?
DEMETRIUS: That's right.
PONTIAC: Thank God.
PONTIAC: You know the person whose van was driving was my very good friend. Also Indian. You get me?
DEMETRIUS: No.
PONTIAC: He's also worried, because in this country, people are suing all the time.
DEMETRIUS: Oh—I got you know. Yeah, this *is* good tea. [Laughing] Oh, I didn't mean to laugh. You can tell your friend he ain't got nothing to worry about.
PONTIAC: [Exhales] I told him he didn't have to worry. You are a good man. All of us people of color must stick together. [Stands up.] United we stand, divided we fall!
TYRONE: That's right, brother. Power to the people! (Nair, *Mississippi Masala*, 1991)

Pontiac's approach to Demetrius and Tyrone here is awkward on multiple levels. He tries to gloss over his ignorance of the ethnic background of American athletes by lumping all the racial groups he can think of into one, rather odd list ("Black, brown, yellow, Mexican, Puerto Rican, all the same"). After Pontiac brings up the matter of the accident, Demetrius realizes what the conversation is really about, but again demurs from taking offense, and

Mississippi Masala. A gracious response to racial insensitivity.

amicably (but ironically) says, "Yeah, this *is* good tea." Pontiac's final plea for solidarity amongst "people of color," despite its pseudo-civil-rights-era grandiloquence, does not ring true. The challenges Meena and Demetrius will face as they struggle to find acceptance for their budding romance in the remainder of the film clearly demonstrate just how false that slogan of solidarity really is.

In the end, Meena and Demetrius find they need to leave Greenwood to develop their relationship and perhaps brighten their career horizons. As Kinnu says to Jay, explaining her choice to run away with Demetrius, "She's just like you." If the first generation of migrants put the family in motion, quite often their children find themselves leaving the place where their parents have settled, continuing the pattern of emigration, in a kind of centripetal pattern of continuing dispersion (we also see this pattern depicted in Nair's *The Namesake*). As importantly, Jay returns to Uganda to see his former house and to try and track down Okelo at the school where the latter used to teach. Jay feels welcome in the new, post–Idi Amin Uganda; a driver greets him warmly: "Welcome back, *bwana*." But Okelo was killed by Idi Amin in 1972, and the house where he formerly lived is now derelict. All the same, the burden that has been on his shoulders since the expulsion has lifted, and he no longer feels haunted by the loss of home. Nair ends the film with Jay in a market square in urban Kampala watching an African woman dance before a crowd. As Jay is watching, a small African boy touches his cheek, suggesting the healing of some old wounds.

Mississippi Masala. Jay returns to Uganda; the wounds are beginning to heal.

Nair also dealt with issues of racial tension in the African context in her 1993 short film *The Day the Mercedes Became a Hat*, and it might be appropriate at this juncture to briefly explore the links between it and *Mississippi Masala*. Nair made the film while living in Johannesburg, South Africa, during the country's transitionary period from Apartheid to post-Apartheid government. Like *Mississippi Masala*, *The Day the Mercedes Became a Hat* is about a family on the verge of expatriating from Africa. As with Uganda in the 1970s, South Africa is a nation experiencing major social and political tumult, and the white family at the center of Nair's short film is deeply anxious about its future status. That said, unlike *Mississippi Masala*, in which the Asian community was forcibly expatriated from Uganda by Idi Amin, the departing South African whites appear to be fleeing not so much out of necessity as out of an almost hysterical fear that the wealth and privilege they enjoy may not continue into a post-Apartheid era. In *The Day the Mercedes Became a Hat*, Nair aims to humanize both major parties in the South African conflict—white and black—and is most successful in doing so through the lens of the two children in the film. The young white boy who is on the verge of departing drops his remote-control toy car, a symbol of decadence in a nation where most blacks at the time were living in poverty. Rather than express anger or resentment, the black boy who recovers it simply turns it into a festive, decorative hat. This symbolic repurposing is Nair's way of suggesting a path towards a livable future for a united South Africa, a future marked not by recriminations but by good-spirited appropriation, hybridizing creativity, and hopeful multiculturalism.

My Own Country (1998)

My Own Country (1998) has quite a bit in common with *Mississippi Masala* in terms of the diasporic theme, though the two films do differ in some important respects. *My Own Country* was filmed for broadcast on television on the Showtime channel and, like *Mississippi Masala*, features as a protagonist an Indian settled in Africa who was forced to leave in the early 1970s. That said, while *Mississippi Masala* does engage with historical events and contemporary issues, it is probably best understood as primarily a love story; by contrast, in *My Own Country*, the social and political issues surrounding the spread of AIDS in the United States supersede the personal dimensions of the story. In its approach to representing the spread of AIDS in a rural Tennessee town, Nair's film closely follows Abraham Verghese's 1994 memoir, *My Own Country*. Finally, it should be noted that Nair's film version of *My Own Country* is stylistically and thematically close to some of Nair's recent short films, including the 2007 "Migration," which focuses on AIDS in India, and the 2002 film included in the collection of short films called *11'09"01*—where Nair focused on the plight of a Muslim family settled in New York after the terrorist attacks.

In her adaptation of Verghese's memoir, Nair emphasizes the personality of Verghese himself, including his history of playing guitar in a jazz or rock band in Ethiopia, and in some cases emphasizing aspects of his personal background and narrative that are not given great attention in Verghese's text. The best example of this shift in emphasis can be seen if we compare the opening scenes of *My Own Country* with Verghese's opening. Nair's film opens with a young Abraham Verghese in Ethiopia in 1974, on the receiving end of sharp ethnic hostility. In a restaurant, a man holding a grenade and an automatic rifle asks him menacingly, "You want to buy us a drink, Indian boy?" The scene, which is imaged as a series of suggestive still photographs rather than live video, ends with the sound of a gun being shot. Verghese himself was not injured, but the encounter clearly indicates to him that he has to leave the country. In many ways, this opening sequence echoes the opening scenes of *Mississippi Masala*, where Jay is forced to reckon with direct physical menace from Ugandan Africans and a sense of personal betrayal. Jay, like Nair's Dr. Verghese, was forced to reckon with the loss of home: "When you're forced to leave a country you once called home, it changes everything. You can't enjoy the simple pleasures of life. You envy people who can." None of this is stated quite so explicitly in Verghese's memoir (the sense of racialized hostility directed against Indians in Ethiopia, for instance, is not mentioned as such there).

By contrast to Nair's film adaptation, Abraham Verghese's memoir opens not with reference to Verghese's story but rather with a particularly dramatic incident involving one of the first AIDS patients to come to Johnson City, Tennessee, where Verghese was working and teaching starting in the early 1980s. The central drama in the book is not Verghese's struggle to find a sense of community and home; instead, it is found in the many individual stories of patients and friends dealing with the disease, either personally or indirectly, as it spread rapidly around the country in the early and mid-1980s. The following passage from the same opening section of Verghese's memoir illustrates the central theme of his narrative quite clearly:

> I know this stretch of highway that cuts through the Virginia mountains; I know how the road rises, sheer rock on one side, how in places the kudzu takes over and seems to hold up a hillside, and how, in the early afternoon, the sun glares directly into the windshield. He would have seen hay rolled into tidy bundles, lined up on the edges of fields. And tobacco plants and sagging sheds with their rusted, corrugated-tin roofs and shutterless side-openings. It would have all been familiar, this country. His own country. (Verghese 1994: 9–10)

These novelistic touches are remarkably effective at bringing the reader to identify with the unnamed AIDS patient, returning home from New York to Tennessee while deathly ill—just hours away from passing out and being taken to the hospital, where he would soon die of complications of the disease. Even in the midst of that acute medical crisis, Verghese's narrative aims to draw the reader's attention to small details—and away from himself. And yet one cannot help but apply a diasporic lens to the way Verghese relates his account of a young man returning home to die, on roads he knew from long experience, from his life in the broader world. Like Verghese, the young man is an immigrant of sorts—an expatriate from rural Tennessee who has spent his adult life in New York City. His last act is an enactment of many emigrants' fantasy: he came home.

When Verghese does introduce himself as the central character in the memoir, he creates a curious homology between his own arrival in the United States in 1980 and the arrival of the disease with which he would be directly professionally associated throughout the 1980s and '90s:

> I had arrived in America as a rookie doctor in 1980.
>
> At about the same time, HIV, the virus that causes AIDS, landed in the port cities of the United States: New York, San Francisco and Los Angeles. The virus arrived from Africa (perhaps via Haiti) carried in the bloodstream of one or more unsuspecting people who had then passed it on by sharing needles or through sexual intercourse. Like recipients of a biological chain-letter, the number of carriers mushroomed. Quickly, but without commotion, the virus took root in the immune system of thousands of urban individuals. (Verghese 1994: 16)

The above passage is in the same vein as the opening passages, where Verghese seems to downplay his presence. Here as before, Verghese focuses on the disease that arrived around the same time as he did and that has destroyed so many lives. Verghese gives his own narrative history one sentence, but he gives the disease four.

Another of the recurring themes that Nair gives greater attention to than does Verghese himself is his struggle to be accepted and succeed as an immigrant physician in the US. He quickly rises through the ranks at an inner-city hospital; inner-city hospitals were among the few American hospitals that accepted foreign medical graduates in the 1970s and 1980s. However, Verghese does not seem to harbor resentment about this somewhat shabby welcome to the Land of Opportunity, and he retains a remarkably positive attitude. For instance, after coming to Johnson City as a specialist in infectious diseases and as an assistant professor of medicine at East Tennessee State University, Verghese (in Nair's film) is seen seen brushing off a rude racial remark from a patient:

> DR. VERGHESE: If you don't stop smoking, you're going to be in trouble.
> PATIENT: I fought for my country. You foreigners come over here and tell me what to do, make money off us? I'm going to write my congressman.
> DR. VERGHESE: You do that. [Starts to walk off]
> PATIENT: Hey Doc, can y'all get me some American doctors? Just like her? (Nair, *My Own Country*, 1998)

Ironically, the young female doctor the patient is pointing to at the end of this scene in Nair's film has just been identified, in the previous scene, as a Dr. Shaheen Ali. The patient wants to be treated by an "American" doctor, and he's ironically correct despite himself (i.e., she *is* American—South Asian American).

As mentioned, the Dr. Verghese of Nair's film, like the personality Abraham Verghese seems to embody in his memoir, seems remarkably able to connect with people outside of his ethnic comfort zone. This openness extends well beyond Dr. Verghese's workplace demeanor; one of the Vergheses' closest friends both in Nair's film and in Verghese's memoir is Allen, a local man who runs a gas station and is very much a part of eastern Tennessee mountain culture. His openness to cultural difference also makes Dr. Verghese a good candidate for doing outreach with gay populations in rural Tennessee. In *My Own Country* Verghese suggests an intriguing correlation between the immigrant struggle to adapt and fit in and the experience of gay men in a heterosexual-centered culture, where the ability to adapt and survive in disguise is often essential:

> As I got to know more gay men, I became curious about their life stories, keen to compare their stories with mine. There was an obvious parallel: society considered them alien and much of their life was spent faking conformity; in my case my Green Card labeled me a "resident alien." New immigrants expend a great deal of effort trying to fit in: learning the language, losing the accent, picking up the rituals of Monday Night Football and Happy Hour. Gay men, in order to avoid conflict, had also become experts at blending in, camouflaging themselves, but at a great cost to their spirit. By contrast, my adaptation had been voluntary, even joyful: from the time I was born I lacked a country I could speak of as home. My survival had depended on a chameleonlike adaptability, taking on the rituals of the place I found myself to be in: Africa, India, Boston, Johnson City. I felt as if I was always reinventing myself, discovering who I was. My latest reincarnation, here in Johnson City, was my happiest so far. (Verghese 1994: 51)

This suggestive linking of the idea of self-invention as experienced by immigrants and gay men isn't developed extensively in Nair's film version of *My Own Country*, though it does arise in various ways, especially in the relationship between Dr. Verghese and his wife, Rajni. In Verghese's memoir, there are some hints of challenges that arise in the relationship because of the overwhelming pressure Dr. Verghese feels, as the only "AIDS expert" in the area, when the epidemic expands. By contrast, in Nair's film, the growing tension between Abraham and Rajni becomes the central narrative tension in the story, and Nair and Taraporevala (working together for a third time) focalize a moment of narrative crisis around Rajni's going into labor at the time one of Abraham's patients comes into the hospital in a state of collapse. Nair and Taraporevala's choice to make the marriage of Dr. Verghese and Rajni the central focus of the film adaptation is a departure from Verghese's memoir, which is more circular, episodic, and structurally complex.

As she did in several other films made in this period of her career, Nair herself makes a strategic cameo in *My Own Country*. Here, she reprises in some sense the gossiping "auntie" role she assigned herself in *Mississippi Masala*. In her first appearance, she is standing in line with Rajni at the traveling Indian grocery truck (a predecessor to the establishment of proper Indian grocery stores). Here she asks: "Is the baby kicking? How's your husband and his AIDS?" The slightly ungrammatical question is by design, as the phrasing suggests that one of the points of embarrassment for Rajni is Abraham's obsessive interest in and public association with AIDS. In their small town, people think of AIDS as "his" disease and the gay patients as "his" as well. Even as a medical professional dedicated to fighting the disease, Abraham is stigmatized by it.

The Perez Family (1995)

Nair's *The Perez Family* is a film adaptation of a novel by the same name by Christine Bell (1990) about a family that was separated at the time of the Cuban revolution and has the potential to be reunited during the Mariel boatlift of 1980. As is well known, the boatlift brought more than one hundred thousand Cuban refugees to the United States in the span of just a few months, with the full, if tacit, approval of both Castro and the US government. Though Nair's film received mixed reviews upon its release, *The Perez Family* has an intriguing take on the problem of diasporic identity that complements Nair's other films from this period. As with *Mississippi Masala* and *My Own Country*, the moment of leaving is here wrapped up in a historical (and personal) trauma: in the other films, the trauma was associated with the racial exclusivism of Idi Amin and the political violence in Ethiopia. In *The Perez Family*, the threat is Fidel Castro's suppression of dissenting voices and ideas, including both political and sexual dissidents.

The Perez Family is one of the films Mira Nair sometimes distances herself from in interviews (see Maira and Srikanth 1996: 136–37), in large part because she had to work within the constraints created for her by the Hollywood studio backing the project. Some of the negative reviews of the film, which we will acknowledge and discuss below, do make salient points, especially regarding the problem of "authenticity" in Nair's film, and it might well be appropriate to say upfront that *The Perez Family* is an idiosyncratic film, far from a definitive account of the Cuban American experience. That said, Nair did win an award from the Spanish Film Critics' Association for *The Perez Family*, and Nair has asserted that the film has remained popular with Cuban Americans, who see it as a contribution to a growing genre of memoirs, novels, and films representing a broad range of experiences associated with aftereffects of the Cuban Revolution. As a film about the diasporic experience, *The Perez Family* covers some of the same ground as *My Own Country* and *Mississippi Masala*. Despite its flaws, therefore, it has merits that make it a compelling film—and one that merits some close attention.

The key context for *The Perez Family* is quite clearly the vexed relationship between Cuba and the United States following the communist revolution of 1959. The collapse of the old US-friendly but deeply corrupt government led by Fulgencio Batista led to an initial wave of Cuban expatriates in the United States in the early 1960s, many of them business owners whose property and assets were under threat of nationalization by Castro (for an in-depth account of the causes and impact of the Boatlift, see Doss 2003). Until the late 1970s, there was very little diplomatic contact between the United States and Cuba, but beginning in 1978, US president Jimmy Carter began to make overtures to Cuba. Both Cuba and the US agreed to relax restrictions on family visits to Cuba, leading a number of Cuban expatriates to return to visit the island. These returning expatriates offered a picture of life in the United States to their countrymen very much at odds with the propaganda about America generated within Cuba itself. Possibly because of this increased contact, beginning in the spring of 1980, large numbers of Cubans began to petition their government to allow them to emigrate. Castro complied by opening emigration from the port of Mariel for several months; he also used the ensuing mass exodus as an opportunity to dispense with hundreds, if not thousands, of Cubans his regime found to be undesirable: political prisoners who dissented from Castro's government, regular criminal convicts, prostitutes, homosexuals, and the mentally ill (see Aguirre, Saenz, and James 1997).

Within the United States, public sentiment quickly turned against the Mariel boatlift, as it was called, in large part because it quickly became clear that Castro was using the mass emigration in part to clear his own jails (as Angel Perez puts it in Nair's film, "Castro has flushed his toilets on us!").

Historians of Hispanic communities in the US have even suggested that the event marked the beginning of an anti-Latino sentiment in American political discourse (Aguirre, Saenz, and James 1997: 487). However, though the "Marielitos" acquired a local reputation as criminally inclined after the boatlift led to a limited spike in crime in the Miami area, this stereotype was dramatically exaggerated by media representations of Cuban gangsters in films like Brian De Palma's *Scarface* (1983). Christine Bell's novel and, after it, Nair's film adaptation give a more balanced depiction of the demographics of the new Cuban immigrants and can, consequently be seen as a kind of corrective to the sensationalism of De Palma's account. The central protagonist in both Nair's film and Bell's novel is Juan Raul Perez, a political prisoner who has been separated from his wife and daughter for twenty years; he sent them away to the US at the beginning of the revolution while he stayed and was put in prison by Castro. The exact reason for Juan Perez's imprisonment is never directly specified, though in Nair's film he refers to an act of overt resistance to Castro ("I set my sugar cane fields on fire. Instead of giving them to him, to Fidel"). Juan Perez is an undeniably positive image of a Cuban immigrant—a former Cuban property owner who is sharply at odds with the communist government. However, both Bell and Nair do acknowledge the presence of prostitutes amongst the immigrants via Dorita "Dottie" Perez (played by Marisa Tomei in Nair's film adaptation). Rather than moralize over Dottie's former profession, both Bell and Nair embrace and foreground her sexuality, which becomes a creative and transformative force in the new world of Florida after the influx of waves of immigrants. In its foregrounding of female sexuality and its use of a coprotagonist who has been involved with the sex trade, Nair's *Perez Family* has links to other important Nair films, especially *India Cabaret*, *Salaam Bombay!*, and *Kama Sutra: A Tale of Love*.

Among the most anti-Cuban voices in Bell's novel and Nair's film are other Cubans, namely the earlier wave of immigrants who are now well-settled around Miami and who have little interest in being associated with the stigmatized Marielitos. The key figure is the character Angel Perez, who repeatedly refers to the Marielitos as "human scum" and makes repeated gestures to Carmela regarding her own security, including giving her an unlicensed handgun for her own protection and then later installing a security system in case of intruders. Angel's obsession with security, triggered by the crime wave associated (wrongly) with the Mariel boatlift, has to be seen as pathological: the invaders whose intrusion he is most paranoid about are his own people.

As mentioned, numerous connections can be drawn between *The Perez Family* and the other films Nair made about diaspora in the early and mid-1990s. Some of the parallels are cross-cultural analogies (i.e., the arguable similarities between Cuban exiles and Asian Ugandans forced out of East Africa), but *The Perez Family* does contain at least a few references to the Indian diaspora community, which form a leitmotif not present in Bell's novel. On the one hand, this adds to the image of a "real" United States that is considerably more complex and diverse than the John Wayne movies Dottie expects. Rather than a "real United States freedom hero," the person who is most helpful to Dottie Perez is himself an immigrant, an Immigration and Naturalization Service (INS) official played by Ranjit Chowdhry (memorable as "Mundu" in Deepa Mehta's *Fire*; Chowdhry also had a role in Nair's *Misssissippi Masala*).

There is something ironic about an Indian immigrant serving as the "model" for the Americanization of a Cuban ("I am going to have to tell you what to do!" he says, at one point), but in fact cross-cultural dynamics like these have shaped wave after wave of immigration in American history; the culture of the United States is in a fundamental sense constituted by the experience of immigrant communities and the processes of acculturation, assimilation, and hybridity. Along these lines, it's quite appropriate that it is Chowdhry's character who reveals to Dottie that John Wayne, for her the very embodiment of a sexy, heroic America, is in fact dead. It's also his "hint" that families will get sponsored more quickly than singles that leads Dottie to stick to Juan Perez, their "son" (a street kid they come across named Felipe), and a mentally ill "father" (Papa) to move things forward.

In Nair's film adaptation of *The Perez Family*, both Juan and Dottie experience, in very different ways, profound confusion and bewilderment in the country in which they have found themselves. The United States that had been projected for them within Cuba was quite different from the actual society they encountered upon arrival. For Juan Perez, who has had almost no contact with the outside world for twenty years, and who is, further, deeply traumatized by his experience in prison, it is exceedingly difficult to think of beginning a new life. Even the rather elementary task he faces, of contacting his wife Carmela and daughter Teresa, are beyond him initially.

For her part, Dottie is much more assertive and able to immediately engage with America and Americans, though she has to overcome a perception of life in America distorted in part by the Hollywood image factory. Unlike Juan Perez, Dottie actively petitioned to be sent to the United States, as shown in an early dialogue between herself and a Cuban police officer on a farm in rural Cuba for rehabilitating "deviants" like herself:

> DOTTIE: I am waiting two months. When can I go on the boatlift?
> OFFICER: You are a whore, no? You like it, eh? [Makes suggestive gesture.]
> DOTTIE: I am like Cuba, used by many, conquered by no one. A man like you changes uniform with each regime. Batista, Fidel. But I am *siempre la isla* [always the island].
> SOLDIER: What do you want in America that I can't give you here?
> DOTTIE: I love Elvis Presley. I dig rock 'n' roll. I want to *fuck* John Wayne! (Nair, *The Perez Family*, 1995)

Though the language here is over-the-top ("I want to *fuck* John Wayne"), it is representative of the way Dottie understands the free expression of sexual desire as central to the idea of American "freedom" she has come to pursue.

Later, when Dottie begins to date a well-built blond security guard assigned to watch over the refugees at the Orange Bowl, she gasps with pleasure, "My hero, my United States freedom hero," again suggesting her cartoonishly sexualized image of life in America. As their boat is arriving at Key West, Dottie makes a powerful symbolic statement by jumping out of the boat, only to reemerge as a new woman. In Nair's film, her emergence from the water is figured as a glamorous, "Hollywood" moment.

Dottie's attempt to redefine herself in America in the model of an artificial, Hollywood image-factory version of Americanness continues in her interview with the US Coast Guard, where she states that she wishes to disavow her given names (Dorita Evita Perez) and simply become "Dottie." When the officer objects that her application for political asylum should be her first priority and a legal name change can come later, she makes a trademark statement regarding what *she* wants from her new life: "I don't want no political asylum. I came here to get away from political asylum. I don't want *no* government."

The image of America Dottie has projected, centered around liberal sexuality and the over-the-top Hollywood masculinity of Elvis Presley and John Wayne, is at odds with the actual experience of Cuban refugees in the Mariel boatlift. While a number of the refugees were quickly sponsored by family members, quite a number were sent, involuntarily, to resettlement camps at various sites around the country. Most Marielitos came to the US to be "free," but, at least initially, their freedom was sharply circumscribed

The Perez Family. Emerging from the water.

by US immigration authorities. Nair's film underlines this with a rather forbidding-sounding voice-over by the Indian American INS officer (Chowdhry), broadcast over the PA system at the Orange Bowl:

> Welcome to the Orange Bowl Football Stadium. You are permitted to leave the premises between 8 a.m. and 9 p.m. After 9 p.m. is curfew, but remember, when you go out you are on your own. If you do not return, you will be deemed illegal. So be careful. Obey the rules of the United States Immigration Service. Welcome to freedom. (Nair, *The Perez Family*, 1995)

The new immigrants are first subjected to a long list of restrictions and rules of conduct backed by threats ("you will be deemed illegal"), only to be then told, "Welcome to freedom." It is perhaps not terribly surprising that many of the Marielitos were, as a result, confused as to whether they were in fact prisoners or merely refugees.

While Dottie is ready to dive into a new life (literally) in the United States, both Juan Perez and the wife he has not seen in twenty years, Carmela, remain adrift. They have spiritually and physically left Cuba behind, but they have not found it easy to engage with their new lives in the United States. They are in rather different positions socially—Juan Perez is attempting to reconnect his life from the bottom up, while Carmela is comfortably settled—but they are seen in both Bell's novel and Nair's film as effective mirror images of one another. Until they resolve the status of their relationship to one another, they simply cannot move on.

The opening of Nair's *The Perez Family* establishes the oceanic metaphor for the Perezes. The opening shot is, it is later made clear, a dream sequence. The camera pans slowly across a beach in Cuba, before the revolution. Elegantly dressed men and women in white suits sit at tables drinking cocktails, as a waiter (again, formally dressed) makes his way through. The music, traditional Cuban Son (the music for the film as a whole is composed by Arturo Sandoval), adds an air of Old Havana nostalgia. The pan ends on the headlights and grill of a vintage 1950s Cadillac—symbolizing, without a single line of dialogue, how the Cuban story was in some sense *always about* the United States, even before the Cubans emigrants left home.

After the Cadillac, Nair cuts to Juan Perez (Alfred Molina), who is watching as his young wife, Carmela, wades into the water with their daughter. She's leaving—and it is here that it becomes clear that this surreal scene is a dream sequence—where he'll be left behind. While water represents, for Dottie, an opportunity to be reborn, for Juan Perez it is a fundamental barrier, sundering him from his family and the beautiful life he had begun to have with them before the revolution.

Carmela (played by Anjelica Huston) has a relationship to water that closely mirrors her husband's. While Juan is seen as effectively unable to cross the water separating him from his family, Carmela feels as if she remains adrift at sea, despite the solidity of her new material world. Here, for instance, is her confession to her daughter Teresa at a moment when she begins to come to terms with the idea that Juan may not ever be coming:

> I feel like I'm floating. Twenty years ago, I lay alone in my bed each night. In the morning, my pillow would be wet with tears. Each I day I put you in the most beautiful embroidered dresses, just in case there was a day he would come. The waiting is familiar now. It's become a friend. It's like breathing. It's part of my life. He's never coming. (Nair, *The Perez Family*, 1995)

As it turns out, Juan is in fact present in Florida, only unable to reach his wife for a variety of reasons, some of them accidental and some of them contrived by her brother Angel, who disapproves of what Juan has become. Just as "freedom" is a complex concept for the Marielitos camped out (or imprisoned) in their resettlement camp, Carmela too does not feel entirely free. In Christine Bell's novel, Carmela is described at various points as "imprisoned" in her

The Perez Family. Nineteen-fifties Americana on a Caribbean beach: Old Havana nostalgia.

house, and her brother Angel is her "warden" (Bell 1990: 246); Nair captures this visually in her film adaptation in the scene where Carmela wakes up after dreaming of Juan only to find men installing bars on her windows, ostensibly for her own protection.

When Carmela and Juan Perez finally do reunite, they find that the time and distance have changed their relationship, and both Bell and Nair make the surprising choice to have this epically belated romantic reunion lead to something other than a conventional happy ending. Though the surprise of this denouement is dramatically disorienting, the choice makes symbolic sense. The choice both Juan and Carmela make, to pursue new romantic interests, is a way of allowing both of them access to a new romantic landscape—a landscape not determined by prerevolutionary Cuba, but rather one that emerges on its own in the United States.

By way of concluding this section, it seems appropriate to refer to some of the criticisms made of Nair's film. Though not all the reviews of *The Perez Family* were negative (*Time* magazine called *The Perez Family* a "delightful, unexpected treat" [Schickel 1995]), the film did earn Nair some of the harshest reviews she has ever received. *Hispanic Magazine* declared *The Perez Family* the "worst" film of 1995 in its December issue, stating,

> The story deals with the experiences that Cubans in the Mariel boatlift encountered upon their arrival in Miami. Unlike *Mi Familia*, the director, writer, and most of the actors in *The Perez Family* were non-Hispanic. And the normally thin Marisa Tomei wore a bronzing

product and put on eighteen pounds because the producers didn't think she was dark or plump enough to play a Cuban prostitute. The main weaknesses of the film, however, were a hokey script and uninspired direction. (Macias 1995: 16)

I do not contest that *The Perez Family* is a flawed film—its script has numerous implausible elements, and it is derived from a somewhat lackluster source (that is to say, Christine Bell's novel). But what is really worth remarking on in Macias's critique is the authenticity issue—the fact that non-Cubans were cast for most of the key roles. (That Marisa Tomei was asked to gain weight for the role is verified by Nair, though it should be noted that Dottie is clearly specified as voluptuous in Christine Bell's novel.) Though the nontraditional casting of *The Perez Family* is perhaps not in itself a problem, the fact that so many of the actors did not have a personal connection to Cuba does weaken the sense of documentary realism one expects from Nair. That said, the critique of a certain Hollywood image of the United States in Nair's *The Perez Family*—as seen in the satirical allusions to John Wayne and in the demystification of the myth of American "freedom"—is notable, especially since it serves as a point of balance for the extensive critiques of the *Indian* film industry in other Nair films (especially *Salaam Bombay!* and *Monsoon Wedding*, discussed in previous chapters). Thus, despite its limitations, *The Perez Family* does have enough going for it to have a place in this study among Nair's other major diaspora vérité films.

After a bruising experience with the critical response to *The Perez Family*, it should be noted that Nair has generally avoided making contemporary films focusing on communities to which she does not herself have a strong personal connection; even her recent film *Queen of Katwe*, which is set in Uganda, is built on a cultural framework she has developed over decades through her and her family's longstanding connections to that country.

That said, Nair has made other ambitious, big-budget films with mainstream studio backing (namely *Vanity Fair*, *Amelia*, and *Kama Sutra: A Tale of Love*) where she has intentionally departed, at least in some ways, from the aspiration to a documentary realist aesthetic that defined her work up through the mid-1990s. Though not all of these films have been successful either, their ambition and the controversies they have often provoked (especially *Vanity Fair* and *Kama Sutra*), along with the ongoing interest in themes related to diaspora as well as gender and sexuality, lead us to take a closer look.

Chapter 6

FEMINIST PERIOD PIECES

Vanity Fair (2004) and *Kama Sutra: A Tale of Love* (1996)

In three recent films, Mira Nair took a step away from her longstanding focus on contemporary global, diasporic communities—*Vanity Fair*, *Kama Sutra: A Tale of Love*, and *Amelia* (2009). All three films contain strong women protagonists and female-centered narratives (even *Kama Sutra*) and should be considered, first and foremost, as films whose feminism is their most prominent characteristic. Moreover, all three feature narratives involving exile and travel in some way, meaning they are thematically linked to Nair's larger filmic project. While this assertion may seem like a stretch—since most scholars of diaspora often limit themselves to patterns of migration in the twentieth century—all three of these films do retain the emphasis on geographic movement and exile as tied to personal liberation that has been one of the key features of the diaspora vérité concept I have been developing throughout this study. Nair's Becky Sharp, in short, has perhaps more in common with Meena of *Mississippi Masala* or Aditi of *Monsoon Wedding* than she might with other heroines of Victorian novels rendered on film. Our attention to Nair's diaspora vérité inspires a distinctive way of reading her films, but it also enables us to see patterns emerging within her body of work that might not be as easily visible without an awareness of the broader oeuvre of the filmmaker.

It should also be noted that all three of these films are adaptations. Of the three, however, only *Vanity Fair* stands up as a strong film now, more than a decade after its release. *Kama Sutra: A Tale of Love* does have some intriguing aesthetic and historical elements and an ambition to provoke, which will be discussed below, as will Nair's struggle with the Indian Central Board of Film Certification (popularly known as the Indian censor board).

As for Nair's 2009 film *Amelia*, despite its thematic overlaps with Nair's other films (especially its incontrovertible feminism), it suffers from being both relatively bland and lacking in a strong diaspora vérité orientation, and as a result we will not discuss it at length here.

The move into historical films involves some adjustments in approach both for the filmmaker and the critic. *Vanity Fair* and *Kama Sutra: A Tale of Love* are adaptations of complex texts from historical periods—texts that are notoriously difficult to represent on film (*Vanity Fair* in particular is so long and involved that the television miniseries format might be a more natural format). Both films are lavish productions with elaborate costumes and sets made with budgets larger than many of Nair's films set in the present day, especially the low-budget *Monsoon Wedding* and *Salaam Bombay!* Because of their budgets and elaborate sets and costumes, these films reflect a partial departure from the realist, documentarian impulse that has been dominant in Nair's filmmaking. That said, making each of these films did involve considerable research on the part of Nair and her writing and production team, and there is a strong (though not absolute) emphasis on accuracy to the respective historical periods invoked in both films.

With *Kama Sutra: A Tale of Love*, an integral part of the story of the film is the response the film engendered, specifically the censorship battles Nair went through in order to have the film distributed in India. Though the censorship case was extremely taxing to the filmmaker, the controversy was not entirely surprising given the history of Indian censorship, and some of that history is related briefly below. In effect, Nair's transgression of the codes governing the representation of sexuality in Indian cinema is at the core of her project in *Kama Sutra*; the film extends and intensifies a pattern of critique we have been seeing in earlier films such as *India Cabaret* and *Salam Bombay!* *Vanity Fair* is a slightly narrower intervention in the sense that its major distinguishing feature is Nair's careful exploration and enhancement of the India-related themes in Thackeray's famous satire of Victorian class and gender relations. However, *Vanity Fair* too might be read as transgressively feminist in that it challenges many of the expectations governing how heroines in British "period pieces" can and should act in their own self-interest. Granted, some of the seeds of Nair's transgression are already present in Thackeray's complex and ambiguous novel. How and whether we accept Nair's interpretation of *Vanity Fair* depends on how one reads Thackeray; below, there will be some consideration of the source texts that have inspired both films alongside interpretation of the films themselves.

The commonalities between *Kama Sutra* and *Vanity Fair* do not end with the fact that they are both female-centered period pieces. Both are, for one thing, about friendships between women of unequal status—Becky Sharp and Amelia Sedley in the Thackeray adaptation, and Princess Maya and Princess Tara in *Kama Sutra*. Also, in both films there is a clear sense that the woman who comes from an impoverished background is more talented and passionate than her social superior, and both films explore, in slightly different ways, how the two protagonists (Maya and Becky Sharp, respectively) negotiate their social ambition without sacrificing their friendships with other better-situated women. Crucially, both films feature love triangles involving the husband of the protagonist's female friend—another good reason to consider the two films together in this section of our study. But perhaps most importantly, both films centrally feature a narrative of geographic displacement, as the protagonists are forced to give up their attachment to home and society in response to transgressive actions taken early in the films. Maya and Becky Sharp become, in short, diasporic feminist subjects. And while the connection to what I have been calling diaspora vérité is necessarily a little more oblique in these studio-backed historical period pieces, I will argue that they do in fact fit the pattern we have been seeing in Nair's other films up to this point in her career.

Kama Sutra: A Tale of Love (1996)

Kama Sutra: A Tale of Love is, like *Vanity Fair*, a period piece and a literary adaptation. Perhaps surprisingly, given the title, the most *direct* source of the adaptation, more than Vatsayana's *Kama Sutra*, is in fact an Urdu short story by Wajida Tabassum, "Utaran" (Castoffs), which provides Nair with the basic plot for the story depicted in the film. Through the film, which became as much a political and social statement for Nair as a work of art in itself, Nair extended a line of films challenging the conservativism of the Indian media, as well as the media's double standards over representations of sexuality, beginning with *India Cabaret* and continuing to *Salaam Bombay!* and then, after *Kama Sutra*, *Monsoon Wedding*. The film itself weaves together, as a kind of cross-historical collage, ancient Indian erotic literature (the *Kama Sutra* itself), the erotic sculptures adorning several important medieval Hindu temples in eastern India including Konark and Khajuraho, the Hindu tradition of Tantric art (where sexual expression is intertwined with religious ritual and sacralized), the classical Indian dance form known as Odissi, and the Mughal/Indo-Islamic traditions of courtly love.

As has already been mentioned, Nair's *Kama Sutra* is not a direct historical adaptation of either Vatsayana or Wajida Tabassum but rather an amalgam of several different historical traditions and narratives. As Vatsayana's text is a book of lessons rather than a narrative, it does not lend itself well to a direct fictional adaptation—hence the introduction of a romantic plot drawn from Tabassum. While Tabassum provides the narrative frame, then, the thematics of *Kama Sutra: A Tale of Love* do clearly derive from Vatsayana's classic Sanskrit text. Contrary to popular conception, the *Kama Sutra* is not merely a book about sexual positions; it is rather, as Sudhir Kakar writes, a book "about the art of living—about finding a partner, maintaining power in marriage, committing adultery, living as or with a courtesan, using drugs—and also about the positions in sexual intercourse" (Kakar 2008: n.p.). Scholars now believe *The Kama Sutra* came into its current written form around the second century CE; it may have first been composed in the second or third century BCE. As is well known, Vatsayana takes an almost scandalously open-minded view of the sexual act and sexual pleasure—particularly as it relates to women—sharply at variance with other ancient Sanskrit texts, most especially the *Manusmriti*, but also roughly contemporaneous texts like the *Arthashastra* (Doniger 2009: 304–38). For most of the modern era, the *Kama Sutra* was unknown to most Hindus as well as Western scholars in India; it was brought to the world's attention following its translation into English in 1883 by Richard Burton, and it has since become one of the best-known texts associated with ancient India outside of India itself. However, its impacts on mainstream conceptions of sexuality in Hindu culture have continued to remain marginal—especially against *Manusmriti*, which remains in many ways the foundation for ideas about gender relations and caste relations for many Hindus today.

At certain points in the film, Nair quotes directly from Vatsayana's *Kama Sutra*, and the pedagogical idea of "lessons in love" (*kama sutra*) is important in the overall fictional plot in the film. On the eve of Princess Maya's wedding, for instance, one of her "aunties" quotes roughly from Vatsayana as follows:

> The wisdom of the *Kama Sutra* is such—it teaches us not to rush. For the first three days after marriage, the girl and the boy should refrain from sexual pleasure. On the tenth night, the king will begin gentle love play, to create confidence in you. . . . You should at this time accept his embrace, and allow him to put betel nut in your mouth. (Nair, *Kama Sutra: A Tale of Love*, 1996)

This monologue in Nair's film is loosely adapted from Vatsayana's *Kama Sutra* (Burton's translation), part 3, section 2, "On Creating Confidence in a Wife":

> For the first three days after marriage, the girl and her husband should sleep on the floor, abstain from sexual pleasures, and eat their food without seasoning it either with alkali or salt.... On the night of the tenth day the man should begin in a lonely place with soft words, and thus create confidence in the girl.... He should embrace her first of all in a way she likes most, because it does not last for a long time. He should embrace her with the upper part of his body because that is easier and simpler. If the girl is grown up, or if the man has known her for some time, he may embrace her by the light of a lamp, but if he is not well acquainted with her, or if she is a young girl, he should then embrace her in darkness. When the girl accepts the embrace, the man should put a "tambula" or screw of betel nut and betel leaves in her mouth. (Vatsayana 1883: part 3, section 2)

While many of Vatsayana's ritualistic prescriptions may seem highly rarefied today, what is striking about passages like this is the emphasis on the sexual pleasure of the woman. The rituals described may seem to some readers a mark of exoticism, but in many ways they are designed to ensure a kind of thoughtfulness and self-consciousness on the part of men and women entering into sexual relationships, and this is something that Nair is clearly interested in trying to develop in her feminist adaptation of the ancient Sanskrit text.

Tabassum's short story, for its part, does not mention *The Kama Sutra* at all (not surprising, given that it's a short story by an Urdu-speaking writer from a Muslim background); it is set in a wealthy Muslim household during the British colonial era and has a distinctively sensual, irreverent style, which might be familiar to readers of Ismat Chughtai. "Utaran" begins with a scene of two girls bathing together, a servant girl named Chamki and her mistress, Shahzadi Pasha. While in Nair's film Princess Tara is simply somewhat disconnected and overshadowed by the servant girl Maya, in Tabassum's story, Shahzadi Pasha (the princess figure) is unlikable and somewhat abusive of her friend. Chamki's mother is the royal wet nurse Anna Bi, and it is really her job to keep Chamki in line so she doesn't offend Shahzadi Pasha:

> According to Anna Bi's reckoning, it was a matter of great good fortune that she had been hired as a wet nurse to the young mistress.

> She was given food and drink from the table of the mistress. After all, she was nursing the Nawab's only daughter at her breast. Nobody could keep count of the clothes she received—they had to be clean and fresh for one who nursed the child. And the greatest boon was that her own child received all the clothes discarded by the young mistress. There was really nothing more one could ask for. The beauty of it was that often even silver jewelry and toys were given away as used or discarded goods. And here was this stubborn wretch who, ever since she reached the age of discretion, had obstinately been asking why she should wear the mistress's used clothes! Sometimes she would look into the mirror with a knowing air, and say, "Ammanni, I'm far prettier than Bi Pasha, am I not? Then why shouldn't she wear *my* used clothes?" (Tabassum 1993: 413)

Chamki is a girl who simply will not take what she's given. While Maya is depicted for the most part in the film as being pleased with the castoffs derived from Princess Tara, in Tabassum's story, Chamki clearly values her one simple cotton dress over the elegant secondhand clothes she must wear: "This one set of clothes freed her from all sense of inferiority, and made her feel supremely exalted. It was not anybody's castoff" (415).

One of the most memorable scenes in Nair's film, Maya's devastating admission to Tara the day after she's seduced Tara's husband, come directly from the closing lines of Tabassum's short story. In Nair's film version, Tara approaches a sleeping Prince Raj and seduces him the night of the wedding—before he's consummated his marriage with Maya. The closing lines of Tabassum's story, which run as follows, form a direct inspiration for Tara's subsequent humiliation of Maya (in Tabassum's story the character names are different):

> The day after the wedding, when in accordance with the customs of the house, Shahzadi Pasha gave her used bridal costume to her nurse's daughter, her playmate, Chamki smiled and said, "Pasha—I—I—I— All my life I kept wearing your castoffs, but now you also . . ."
>
> And she began to laugh like one possessed. "Something I have used you will also—for the rest of your life. . . ." There was no stopping her laughter. Everyone thought that the sorrow of parting from her childhood companion had temporarily driven Chamki out of her wits. (Tabassum 1993: 416)

While the sensuality in Nair's film derives mainly from Vatsayana's *Kama Sutra*, along with the sculptures of Khajuraho and classical Odissi dance, it is Tabassum's story that provides her film its most accessible human drama. Furthermore, Nair's use of Tabassum enables her to transform a text written by a man and largely (though not entirely) addressed to men into a woman-centered narrative focused as much on friendship and intimacy between women as on erotic relationship between men and women.

As with Nair's other major films, the experience of exile plays a key role in furthering the plot and the personal development of *Kama Sutra*'s main protagonist, Maya (who plays the role of Tabassum's "Chamki" in the passage quoted above). While Tabassum's story ends with the laughter of the mistress, Nair's film interpretation continues the story and adds complications and characters, including a jealous brother to the prince, Biki (played by Khalid Tyabji), a sculptor named Jai Kumar (Ramon Tikaram), who becomes Maya's lover in her time in exile from the kingdom, and Rasa Devi (played by the Bollywood superstar Rekha), who becomes Maya's teacher. As with other, more explicitly diasporic films in Nair's body of work, the experience of exile gives Maya opportunities for social mobility she otherwise would not have had. She meets Jai Kumar, who introduces her to Rasa Devi—who in turn teaches Maya about *The Kama Sutra*, which is reframed in Nair's film in feminist terms as a toolkit for the exploration of female sexual empowerment. After gaining her education outside the kingdom, Maya can close the diasporic circle and return "home" as a preferred courtesan to the king—a much more secure position than her earlier status as a servant girl and playmate to Tara. Maya's ability to grow and adapt while in exile "abroad" for her earlier sexual transgressions suggest similarities to other Nair protagonists, most notably the other major protagonist for this chapter, Becky Sharp (to be discussed in greater detail below).

While *Kama Sutra: A Tale of Love* is a far cry from those of Nair's films that are more firmly rooted in the documentary realist tradition, the film does evince a careful attention to historical representations related to gender and sexuality in the Indian tradition; there is something to be learned from the film if the viewer knows where to look. Traditions informing the concept behind Nair's *Kama Sutra: A Tale of Love* include the Tantric strain within the Hindu tradition and the erotic temple sculptures found in eastern India at Khajuraho and Konark, built during the middle ages (both are cited by Nair herself in the DVD director's commentary; the erotic sculptures at Khajuraho are directly visually cited in her film). The Tantric tradition, for its part, is quite ancient, dating back thousands of years, and is thought of by scholars to be a parallel textual tradition alongside, and sometimes competing with, the dominant Vedic textual tradition that has produced mainstream Hinduism. The Tantric cosmology is complex and beyond our ability to briefly summarize; for now, it will have to suffice to say that the ritualized expression of sexuality in pursuit of transcendence is one of the Tantric tradition's central precepts (Mulchandani 2006: 140).

In the end, the different erotic discourses in the various classical Indian traditions are intertwined. In the oldest known Vedic text, the *Rg Veda*, there are sensual stories (such as the romance between Puruvasa and the nymph Urvashi); a strand of sensuality is also present in the *Mahabharata* (where King Pandu encourages his wife, Kunti, to have children by other men since he is impotent). There are also many other classical-period Indian writers who explored sex and sensuality in their works, including most famously the poets Kalidasa and Amaru. But this thread in the Hindu tradition has now been widely, though not completely, forgotten by many in contemporary India, mainly because a much more sexually conservative version of the tradition came to dominate starting in the medieval period (see Mulchandani 2006: 117–18).

According to Mulchandani's account, it may have been the growing conservativism of mainstream Hinduism itself that provoked the efflorescence of erotic sculpture in temples in eastern India in the ninth and tenth centuries—as a kind of reactive gesture. Also, while they are not directly historically connected (though some friezes at Khajuraho do depict catalogues of sexual positions specifically described in *The Kama Sutra* [Kakar 2008]), the Tantric tradition and the erotic temples of Khajuraho share an emphasis on the link between sexuality and spiritual devotion; the sensuality of Tantra, one may presume, found at least an oblique expression in the famous sculptures of Khajuraho. (The art historian Ajit Mookerjee, who is also directly named by Nair in her director's commentary to *Kama Sutra*, includes some images of these medieval sculptures as representing ideas in Tantra in his influential book, *Tantra Art* [1966].) Through the character of the sculptor in her film, Jai Kumar, Nair has imagined an artist actively engaged in representing eroticism and desire via his art, attempting to bring to life the kind of creative energy that animated the sculptors of Khajuraho, and at times Nair uses actual images from Khajuraho in her film to underline this point.

Of course, more than anything else, the references to the classical and medieval Indian tradition, including *The Kama Sutra*, Khajuraho, and Odissi dance, are all included in Nair's film as part of a larger historical point Nair

Feminist Period Pieces: *Vanity Fair* and *Kama Sutra: A Tale of Love* 141

A Khajuraho frieze in *Kama Sutra: A Tale of Love*.

wishes the film to make—that representing sexuality is not a "Western" art but something that is deeply ingrained in the Indian tradition. Eroticism is not only to be found in a single, idiosyncratic ancient text (Vatsayana's *Kama Sutra*) but is rather also present in the Tantric tradition, in living dance arts such as Odissi, and in the modern Urdu short story. All of the classical and medieval reference points add to Nair's contention that sexuality can and should be part of the work of making serious, authentically "Indian" art.

Unfortunately, even the weight of this evidence was not enough to convince the Indian censor board to allow the finished film to be shown uncut to adult audiences, as Nair had initially hoped it would be. Controversy, of course, must be part of the point of any serious film with the title *Kama Sutra*; just as the fatwa on Salman Rushdie has become in effect an ex post facto part of his novel *The Satanic Verses*, the controversy that followed the release Nair's film cannot be disentangled from the polemical force of Nair's invocation of the representations of sexuality in ancient and medieval Indian traditions within the film itself.

Kama Sutra was released in the United States as an unrated film in 1996, and it did fairly well in limited theatrical release. Critical reaction to the film was muted; many critics who had favorably reviewed earlier Nair films declined to comment on this effort. The silence is understandable, given the film's aesthetic flaws: while Declan Quinn's cinematography is excellent, dialogue in the film is often hampered by problems aligning the actors' various accents and differential acting abilities. Alongside accomplished Indian American actors like Sarita Choudhury and veteran Bollywood stars like

Rekha, Nair's choice to cast Indira Varma, best known at the time as a British fashion model with limited training and a less-than-convincing rendition of an Indian accent, seems like a mistake (Varma has since earned her chops by acting in prestige television series like *Rome*, *Game of Thrones*, and *Paranoid*).

In India, the Central Board of Film Certification (CBFC) initially demanded fifty-nine cuts, and Nair decided to fight the decision, a process that dragged on for nearly a year and a half. The film was finally released in 1998 in India and was a clear commercial success, though Nair has stated that she has understood that the film was even more widely circulated in pirated form, which seems plausible but is impossible to confirm. Interestingly, the versions of the film released in Hindi and in English were differently censored; the Hindi-language version of the film had more severe cuts, while the English-language version had fewer cuts. No explanation of the rationale for that difference from the CBFC itself was released, though the Indian distributor of *Kama Sutra* did comment that he interpreted the move as implying that "the audience of an English film is more liberal and mature than that of a Hindi film. A notion which is completely unjustified" (cited in Pendakur 2003: 74).

Nair's comments on the censorship controversy in her director's commentary are worth quoting at length, as they bring together her aesthetic ambitions for the film with the problem of the censorship of sexuality by the CBFC:

> Our country, despite having created *The Kama Sutra* and created the most extraordinary erotic temples of all time, and having such a rich tradition of love poems and epic poems that celebrate the erotic as divine—despite this tradition, we are now in a time when the culture is highly repressed. Sexuality is not spoken of, it's certainly not an open part of our everyday life. And in this context, to show a film like *Kama Sutra*, I knew would be an uphill battle. But what I did not knew was that the film would be devouring more than two years of my life after its completion.
>
> I first submitted the film to the censor board in October 1996, and the film was finally released in February 1998. I have gone through lawsuits, I have gone through about 8 or 10 screenings with different censor committees, I have gone through taking the censor board to the highest court of India and winning that battle, and still having the board not adhering to the court's decision. . . . Until finally, with a number of compromises and a number of cuts, I could finally

release the film in February 1998. . . . People who see it in India are aware of the absolutely ridiculous censorship of the censor board and, while they have enjoyed the film, have really realized how censors can ruin a work. (Nair, *Kama Sutra: A Tale of Love*, 1996, DVD director's commentary)

Given the trajectory of her career (specifically, her investment on pushing the boundaries regarding the representation of women), and also given the emphasis she has always placed on having her films based in India actually screened within India, it's understandable that Nair would fight as hard as she did to ensure that her film be released in India in something like the form she had intended.

A few words about the nature of film censorship in India might be helpful at this point. First, Indian film censorship has a long history going back to colonial era. The first legal justification for censorship took effect with the Cinematographic Act of 1918, where the focus was in fact devoted to screening out what was deemed to be subversive political content (see Barrier 1974). Some early Indian films did in fact have somewhat suggestive content (including lip-to-lip kissing, which was first depicted in an Indian film in 1933 (Devika Rani and Himanshu Rai in *Karma*). The modern era of film censorship began with the formation of the CBFC (then known as the Central Board of Film Censors) in 1951, and the Indian government has repeatedly reviewed and reaffirmed the film censorship system over subsequent decades, most importantly in 1969 (with the Khosla Commission Report) and in 1980 (with the Report of the Working Group on National Film Industry).

Throughout its history, the CBFC has been attacked, often by filmmakers themselves, for lacking a clear principle for censorship. As C. K. Razdan put it in an early polemic: "The range of their whims and idiosyncrasies is so absurd and unpredictable that one never knows what they will censor next" (Razdan 1975: 1). However, a number of serious filmmakers have also defended the practice of film censorship, including the art film director (and head of the NFDC), Hrishikesh Mukherjee. Mukherjee supported Justice G. D. Khosla's decision to ban Stanley Kubrick's *A Clockwork Orange* in 1984 (Pendakur 1996; quoted in B. Bose 2006: 19), along the lines that its use of sexualized violence did in fact make it "obscene" by the standards of middle-class Indian culture. Similarly, Tejaswini Ganti gives excerpts from interviews with two commercial Hindi film directors, Subhash Ghai and Ramesh Sippy, both of whom support an evolving censorship regime, in part because they feel Indian audiences are not "mature" enough to handle uncensored material (Ganti

2004: 194–96). However, the many instances of the censor board being used to suppress politically controversial films suggests that the censorship regime is important to the Indian state's need to maintain control of representations particularly of its own role in Indian society. A short list of films censored (sometimes unsuccessfully) with politically controversial content include: *Garam Hawa* (1974), *Naxalites* (1980), *Maachis* (1996), *Bandit Queen* (1994), *Such a Long Journey* (1998), *Zakhm* (1988), *Godmother* (1999), and *Paanch* (2003). While some of these films certainly do have material that might be offensive or shocking to some viewers, others appear to have been censored simply because they might have made some government bureaucrats feel a bit uncomfortable about the course of modern Indian history.

As is widely known, kissing was for many years effectively banned from popular Indian cinema, though this ban was in large part a result of self-censorship, since in the actual statutes related to film censorship, kissing has never been technically banned; according to Kobita Sarkar, the Khosla Committee Report allowed "aesthetic," as opposed to "lascivious," kissing (Sarkar 1982: 118–25). Nair herself challenged the restriction on kissing in *Salaam Bombay!*, though she did not encounter any difficulties with the censor board over the kiss between Baba and Rekha in that film. This is not to say that eroticism has been absent in Indian cinema, either in the art or parallel cinema tradition or in commercial Indian films. As Rachel Dwyer puts it, "Hindi cinema has evolved its own code of showing the erotic and, to some extent, the intimate, though self-censorship or fear of cuts that might be imposed by the censor boards. These include the famous 'wet sari sequences' where the heroine, and increasingly the hero, are soaked by water, usually rain, and sing songs of love, longing and desire" (Dwyer 2006: 291). Scholars like Dwyer and Ganti have shown in their respective studies how standards for depicting sexuality have liberalized considerably in commercial Hindi cinema in the past two decades, though some of the conventional elements (such as the taboo on kissing) have remained largely in place in family-oriented commercial films.

Two noteworthy controversies immediately preceded Nair's *Kama Sutra* in the 1990s, one involving Subhash Ghai's *Khalnayak* (1993) and another involving Shekhar Kapur's *Bandit Queen* (1994). With *Khalnayak*, the entire issue came down to one song, "Choli ke peeche kya hai" (What is behind the blouse?). A private citizen named R. P. Chugh sued to have the song banned and the picturization of the song removed from Ghai's film, even though most Indians did not apparently find the song obscene (see D. Bose 2005 and M. Mehta 2008). The case was dropped on a technicality, though the incident did raise awareness that a slippage was emerging in which the technical restrictions required by the CBFC (on nudity especially) were being rendered obsolete as a new generation of filmmakers worked around those restrictions to bring sexually suggestive content to audiences that had themselves become more liberal.

A second controversy prior to *Kama Sutra* involved the filmmaker Shekhar Kapur, a director who, like Nair, has had one foot in the American film industry and another foot in Indian cinema. Kapur's *Bandit Queen* was screened at Cannes in 1994 and released commercially in the West in 1995, where it was well-received. In India, the film was the subject of a major censorship battle over the graphic and intense depiction of the gang-rape of a woman, Phoolan Devi—though other elements were also involved in the controversy, the depiction of caste groups (the Gujjars in particular), as well the fact that the subject of the film—Phoolan Devi herself—objected to the film. By May 1996, the film was granted a certificate for screening within India, with relatively minor cuts. Some feminist activists and scholars (such as Ratna Kapur) strongly argued that the film be allowed, while others (Arundhati Roy among them) sharply criticized the film's depiction of rape, caste conflicts, and apparent inaccuracies in the historical record (see Kosambi [1998] 2006; Roy 1994). Even after the film was legalized, it continued to be controversial in India, as the graphic gang-rape scene apparently incited some men in audiences around the country to make obscene gestures and harass women in the audience (the phenomenon led theaters in Bombay to introduce "ladies-only" screenings). The feminist scholar Ratna Kapur, who defended the film during the controversy and has subsequently written on censorship issues, astutely points out the irony of the film's becoming a pretext for sexual harassment and titillation: "The extraordinary paradox is that this film, which in part is about the horrifying nature of sexual violence against women, poor, rural, lower caste women in particular, has come to be associated with 'sex' and 'titillation' at the level of popular discourse" (Kapur [1996] 2006: 222).

This is the context and climate in which Nair made *Kama Sutra: A Tale of Love*. In terms of its depiction of sexuality, Nair's film ought to be less controversial than Kapur's *Bandit Queen*, since all sexual encounters depicted in the film involve consenting adults and there are no caste issues or conflicts associated with depicting people—especially survivors of rape—who are still alive. However, while it did not generate the same level of controversy as did Kapur's *Bandit Queen*, Nair's film was censored no less aggressively. The reasons are understandable: by calling itself *Kama Sutra*, Nair's film clearly indicates symbolically that it is centrally *about* sexuality—it is not simply a film that happens to have some sexual content in it. In effect, the choice of title and subject constitute a "full-frontal" attack by Nair on the institution of film censorship in India as a whole; if a film called *Kama Sutra* can be permitted, the very concept of censorship along the lines of sexual content in Indian cinema seemingly comes into question.

Since the film was finally legally released in Indian movie halls in 1998 (with several cuts), Nair technically won the battle, though, as we have seen, it was not without compromise. The controversy over Nair's film as well as several others suggested that the overall culture of Indian cinema seemed to be changing by the late 1990s, and these changes were reflected in the move in 2002 by CBFC head Vijay Anand to reform the system in light of the liberalization of Indian culture that had evidently occurred in the 1990s (D. Bose 2005: 27–33; Ganti 2009). However, with the rise of the conservative Bharatiya Janata Party (BJP) government, Anand's attempts to radically reform the censorship regime were stymied (and Anand himself was abruptly forced to resign), and subsequent CBFC heads, such as Anupam Kher and Sharmila Tagore (one of the leads in Nair's own *Mississippi Masala*!), have not been nearly as aggressive in pushing reforms. Nearly two decades after Nair's struggle with the censor board over *Kama Sutra*, the essential apparatus of Indian film censorship remains intact. And the problem of film censorship has not gone away; if anything, it has only intensified, with subsequent controversies (over variously political, religious, and sexual content) over Deepa Mehta's *Fire* (1996), *Water* (2005), *Such a Long Journey* (1998), *Elizabeth* (1998), *Godmother* (1999), *Gajgamini* (2001), *Paanch* (2003), *The Final Solution* (2003), *Jo Bole So Nihaal* (2005), and *Love, Sex Aur Dhoka* (2010), to name just a few (for a comprehensive treatment of censorship practices in South Asia through 2008, see Mazzarella and Kaur 2009: 1–28).

Vanity Fair (2004)

Nair's adaptation of *Vanity Fair* is a large-scale Hollywood studio production, costing $23 million to make, with a marquee star in Reese Witherspoon. The film received mixed reviews, with some critics appreciating its originality and energy and others complaining about the compression of Thackeray's expansive story and Nair's seeming departures from Thackeray's novel (a theme to be explored in depth below). *Vanity Fair* was also somewhat of a commercial disappointment for Nair, earning about $19 million worldwide.

Any analysis of Nair's *Vanity Fair* must address methodological questions regarding the director's sometimes unconventional approach to the adaptation of Thackeray's novel, and we will spend some time in the section below looking at the parallels and divergences between Nair's adaptation and the Thackeray source text. However, it is no less important to engage Nair's emphasis on the Indian and colonial material in Thackeray's novel, which is one of the primary ways in which we can see this film as part of Nair's larger diaspora-oriented filmmaking project.

Nair's *Vanity Fair* is "diasporic" in at least two ways. First, because of its strategic deployment of historical thematics related to the history of British colonialism, the film offers an Indian diasporic director and her collaborators a chance to revisit that history from a unique vantage point. The India theme might have seemed marginal or merely "colorful" to earlier generations of readers, but in Nair's hands it can be rearticulated as central and defining. We can see surprising through-lines and connections in the novel. Not only is Becky Sharp a protagonist who, as a result of her transgressions in England, is forced to live much of her adult life abroad, but she is not the only one forced to go abroad. Jos Sedley, too, can be seen as part of an English "diaspora"—a large community of colonial subjects who went abroad during the heyday of British colonialism in pursuit of economic opportunities. Looking more broadly at Nair's career, Becky Sharp reminds one, first, of Maya's similar journey in *Kama Sutra: A Tale of Love*, but also of Meena in *Mississippi Masala* and Aditi in *Monsoon Wedding*—both heroines who use their power to leave difficult situations (in Aditi's case, her willingness to marry Hemant also signals her intention to leave India and go abroad). With all of these parallels in mind, Nair's *Vanity Fair* seems very much of a piece with her broader diaspora vérité filmmaking project.

Adapting *Vanity Fair* to a two-hour feature film is likely to be a challenge for any filmmaker. First, it is difficult to do something new with a story that has been filmed so many times, though admittedly the field is not nearly as overplowed as it is with Jane Austen. Nair's version of *Vanity Fair* is at least the seventh major film version of the film in English, and the tenth version if one counts the three miniseries adaptations of the novel made for British television since the 1960s. In fact, the reception of Nair's film version may have suffered somewhat because Nair's 2004 film came rather soon on the heels of a popular 1997 miniseries version of *Vanity Fair* made for the BBC starring Natasha Little as Becky Sharp. Though the BBC *Vanity Fair* is well-acted and scrupulously faithful to Thackeray's novel, because of its highly mannered and dynamic visual style and ambitious production design, Nair's

Vanity Fair. Victorian "vérité": a gesture towards urban realism in a period film.

film has little in common with the straightforward approach taken by the BBC. Though Nair's adaptation does suffer at times from overcompression, Nair, working with scriptwriter Julian Fellowes (who has also written scripts for *Gosford Park*, *The Young Victoria*, and more recently *Downton Abbey*), does manage to preserve the central characters and dramatic events of Thackeray's 1847–48 novel—while reinventing the novel in her own cinematic idiom. To invoke Dudley Andrew's terms, Nair's adaptation is partly a *borrowing* (with a significant investment in period fidelity), partly an *intersection* of Thackeray's text with Nair's creative vision, and partly an intentional *transformation* of Thackeray's novel—especially its ending (Andrew 1984: 98–100).

In that it is a "period" piece, Nair's *Vanity Fair* resembles *Kama Sutra: A Tale of Love*, but unlike that film, here Nair strives to maintain her emphasis on cinematic realism, and she does this by giving as much attention to the marginal, poverty-stricken characters and settings of Victorian London that are described in Thackeray's novel as she does the glamorous life of the aristocracy.

As she puts it in her director's commentary, "one of the things I loved about [Thackeray] is that he wrote the cinéma vérité of his day." While this statement renders Thackeray perhaps more earnest than the literary critical consensus might allow—Thackeray's *Vanity Fair* is above all a satire of Victorian opportunism, hypocrisy, and snobbishness, not a statement of social realism—the reference to cinéma vérité is helpful for us, as it suggests Nair's angle of approach, while also connecting her work her with earlier points in her career, including her documentary work and *Salaam Bombay!*

Of course, what is most striking about Nair's adaptation of *Vanity Fair* is not so much the "upstairs downstairs" portrayal of personal ambition in Becky Sharp as she catapults her way up the British class ladder—though

Feminist Period Pieces: *Vanity Fair* and *Kama Sutra: A Tale of Love*   149

Vanity Fair. Peacock in opening credits.

there are interesting parallels evident along those lines between her adaptation of *Vanity Fair* and Nair's earlier *Monsoon Wedding* (in both films, the servants are on their way up, while the masters can be seen as on their way down). Rather, the aspect of Nair's film that has elicited the most comment from skeptical critics is Nair's intentional emphasis on the colonial contexts that surface periodically in William Makepeace Thackeray's novel and that are also part of Thackeray's own life story. The colonial symbols first appear in the opening credits, with shots of an Indian peacock, pearls, and richly embroidered, sari-like fabrics, all of which represent for Nair "the colonies, and money coming from colonies into the empire." The peacock might also be read as a metaphor for performance and showmanship—which are hallmarks of Becky Sharp's character—though one has to keep in mind the gendering of the peacock's display (male peacocks have grand displays to attract females).

Many critics of Nair's *Vanity Fair* felt the filmmaker was making the India connection too strong. A representative example might be Stephen Holden in the *New York Times*, who wrote,

> Ms. Nair, the Indian-born director of "Monsoon Wedding" also can't resist embellishing the novel's connections to her South Asian roots and slaps on a contemporary multicultural gloss. Two outlandish Bollywood-flavored production numbers in the second half of the film come off as jarring digressions that seem shoehorned in from another movie. In the first, Ms. Witherspoon, flanked by dancers, does a grinding Indian-flavored hoochy-cooch, worthy of Britney Spears, at a party given by her social mentor, the Marquess of Steyne (Gabriel Byrne). (Holden 2004: n.p.)

150   Feminist Period Pieces: *Vanity Fair* and *Kama Sutra: A Tale of Love*

Vanity Fair. Becky eating an Indian chili.

We will have more to say about the "Bollywood" numbers below. However, on the question of authenticity to Thackeray's text, in fact the colonies, and India in particular, are important in the source text—and all but one of Nair's visual references to India or the Orient derive straight from the Thackeray text. (The exception is Nair's decision to end the film with Becky and Joseph Sedley leaving Baden-Baden for India; Thackeray's novel, by contrast, ends in Europe.) Nair herself defended the emphasis on India in interviews around the time of the film's release: "People who don't know the novel may think, 'Oh, here's an Indian director, she's imposed her India on it,' but it's the politics, the aesthetics—it was all given to me (in the novel)" (McDonald 2004: n.p.).

In a very early scene present in both the Thackeray novel and Nair's adaptation of *Vanity Fair*, Becky attempts to attract the attention of Joseph Sedley, wealthy and recently returned from India, by boldly eating an entire green chili—and then suffers a small public humiliation when she finds she cannot bear the spice, to Joseph's amusement ("So, Miss Sharp, how do you find your first taste of India?"). The scene can be read as an early foreshadowing of Becky's future: her daring may be briefly rewarded (Jos is interested, though he will be later warned off by George Osborne), but it does not come without a price. Incidentally, some of the costume choices in these scenes derive quite directly from Thackeray's novel. Thackeray's Jos Sedley, for instance, is described as dressing extravagantly, and it is not too far-fetched to speculate that he may have used Indian fabrics and embroidery: "His valet made a fortune out of his wardrobe: his toilet-table was covered with as many pomatums and essences as ever were employed by an old beauty: he had tried, in order to give himself a waist, every girth, stay, and waistband then invented. Like most fat men, he would have his clothes made too tight, and took care they should be of the most brilliant colours and youthful cut"

Vanity Fair. Nair uses Duleep Singh's palace at Elveden: India in England.

(Thackeray [1847–48] 2001: 19). Amelia's Indian-inflected dress in the dinner scene at the Sedleys' house is also based on details in Thackeray; Jos brings back cashmere shawls as presents for her.

The scope of Nair's subversive intent in *Vanity Fair* emerges as it is revealed that many shots presumed to be in England were in fact filmed in India (including some shots of Miss Pinkerton's school, as well as an intimate scene featuring Becky Sharp and Rawdon Crawley), the latter being filmed at Umaid Bhawan in Jodhpur, which is also coincidentally the palace shown at the end of Nair's film. In other cases the reverse is true—some scenes set in India within the narrative of the film were actually filmed in England. One scene showing Dobbin in exile in India was actually filmed in Colchester, while another was filmed at Elveden in Norfolk, where the exiled Victorian Maharaja Duleep Singh had added a dome and minarets to the old English castle. Especially in the latter scene, Nair's interest in the historical roots of the Indian diaspora is evident, and provocative: Indians have been involved in English culture for hundreds of years, and India is as central to the story of modern England (and modern English*ness*) as England is to the story of modern India.

Finally, one of the most provocative scenes in Nair's adaptation is the "Bollywood" dance sequence standing in for the dumb charade play in the court of King George in Thackeray's novel. Though the scene was singled out by reviewers like Holden (quoted above) as clearly anachronistic, here we will argue that Nair's adaptation embodies a mix of features that reflect elements of both faithful interpretation of the text and her own creative vision—or what film theorist Dudley Andrew would describe as an "intersecting" mode of adaptation. Where in Thackeray Becky plays the Greek mythological figure Clytemnestra, in Nair's imagination she is a slightly "goth"-looking Arab princess—and this adjustment appears to have been especially galling to the reviewer quoted above. However, another performance in the same scene in Thackeray's novel does contain strongly Oriental content, and it can be surmised that Nair's interpretation of the scene melds the role given to Becky in the third charade in Thackeray's text with the role given to Bedwin Sands in the first charade in the sequence. Here is a brief excerpt from Thackeray describing the first charade:

> A Turkish officer with an immense plume of feathers . . . was seen couched on a divan, and making believe to puff at a narghile, in which, however, for the sake of the ladies, only a fragrant pastille was allowed to smoke. The Turkish dignitary . . . claps his hands and Mesrour the Nubian appears, with bare arms, bangles, yataghans, and every Eastern ornament—gaunt, tall, and hideous. He makes a salaam before my lord the Aga.
>
> A thrill of terror and delight runs through the assembly. . . . "Bid the slave-merchant enter," says the Turkish voluptuary with a wave of his hand. Mesrour conducts the slave-merchant into my lord's presence; he brings a veiled female with him. He removes the veil. A thrill of applause bursts through the house. It is Mrs. Winkworth (she was a Miss Absolom) with the beautiful eyes and hair. She is in a gorgeous oriental costume; the black braided locks are twined with innumerable jewels; her dress is covered over with gold piastres. The odious Mahometan expresses himself charmed by her beauty. She falls down on her knees and entreats him to restore her to the mountains where she was born, and where her Circassian lover is still deploring the absence of his Zuleikah. No entreaties will move the obdurate Hassan. He laughs at the notion of the Circassian bridegroom. Zuleikah covers her face with her hands and drops down in an attitude of the most beautiful despair. (Thackeray [1847–48] 2001: 492–93)

Becky, for her part, plays Clytemnestra, a woman who, in Aeschylus's *Oresteia*, murders her husband, Agamemnon. Becky's performance is, as Lord Steyne says, "killing"; here is how Thackeray describes the initial audience response: "Rebecca performed her part so well, and with such ghastly truth, that the spectators were all dumb, until, with a burst, all the lamps of the hall blazed out again, when everybody began to shout applause." After subsequent performances, including Becky singing, the audience declares Becky as the clear centerpiece of the evening. It is, as it were, a "crowning" moment

Feminist Period Pieces: *Vanity Fair* and *Kama Sutra: A Tale of Love*   153

Vanity Fair. Becky's "Bollywood" dance.

for Becky in Thackeray's novel, though unfortunately the sense of triumph does not last, and the symbolic implication of playing a woman who kills her husband is borne out as her real husband, Rawdon Crawley, soon finds himself in debtor's prison. But again, here is Thackeray: "She had reached her culmination: her voice rose trilling and bright over the storm of applause, and soared as high and joyful as her triumph." Given the spectacular power Becky seems to have over her audience as she stands at the center of the stage, and given the Oriental motifs that Thackeray himself writes into the scene, it does not seem to be such a great departure for Nair to here inject a kind of showstopping dance, set to an Arabic song, with scantily clad female dancers and an overall harem-like quality.

Though Nair remains true to Thackeray's use of a Middle Eastern (notably, *not* Indian) theme in the "charade" sequence, to term it a "Bollywood" dance is nevertheless not entirely inappropriate. Nair's choreographer for this dance is Farah Khan, a major figure in the commercial Hindi film industry (who also, incidentally, choreographed the "Chunari Chunari" song sequence in *Monsoon Wedding*). Ironically, if "Bollywood" has come to signify relatively curtailed sexuality in contrast to contemporary American cinema, when it is inserted into Thackeray's conception of Regency England, the dance and revealing costumes are interpreted as a highly inappropriate "hoochy cooch," as Holden puts it.

India is by no means the central theme in Thackeray's vast body of work, but it is important in several of his novels, most notably *Vanity Fair* and *The Newcomes*. As is widely known, William Thackeray himself was born in India in 1811, and he came from a family that had long worked for and benefited from the British East India Company. Thackeray's grandfather, to begin with, was in service in India in 1766, and four of his sons, including

Thackeray's father, also worked for the company in India (Taylor 1999: 19–20). On Thackeray's mother's side, the Becher family also had a strong familial investment in India: fifteen of Anne Becher's family members were connected to the Indian subcontinent (Taylor 1999: 21). The fortunes of the entire family in effect rested on the connection to India. Thackeray's father and mother met in Calcutta and were married there.

That said, Thackeray himself did not spend very long in India. As was common at the time, he was sent away to England to be educated at age five and never managed to return, though he did apparently think of visiting later in life (Taylor 1999: 24). His social circle in London, through his extended family connections, did involve several "Anglo-Indians," and it is thought that they gave him access to the common Victorian tendency to insert Hindustani terms into their spoken English. One of the dishes eaten in *Vanity Fair* is pilau (which might also be spelled by the Victorians as "palau" or "palao"), and *The Newcomes* is replete with Indian English terms like "bahawdurs" and "mohurs." (Victorian readers did not get glossaries to explain what these things were; presumably they did not need them.) A recent Thackeray biographer, D. J. Taylor, summarizes the role often played by India in Thackeray's fiction as follows:

> India features in his novels as a place of mystery and excitement, the source of wealth and exotic gifts, like Miss Honeyman's embroidered shawls and ivory chessmen in *The Newcomes*, and of disaster. Bad news has a habit of coming from the East in Thackeray, either in human form (Amory, inevitably, is an old India hand) or in the shape of financial meltdown: the collapse of the Bundelcund Bank rubs out Colonel Newcome's patiently acquired fortune just as, twenty years before, the collapse of the Indian banking houses was to obliterate what remained of Thackeray's own. . . . India remains a signature mark in Thackeray's fiction: its appearance is generally the signal for a raising of the emotional temperature and the thought of danger. The moment the narrator of "A Gambler's Death" in the *Paris Sketch Book* mentions that "Jack was in India, with his regiment, shooting tigers and jackals," the reader knows exactly what to expect. (Taylor 1999: 24–25)

In Thackeray's *Vanity Fair*, the key ongoing connection to India is through the character of Jos Sedley, who is shown just after returning from there at the beginning of the novel, and then returns there after George Osborne's death in battle in the middle of the novel. India is, in effect, the only reliable place where a young person can earn an "honest" income in the world of Thackeray's *Vanity Fair*; in every other case, fortunes are inherited and money invested within England itself is subject to either devastating losses or coercive business practices—along the lines of what happens to the Sedley family.

It is with her radical approach to the conclusion of *Vanity Fair* that Nair moves from "intersecting" with Thackeray's vision to a mode of adaptation that Andrew would refer to as "transformation"—an assertion of a creative vision that runs contrary to Thackeray's own. Nair ends her film "happily," with Jos Sedley and Becky Sharp together in India—taking what is usually seen as a tragic ending in Thackeray and turning it into a kind of victory for Becky Sharp. Nair's clear sympathy for Becky Sharp (she allows her to end up with a living Jos Sedley, rather than as Jos's presumed murderer, as in the Thackeray novel) is certainly Nair's greatest departure from the Thackeray, and it is perhaps the only departure that meaningfully changes Thackeray's story.

As with the general turn towards an Indian theme, Nair's departure from Thackeray's ending galled many critics after the film's release. Michael Wilmington of the *Chicago Tribune* thought Nair was too upbeat and anachronistically feminist in her adaptation:

> In Thackeray's "Fair," we see an initially poor but pretty, witty lass clawing up to the British elite, pitting herself against its fools, fops, frauds and fellow schemers. The mostly unsentimental Thackeray thought she was a villainess. But was Becky good or evil—or somewhere in between? Heartless schemer, social climber and conscienceless seductress—as the great novelist kept insisting? Or a kind of prefeminist pragmatist fighting for her rights to rise in an amoral society forcing her to be "bad"—as Nair seems to feel? The book sees it one way, the film another. Here's my vote, though, for the bad Becky, the one the brilliant Nair suggests, yet can't quite bring herself to reveal. (Wilmington 2004: n.p.)

In fact, the actual attitude to Becky Sharp in Thackeray's novel is a good deal more complex than Wilmington here allows. While she is certainly "conscienceless," it is not really until the very end of the novel, when she is virtually spent, that Becky commits an action that might merit the term "villainess." Along these lines, Thackeray's critic and biographer Catherine Peters writes, "We may even feel that Becky, with her energy and inventiveness, and her capacity to accept the down-turns of fortune with good humour, comes off best after all, since even the least ambiguous spokesmen for the 'humble-mindedness' Thackeray admired—Dobbin and Lady Jane Sheepshanks—do not obtain happiness through behaving correctly" (Peters 1987: 151). For most of Thackeray's novel, it can be argued, there is in fact considerable sympathy for Becky, who is the most talented, intelligent, and accomplished person in her social circle.

It is the transformed ending of Nair's film adaptation (as a reminder, Nair shifts the setting from Germany to India and alters Thackeray's tragic ending for Becky Sharp with Becky's final triumph) that is really the issue for knowledgeable critics, then—not the eating of the chili or the "Bollywood" dance sequence. On the one hand, it could be argued that Nair, as a contemporary interpreter of a historically situated story, has every right to reimagine that story, and that the criterion for historical authenticity or fidelity to the original text is less important than a sense of coherence in her own vision (for theorists informed by poststructuralism, such as Andrew, this is the only intelligent approach).

That said, many critics do value fidelity for good reasons, especially to the historical period, but also the spirit of the text that is the source of the film adaptation. One could ask, since Nair and her production design team are so rigorous in other respects in creating historically accurate scenes and in fidelity to the spirit of Thackeray's text, why not be "faithful" here as well? Here, one could respond that Thackeray's own vision might simply be too negative to be fully palatable, *either in his own day or ours*. Thackeray was not unaware of the trauma he was inflicting on his readers with the ending he chose for his novel, as he himself wrote, in a letter to Robert Bell, "I want to leave everybody dissatisfied and unhappy at the end of the story—we ought all to be with our own and all other stories" (cited in Iser 1987: 113). It might be, with a vision as unrelenting as Thackeray's ending of *Vanity Fair*, that Nair's final elevation of Becky Sharp—to the top of an elephant, on the way to a hilltop palace—is a better reading of Thackeray's primary argument in *Vanity Fair* than Thackeray himself could provide. If, as Thackeray wrote, "we are for the most apart an abominably foolish and selfish people," why not allow Becky Sharp, selfish opportunist though she may be, to triumph?

It should be added that anachronistic interpretations of *Vanity Fair* have a long history. To begin with, Thackeray's novel is itself not always historically faithful, as Thackeray intentionally inserted references to the London of the 1840s in his novel set in the 1810s, along with jokes that were strictly contemporaneous—designed to amuse the readers of his story as it was being published, serially, in 1847 and 1848 (Taylor 1999: 252). Second, earlier prominent filmic interpretations of *Vanity Fair* have also taken the novel's interest in contemporary fashions and applied them literally. Myrna Loy, in the 1932 Hollywood film version of *Vanity Fair*, is seen wearing backless dresses with plunging necklines fashionable in the late 1920s but unthinkable in early nineteenth-century London. (The production as a whole is updated to the 1920s; Becky and Amelia leave Miss Pinkerton's at the beginning of the film in a motorcar rather than a coach, and the references to war are entirely absent; George Osborne, instead, dies in a riding accident. Finally, Myrna Loy's Becky Sharp is seen smoking a cigarette in the scene in Queen's Crawley where Sir Pitt Crawley propositions her.) Though the often-praised Technicolor version of *Vanity Fair* starring Miriam Hopkins (*Becky Sharp* [1935]) is set in the Victorian period, it too makes numerous changes in character relations and plot trajectory, often seemingly arbitrarily. Though many critics of Nair's film in 2004 complained about what they perceived as its infidelity to Thackeray's text, a closer look at earlier adaptations (and I have not done a comprehensive analysis), suggests that her adaptation of Thackeray may be, surprisingly, the *most faithful* film version to have ever been given theatrical release.

Finally, in the context of the present study, it should be noted that Nair's Becky Sharp becomes, effectively, a diasporic figure, who resembles many other Nair protagonists who attempt to find a space for self-expression and personal freedom by escaping various kinds of repressive environments. In that respect she resembles Meena in *Mississippi Masala*, who leaves home with Demetrius to be free of the judgmental disapproval from her family and community; and Aditi in *Monsoon Wedding*, who by marrying Hemant is escaping the claustrophobic confines of her family's conservatism; not to mention later Nair protagonists, such as the Gangulis of *The Namesake* or Amelia Earhart from *Amelia*. The choice to have Becky Sharp emigrate to India may have been a stretch for some viewers of *Vanity Fair*, but in the context of Nair's broader film career, the choice to end with the protagonist's expatriation is perfectly fitting.

Chapter 7

"EVERY DAY SINCE THEN HAS BEEN A GIFT"

The Namesake (2006)

The Namesake marks a second change in direction for Nair. While in the 1990s she made films that were, at least superficially, further away from the documentary realist exploration of diasporic life that we have been calling her "diaspora vérité," with *Monsoon Wedding*, *The Namesake*, and *The Reluctant Fundamentalist* (all made after the year 2000), Nair seems to have returned directly to the theme and the diasporic community that has pervasively defined her unique vision as a filmmaker. We have explored *Monsoon Wedding* in depth in chapter 4; here we will look closely at Nair's adaptation of Jhumpa Lahiri's *The Namesake*.

Aesthetically and conceptually, *The Namesake* is one of Nair's most accomplished and refined works. Here Nair returns to a set of visual ideas and thematics she had begun to develop in her early documentary films (especially *So Far from India*, discussed in chapter 2). While Nair's early films like *So Far from India* figured the Indian diasporic experience as one of loss, or as largely determined by traumatic experiences in the country of origin (*Mississippi Masala*, *My Own Country*, *The Perez Family*), *The Namesake* aims, first and foremost, to tell the story of post-1965 Indian immigrants as a kind of steady progress and growth—with more gains than losses accompanying the act of migration. More broadly, Nair's film, like the Jhumpa Lahiri novel that is its source text, aims to stand as a kind of documentary milestone—an emblematic and definitive account of the experience of middle-class South Asian immigrants from the 1970s to the 1990s. In *The Namesake*, Nair uses a juxtaposition of textual, telephonic, and visual montages to meditate on the problem of diasporic representation. The (textual) problem of naming that is at the center of Jhumpa Lahiri's novel is, in Nair's film adaptation, attached to a series of visual and aural problems characteristic of the diasporic experience: problems of seeing and being seen, of communicating across great cultural and geographical distance. The treatment of Nair's film in this chapter will be closely intertwined with the novel that is its source text, especially in the exploration of the naming theme. However, as with Nair's adaptations of *Vanity Fair* and *The Reluctant Fundamentalist*, there are some areas where the filmmaker and screenplay writer transform Lahiri's story, and we will explore these as well. Nair's film adaptation shifts the focus from the second generation (the children of immigrants) to the first generation; it also introduces a sensitivity to the gendering of the South Asian diaspora experience (Ashima's point of view) that is not fully developed in Lahiri's novel. Finally, there are numerous ways in which the visual style of Nair's film complements the core ambition of Lahiri's novel—to document the South Asian diaspora experience.

It might be worth briefly contextualizing Nair's *The Namesake* in the context of her broader career as a filmmaker. One big change one sees over the course of Nair's career pertains to the status and accessibility of "home" after emigration. While *So Far from India* seemed to suggest that it isn't possible to go home again, *Mississippi Masala* showed that some exiles can and should go home—Jay returns to Uganda to find closure—even as the pattern of departures seems to repeat itself in the second generation. However, what both *Monsoon Wedding* and *The Namesake* seem to show is that the previously hard line between "home" and "abroad" has diminished, as diasporic subjects now can have continuous interactions with their country of origin in their new homes. The pattern of departure and return continues, but departures need not be final.

Just as *The Namesake* seems to complete a sequence of Nair's films about South Asian diasporic life, it also offers Nair a chance to film in Kolkata (formerly Calcutta), an Indian city she has had a long personal connection to from her childhood in nearby Orissa. Other Nair films have provided distinctive images of Delhi (*Jama Masjid Street Journal*, *Monsoon Wedding*) and Mumbai (*Salaam Bombay!* and *The Laughing Club of India*). Each of those accounts of urban life in India has had its own particular agenda, which we have addressed in previous chapters—*Salaam Bombay!*, for instance, aimed to frame the lives of slum children in realistic shades, while *Monsoon Wedding* provided a glimpse of the new middle class in Delhi. *The Namesake*'s approach to Kolkata is somewhat less sociopolitical, though Nair does show urban scenes and market scenes using camera angles that mirror her street scenes in those other films (interestingly, though much of *The Namesake* is set in the United States, we see far more attention paid to the landmarks and street life of Kolkata than to those of New York). The Kolkata setting also suggests an aesthetic legacy: in this film Nair is interested in offering a window, through visual citations and cameos, into the world of Bengali art cinema.

By way of introducing the plot and thematics of *The Namesake*, it might be worth exploring the links between it and Nair's first full-length documentary, *So Far from India*, as *The Namesake* addresses—almost as a mirror image—the problematic introduced in that earlier film. While *So Far from India* witnesses the beginning stage of an Indian immigrant experience in America, *The Namesake* follows the Ganguli family over a sequence of many years, beginning to settle and adapt to life "far away," in the "cold cities" of the North American East Coast. While Lahiri's novel actually places the Gangulis in Massachusetts, in her film adaptation, Nair relocates them to New York—thereby making the connection to *So Far from India* (with its images of the New York subway, shops, and streets) even stronger.

In Nair's earlier documentary, the symbolism of diasporic life is expressed via directly contrasting images of traditionalism (the folk singer, at the beginning) against the uncertainty of the future (the open road, at the end). By contrast, in *The Namesake*, the symbolic acknowledgment of the universality of travel seems to reverberate everywhere. For instance, Nair focuses quite closely on the centrality of bridges in the everyday lives of residents of both New York City and Kolkata. The metaphorical content of Nair's bridges, of course, is not hard to decode—bridges represent movement in space and the possibility of change—though in Nair's case the emphasis on bridges in *The Namesake* gains added richness in the context of several other films, especially *Hysterical Blindness*, where one sees New York's bridges from the New Jersey side), and Nair's short film included as part of the 11'09"01 collection. Another important metaphor for Nair in *The Namesake* is shoes—Ashima, near the beginning, tries on Ashoke's shoes (which are marked "Made in U.S.A.") before formally meeting him, suggesting her early willingness to follow her husband-to-be in his own journey across continents and cultural frames. Later, after the death of Ashoke, Gogol Ganguli's own embrace of his father's shoes seems to represent a tentative return to a kind of cultural stasis through renewed identification with his family as well as his Bengali heritage.

The primary visual method of Nair's *The Namesake* is photographic montage. The film follows Lahiri's own novelistic method in that it is dramatically minimalist, focusing on telling, but fleeting, bits of dialogue. As Nair herself put it, in a short essay called "Photographs as Inspiration,"

If it weren't for photography, I wouldn't be a filmmaker. Every film I make is fueled by photographs. Sometimes it is a particular image of a photographer, sometimes it is what I have learned by seeing the world through his or her eyes. Either way, photographs have always helped me crystallize the visual style of the film I'm about to make. (Nair and Lahiri 2006: 12)

This emphatic statement of artistic affiliation rings true, especially considering Nair's early connection to the photographer Mitch Epstein (her teaching assistant in a documentary film class at Harvard, and also her first husband), as well as given the historical connection between documentary photography and documentary filmmaking. Elsewhere in "Photographs as Inspiration," Nair names several specific photographers and photographs that influenced her film adaptation of *The Namesake*, including Raghubir Singh, Raghu Rai, Garry Winogrand, Derry Moore, and Manuel Alvarez Bravo. (The photography of Raghu Rai—a master in the documentary photography tradition—was also an influence on Nair in *Monsoon Wedding*; it was his landscape image of a woman praying inside her house, with the Jama Masjid neighborhood surrounding her, that inspired Nair to use the same setting for Dubey's house in her 2002 film.)

The emphasis on photographic tableaus makes *The Namesake* somewhat static visually, even though its subject matter is about movement: "Gradually I began to see that the film would be about movement and crossings. The bridges, the trains, the airplanes, the constant comings and goings of an immigrant." (Nair and Lahiri 2006: 19). The fixed visual framing combined with the constant thematization of the modes and spaces of transportation (airports, train stations, bridges), enables Nair to work through a novel that chronologically spans nearly thirty years, without losing the thread; the essentially discontinuous visual method of *The Namesake* (i.e., montage) actually makes the necessary chronological jumps intrinsic to the story seem less disruptive to the viewer.

From Lahiri's Novel to Nair's Film Adaptation

In general, Nair closely follows the plot of *The Namesake* in her adaptation (working mainly in the "borrowing" mode), though she does make a significant shift of emphasis, expanding greatly the focus on the Ganguli parents' story as well as the proportion of the story that is narrated in India.

But the intersections between Lahiri's novel and Nair's adaptation vastly outweigh the points of divergence, so it seems appropriate to introduce Nair's film with an account of Lahiri's source text. In particular, the textual ambivalence in Lahiri's novel is active in Nair's film adaptation, as the main characters debate names and naming, language and accent, and the problem of communicating across distance. Many of these concerns are translated to the film via dialogue, but Nair is also quite interested in depicting writing at various moments—from the bilingual opening credits thematizing Bengali and English scripts to the numerous scenes in the film that show major characters writing as a way of bridging differences and distances.

The first thematic, Gogol Ganguli's ambivalence about his incongruous name, is largely a textual one. It is presented as a set of personal as well as social and historical allusions in both Lahiri's novel and Nair's film adaptation. Our names are a puzzle: they tell us something about who we are and constitute and aspect of identity that is deeply psychically rooted. Ironically, names are at the same time somewhat extraneous to the self, chosen by one's family members rather than oneself. A second issue associated with naming is the patronymic, the tradition of last names passed down through the father's side of the family, a tradition which has been formally in place in Western Europe and the United States since the 1700s and which is practiced, with some variations, in India as well. Patronymics suggest a sex-gender system oriented to patriarchal authority and often embed certain clues as to socioeconomic status. In the Indian tradition, last names also potentially say something about a person's caste background, as well as his or her religion.

Third, in a multicultural society like the United States, names are a marker of ethnicity. The central family in *The Namesake*, the Ganguli family, has a name that is obviously Indian (though some people might simply hear it as "foreign"). People who know Indian culture might recognize that it is not just an Indian name but a specifically Bengali and Hindu name. To American ears, the name Ganguli sounds quite strange, though for Bengalis it is a common and familiar name. In that it is a foreign name, it is somewhat of a liability and a flag of difference, as we see when the Ganguli family's house is vandalized as "gangrene," which is ugly in part because it connects the name of a respectable family to a tissue disease and also because describing an immigrant family as gangrene—an unwanted growth—reflects a strong prejudice against immigrants. In Nair's film, the name Ganguli is thematized in the first place not as a sign of foreignness, but as a sign of identity in the opening shot of the film—as we see a porter carrying Ashoke Ganguli's trunk in the Kolkata central train station. On the trunk, the name "A. Ganguli" is painted in large block letters—in English. The legacy of colonialism and Anglicization leaves its mark: even within India, in a Bengali-speaking region, the preferred script used for identifying an item of personal property is Roman, not Bengali or Devanagari. Moreover, the name Ganguli is itself an Anglicization of "Gangopadhyay" that dates to colonial administrators' preference for simplifying various Bengali names for their own ease of pronunciation (Bandyopadhyay became Bannerji, Chattopadhyay became Chatterji, and so on). There's a great deal of history packed in the name printed on that trunk.

As a young man growing up in the United States, Gogol struggles with the sound and significance of his name. Gogol Ganguli is a name that would sound strange anywhere, but it is especially marginalizing in the suburbs of New York as they were in the 1970s and '80s (or, in Lahiri's novel, the suburbs outside of Boston during the same period). Not only is his last name the strange, foreign-sounding "Ganguli," but his first name comes from a Russian writer not widely known to his American peers, courtesy of his father's passion for Russian authors. Gogol Ganguli, in short, is a name that is neither here nor there: neither traditionally Indian, because the name Gogol makes him strange within the Indian American community, nor comfortably American.

In Lahiri's novel, there is a divergence between Ashoke and Ashima in their attitude towards Gogol's name. In contrast to Ashoke, Ashima does not initially give naming a priority, because she is struggling with the fundamental problem of imagining how she will raise a child in America without the support of her extended family, seen as essential in India.

> Without a single grandparent or parent or uncle or aunt at her side, the baby's birth, like most everything else in America, feels somehow haphazard, only half true. . . . He needs to be fed and blessed, to be given some gold and silver, to be patted on the back after feedings and held carefully behind the neck. Names can wait. (Lahiri 2003: 24–25)

In a traditional Indian context, naming is a collective and familial ritual, but in the United States the Gangulis must do everything on their own, and it is hard for Ashima to think of naming her child without that familial participation. America is a new world for her, something like a dream, where everything feels "somehow haphazard, only half true." However, for the purposes of the hospital, a name is required, and Ashoke comes up with the name Gogol out of loyalty to his favorite author. The more traditional name "Nikhil" is later added, but by that time, the child has already come to identify first and foremost with Gogol, the name he was first given by his parents.

There is an additional wrinkle to the issue of naming in Lahiri's novel that comes out of traditional Bengali culture. This is the tradition of the "pet name" (*daknam* in Bengali), which is a nickname a family gives to a child early in life. The nickname is not just casual or temporary—it stays with a child, often throughout his life—but it is understood that only family and friends may use the *daknam*. Out in the broader world and on all formal written documents, a child's acquaintances and peers will use the "proper name" (*bhalonam* in Bengali). Here is how Lahiri distinguishes the two kinds of names in the novel itself:

> Pet names are a persistent remnant of childhood, a reminder that life is not always so serious, so formal, so complicated. They are a reminder, too, that one is not all things to all people. They all have pet names. Ashima's pet name is Monu, Ashoke's is Mithu, and even as adults, these are the names by which they are known in their respective families, the names by which they are adored and scolded and missed and loved.
>
> Every pet name is paired with a good name, a *bhalonam*, for identification in the outside world. Consequently, good names appear on envelopes, on diplomas, in telephone directories, and in all other public places. . . . Good names tend to represent dignified and enlightened qualities. Ashima means "she who is limitless, without borders." Ashoke, the name of an emperor, means "he who transcends grief." Pet names have no such aspirations. Pet names are never recorded officially, only uttered and remembered. Unlike good names, pet names are frequently meaningless, deliberately silly, ironic, even onomatopoetic. (Lahiri 2003: 26)

Though there are of course nicknames in mainstream American culture, they are not usually as "sticky" as the Bengali tradition of the *daknam*. Western names are also not usually quite as elevated or poetic as formal naming in the Indian tradition. While some American parents might consider quite carefully who they might be naming a child after (for instance, a grandparent), the names generally do not have a literal meaning, as Gogol's mother's name, Ashima, does.

For Gogol (and this is a dynamic present in both Nair's film and Lahiri's novel), the relationship between *daknam* and *bhalonam* is hopelessly confused almost from the beginning. Traditionally, the name that should have gone on his birth certificate should have been the *bhalonam*, but because that name is given through a ritual that involves family members, and Gogol's letter from his grandmother with the name written on it is lost in the mail, no name is available. As a result, his parents give what should be a *daknam* as his legal name, thinking they'll change it later. But by the time Gogol is of school age, he rejects "Nikhil," when it is introduced, and his teachers and classmates come to refer to him as "Gogol," against his parents' wishes. By the time he is a teenager, however, Gogol comes to hate the strangeness of his chosen first name. As an ordinary American teenager, he has no interest in strange Russian writers, and he resents his father for having chosen such an odd-sounding name for him when his first and foremost desire is to be "normal."

Later, in college, Gogol decides to claim "Nikhil" after all, though by this time his parents have come to accept that his name is just "Gogol" and in fact resist his renaming ("Gogol is your name now," his father says). Though the name "Nikhil" is more conventionally Indian and Bengali than "Gogol," it seems clear that Gogol, as he tries on this new name, is trying on a new *identity*. In other words, while Gogol's renaming as Nikhil might seem like a return to "tradition," ironically it only marks a movement *away from* the cultural identity associated with Gogol's already displaced parents. In that sense, he is like many American students who experiment with various forms of rebellion, both in high school and when they go away to college. Interestingly, throughout the novel, the narrator of *The Namesake* continues to refer to Gogol as Gogol, suggesting that Lahiri doesn't really accept that her character can ever truly re-name himself. And indeed, though Gogol's first serious girlfriend, Maxine, refers to him as Nikhil (and some of their friends refer to him merely as "Nick"), the part of his life where he is exclusively known as Nikhil seems to come to a dead end after his father dies. After he goes through these transition experiences and approaches maturity, Gogol returns to his original name—his original misnomer, as it were—completing the diasporic circle.

Gogol's early ambivalence about his name and the confusion that follows from his subsequent renaming are small dramas, less significant in some ways than the larger human dramas that drive both versions of the story we have been discussing: birth and death, migration, love, marriage, and divorce. But the questions about naming represent a textual kernel—in both the novel and Nair's film adaptation—that stands in for more widespread ambivalence over the diasporic experience at both a personal level (Who am I? What is my "good" name?) and at the group identitarian level (Who are Indian Americans? Where do they belong?).

Nair's adaptation of *The Namesake* follows its source's exploration of hybridity quite closely but expands and transforms that source in two key ways. One is the addition of a visual dimension of cultural hybridity that, for obvious reasons, did not appear in Lahiri's novel. Here Nair experiments with photographic montage, jump-cutting between Indian and American settings, the interplay of Bengali and English fonts and titling, and visual motifs (especially bridges), all of which suggest an idea of diaspora that is culturally rich and fundamentally hybrid. The second form of transformation is more thematic and plot-oriented: Nair's film adaptation focuses much more on Gogol's parents' lives than Lahiri's novel does. Lahiri's novel is essentially a coming-of-age story where the central issue is how the "second generation" (the children of immigrants) come to define themselves as Americans. By making the first-generation immigrants Ashoke and Ashima more central in her version of the story, Nair refocuses *The Namesake* as a narrative about relationships (or more precisely, *communication*) between parents and children. While in Lahiri's novel the defining experiences in Gogol's adult life pertain to his relationships with Maxine and Moushumi, in Nair's film adaptation greater emphasis is placed on Gogol's relationship with his father, and Ashoke's death is much more of a defining experience.

Nair's decision to focus on the Ganguli parents also allows her to develop other themes related to immigration and the emergence of a diasporic identity, one of them being the gendering of the immigrant experience. Indeed, gender is depicted in a provocative way in both Lahiri's novel and Nair's film. While the Ganguli family is traditional in many respects, with Ashoke and Ashima meeting through an arranged marriage, the burden of cultural adaptation falls equally on the shoulders of both husband and wife. The companionate marriage that eventually develops between Ashoke and Ashima reflects a more optimistic vision of diasporic life than was seen in Nair's earlier treatment in *So Far from India*. There, the diaspora was depicted a space where husbands go, while wives stay behind, unable to engage the broader world. The implication is that the opportunity to travel, and to change through movement, is exclusively available to men. By contrast, Gogol Ganguli's birth in a hospital in New York, with a Manhattan bridge in the background outside the window, marks the diasporic experience as a joint project—shared equally between Ashima and Ashoke.

The Namesake. Posing for a family photo in front of the Queensboro Bridge in New York

Indeed, if the starting point in *The Namesake* is Ashoke's rupture with the past, provoked by his traumatic experience of a train derailment, as Nair's film moves forward, it is increasingly Ashima who becomes the focus of cultural transformation. Some of the most powerful scenes of diasporic adaptation and transformation in the film feature Ashima, including especially Nair's visceral use of Ashima's forlorn figure emerging as the automatic garage door slowly opens after the death of Ashoke. The diasporic experience is not uniformly a happy one in the hands of Nair and Lahiri, and there are, it should be acknowledged, moments of profound isolation and suffering in the film, particularly at the moment of the Gangulis' first arrival in America, and then again at the time of Ashoke Ganguli's death. But while Nair's early documentary *So Far from India* seemed to figure emigration as a catastrophic event in the life of the Seth family, in *The Namesake*, diasporic life is at least *livable*, and it offers avenues for growth and personal transformation not seen in Nair's earlier approach to the subject.

Another significant shift in emphasis that is evident in Nair's film is the serious interest in the cultural and intellectual milieu of upper-middle-class Bengali culture—the "bhadralok" community that has also produced some of postcolonial India's most important literary and cinematic figures. Nair inserts a series of allusions to Bengali films, including the films of Satyajit Ray and Ritwik Ghatak, as described by Nair in her director's commentary. At one point, for instance, Ashima's father is seen painting while sitting back with his knees up. This is an homage to Satyajit Ray, who was once photographed painting in a similar posture by Nemai Ghosh (Robinson 2005: 72).

The Namesake. The yawning suburban garage door.

In her director's commentary, Nair also mentions that the sequence where the relationship between Ashoke and Ashima starts to develop (that is, just after their move to the United States) is inspired by Ray's *Apur Sansar* (*The World of Apu* [1959]). Ray's film is about the challenges faced by a couple brought together by traditional circumstances (an arranged marriage, with all the cultural expectations that come with that), but who nevertheless try to define themselves as much as possible as a modern couple in an urban setting. Like Ashoke and Ashima, Apu (Apurba) and Aparna (played by the then very young Sharmila Tagore) marry virtually without knowing each other at all. Apu agrees to marry his friend's sister as a heroic gesture after her planned wedding falls apart. The scenes between Apu and Aparna in the first days of their married life, where they interact with one another shyly but with earnestness and devotion, are directly echoed in Nair's film. Apu's confession to Aparna on their wedding night, that the life he is bringing Aparna into will not be an easy one, and her subsequent assent resemble in many ways the proposal scene in Nair's version of *The Namesake*. Other dynamics in Ray's film, such as the learning curve of a relatively innocent young woman in the big city, are also echoed in Nair's film in Ashima's adjustment to the asperities of life as a new, and relatively friendless, immigrant on the North American East Coast.

As the example of Aparna's adjustment to displacement in Kolkata might suggest, Ray's *Apur Sansar*, an adaptation of a novel by Bibhutibushan Bandopadhyay, covers certain "diasporic" themes that are internal to India. In that Apu and his wife are migrants in Kolkata, having been displaced from their

"Every Day Since Then Has Been a Gift": *The Namesake*

The Namesake. An allusion to Nemai Ghosh's portrait of Satyajit Ray.

village upbringing, Ray's film is itself in some sense a story of emigration. Ray's own filmic education (like Nair's) was partially European, and his early films, as has been often pointed out, are deeply influenced by the naturalism of the Italian neorealist school, which also influenced Nair indirectly through her cinéma vérité background, as discussed in previous chapters.

At this point, it might be helpful to discuss Nair's visual exploration of hybridity in *The Namesake* in somewhat greater depth, as this is one of the key ways in which Nair transforms and expands the range of ideas in Lahiri's novel. As mentioned above, the visual method of *The Namesake* is essentially photographic—which is to say, it is built around still frames that serve as points of narrative fixity for a group of characters disoriented geographically and culturally by life in the diaspora. Nair anchors many of the dramatic scenes in the film with still frames featuring architectural and domestic motifs for movement, travel, and hybridity as visual metaphors, which overlap with the central metaphor in both Lahiri's narrative and Nair's adaptation of it—the metaphor of naming. In the opening credits themselves, Nair uses the flickering letters in the names of actors as a way of visually conveying a sense of the personal and cultural mutability of her main characters: "ইরফান খান" becomes "Irrfan Khan." Several scenes in *The Namesake* are also filmed in transportation centers, including airports and train stations, and Nair repeatedly uses the visual motif of the bridge, including bridges in New York as well as in Kolkata. Finally, Nair also uses images of her characters' shoes as a visual metaphor to suggest movement, migration, and the fluidity of personal identity.

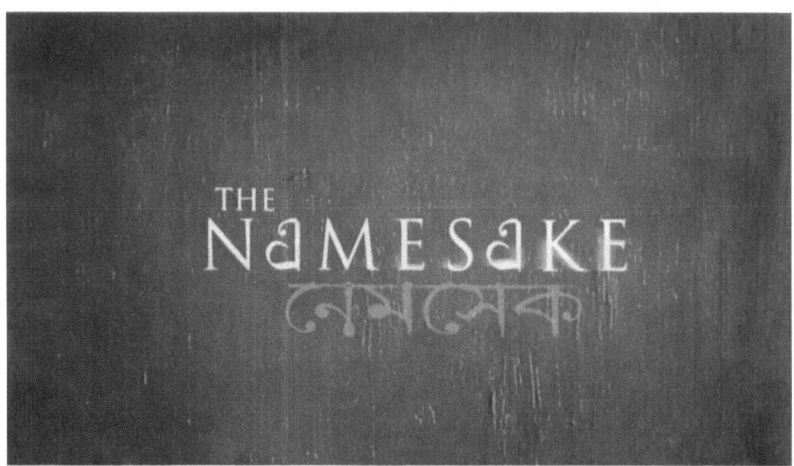
Dual scripts for *The Namesake*.

Every visual element in *The Namesake* seems to communicate an idea about movement or migration. The pattern begins with the opening credits, designed by Divya Thakur, where letters of the actors' names continually flicker and transform from Bengali script to Roman letters, suggesting the various forms of transformation to be experienced by the characters themselves (they are both Bengali and Euro-American). Even the title of the film, *The Namesake*, is shown in dual scripts—notably not English and the Bengali translation of *The Namesake*, but rather a phonetic transliteration of the word "Namesake." The name is pronounced the same in both cases, but it is indicated in two ways. This might seem like a mainly symbolic issue, but it is significant in a film that is, in general, about naming. The film, *The Namesake*, has in the end only one name, though it can be scripted in two ways at once. The flickering between two scripts continues throughout the opening titles for the film, suggesting the hybrid nature of both the film itself and its transnational cast of actors and crew.

Another use of flickering as a visual motif is in the form of Elizabeth Diller and Ricardo Scofidio's permanent installation art at John F. Kennedy International Airport (*Travelogues*). The art appears for the first time as the Gangulis are heading to India for a family vacation. It appears again after Ashoke Ganguli's death, suggesting another moment of transformation. Diller and Scofidio's holographic images, of both individual immigrants and words and ideas associated with travel, are made with a digital lenticular printing process—which allows the images to appear differently depending on the angle of vision (for more on Diller and Scofidio's art, see Scanlon 2000).

"Every Day Since Then Has Been a Gift": *The Namesake*   171

The Namesake. Diller and Scofidio lenticulars at JFK International Airport.

The transformation of images as the passerby moves past them emphasizes the importance of perspective: the Diller and Scofidio images used by Nair in her film show shifts in visual identity. Looked at one way, the traveler (or immigrant) is one kind of person. From another angle, or another cultural context, he is something quite different. And the use of airport flight information boards as a motif is no accident: for the characters in Nair's film, the everyday arrivals and departures figured in the Diller and Scofidio lenticulars are imbued with deep personal meaning.

Another important set of visual motifs are the many bridges and piers that appear in Nair's film. In her essay on *The Namesake*, "Photographs as Inspiration," Nair describes how she aimed to film Kolkata and New York "as if they were one" (19), and indeed, at several points in her version of *The Namesake*, Nair jump-cuts between events taking place in New York and images of life on the streets and in the houses of Kolkata. Both are highly industrialized cities, with pockets of immense wealth and extreme poverty. Both, Nair points out, are also "stitched by rails," (19) and Nair uses several shots of elevated trains in her film, including both elevated New York subway lines and the trains in Kolkata. But above all, Nair uses bridges in both cities to create a visual homology between them. Nair points out that the George Washington Bridge in New York City has a kind of monumental status, which has a correlative in Kolkata in the Howrah Bridge (16), and Nair uses images of both bridges in her film at certain key moments (it appears that Nair also uses the Queensboro Bridge—seen from the window of the hospital room where Gogol Ganguli is born).

The Namesake. The Howrah Bridge as metaphor for change, transformation.

Bridges connect opposing banks of rivers, and they suggest, visually, an ability to find connections between worlds. They are also markers of modernity and industrialization—the Howrah Bridge in Kolkata is a definitive marker of that city's modernity, in much the same ways as are New York's many bridges and tunnels. The Howrah Bridge in Kolkata figures in an important way when Ashoke is in the hospital in Kolkata recovering from the train accident as a young man. Nair also returns to the Howrah after Ashoke's death, as Ashima and Gogol return to Kolkata to scatter his ashes in the Hooghly River in a traditional Hindu ceremony; the Howrah Bridge stands in the background.

In *Ulysses*, James Joyce once described a waterfront pier as a "kind of disappointed bridge." While this is purely a literary conceit (that is to say, when a pier is constructed, it is never intended to work as a "bridge"), the idea translates perfectly to Nari's adaptation of *The Namesake*. While elsewhere in Nair's film the background presence of bridges always seems to suggest that characters have a way out of their present sense of confinement (particularly in the two hospital scenes that feature bridges from the window), the scene at the pier with the young Gogol and Ashoke aims to convey a decided sense of finality; it suggests that the Gangulis have reached their destination and are consequently no longer looking for bridges. The scene is inserted in Nair's film at two moments—first as a fragment from the life of the Ganguli family, and second as a flashback after Ashoke Ganguli has died—and becomes one of Gogol's key memories of his father. As Ashoke and Gogol walk out to the

The Namesake. A rocky pier by the waterfront in the New York area.

end of the pier, they realize they don't have a camera with them. Ashoke tells Gogol he will simply have to create a photograph of the place in his mind, and ends by saying, "Remember that you and I made a journey, and went to a place where there was nowhere left to go."

For Ashoke, the pier is an endpoint in the endless process of migration, the place "where there was nowhere left to go." Fittingly, Nair presents the scene at the beach with bleached colors, as the family shudders against the cold in the middle of winter. The setting and color scheme are minimal, bordering on dismal, but there is an essential warmth within the family. And there is, importantly for Lahiri's novel and Nair's film, a sense of symmetry between father and son: each is on his own respective journey, but those journeys are parallel and apposite to one another much more than Gogol can imagine as a young man. The strong implication is that immigration is never simply one person's story. In a family of immigrants, the story of the parents is effectively repeated in the second generation, as children tend replicate the pattern of emigration set by their parents. In Lahiri's novel and Nair's film, Moushumi Mazoomdar shows this through her move to Paris, while Gogol goes on his own identity journey. His achievement is to find the pattern and to see himself as no longer alone on his journey but rather as continuing in a tradition established by his father for him.

A third visual motif used in Nair's film, which derives directly from Lahiri's novel, involves shoes. Ashima tries on Ashoke's shoes before stepping into the room to meet him. The detail comes directly from the novel, and through it, both Lahiri and Nair can convey ideas about the strangeness of the arranged marriage meeting—the rushed intimacy—as well as the experience of migration and travel:

> Glancing at the floor where visitors customarily removed their slippers, she noticed, beside two sets of chappals, a pair of men's shoes that were not like any she'd ever seen on the streets and trams and buses of Calcutta [sic], or evening the windows of Bata. They were brown shoes with black heels and off-white laces and stitching. There was a band of lentil-sized holes embossed on either side of each shoe, and at the tips was a pretty pattern pricked into the leather as if with a needle. Looking more closely, she saw the shoemaker's name written on the insides, in gold lettering that had all but faded: something and sons, it said. She saw the size, eight and a half, and the initials U.S.A. And as her mother continued to sing her praises, Ashima, unable to resist a sudden and overwhelming urge, stepped into the shoes at her feet. Lingering sweat from the owner's feet mingled with hers, causing her heart to race; it was the closest she had ever experienced to the touch of a man. The leather was creased, heavy, and still warm. On the left shoe she had noticed that one of the crisscrossing laces had missed a hole, and this oversight set her at ease. (Lahiri 2003)

This passage crisply draws together the two intimately associated themes associated with Ashoke Ganguli's shoes. On the one hand, they clearly betray their American origins in the make and style of the shoe, and to the extent that the choice to wear American shoes reflects on Ashoke Ganguli's character, it suggests that he is, after just a few years studying abroad, already somewhat acculturated to the American context—he is already on a path towards the kind of cultural hybridity that is the hallmark of diasporic life. When Ashima sees them—before meeting Ashoke or committing to marry him—she tries them on for herself. This suggests a hint of physical intimacy that she otherwise will not experience when meeting Ashoke via a formal introduction through their respective families. It is through her decision to try on and walk in Ashoke's shoes that Ashima begins to imagine her own future in the United States—as part of the Indian diaspora.

The shoe motif returns several times in Nair's film. At one point, on a return trip to Kolkata, she confesses her appreciation of Ashoke's shoes at that first meeting. It's also notable and symbolically significant that, when Ashima first begins to react to news of Ashoke's death years later, she stands in her

The Namesake. Ashima tries on Ashoke's American shoes.

garage in their suburban American house, utterly barefoot in the middle of winter. Later in the film, Ashoke's shoes become an intergenerational symbol, as we see when Gogol tries on his father's shoes the day he goes to his father's apartment in Cleveland after Ashoke's sudden death there.

Gogol Ganguli and Imperfect Names

Much of our discussion thus far has been on the symbolic attributes of Nair's *The Namesake*, the figures representing movement and migration, and names and identity. However, there is also a more conventional plot in the film that should be addressed. Gogol Ganguli goes to Yale University and becomes an architect, surprising his parents. He later begins to work at an architectural firm in New York City and begins dating Maxine Ratliff. Maxine comes from an established American family with a white Anglo-Saxon Protestant pedigree, and her parents are both affluent and liberal; they are relaxed about all the things the Gangulis never could be. Gogol is taken by their lifestyle and seems to be leaning towards a long-term relationship with Maxine, when news of his father's death changes his priorities, reminding how important his own family is to him—a family that Maxine, for various reasons, cannot really connect with. Gogol then breaks up with Maxine and sometime later is reintroduced to a childhood acquaintance, Moushumi Mazoomdar, now a graduate student in French literature in New York, someone whose approach to life as a second-generation Indian American is quite like Gogol's. After a brief courtship, Gogol and Moushumi decide to marry, making Gogol's mother happy, but somehow a spark is missing from their marriage. After a time, Moushumi begins to have an affair, and the couple split. The film ends with Gogol single again, as his mother leaves for India, where she will pick up singing Hindustani classical music again after a long pause.

Though it is not exactly a "happy" ending, both Nair and Lahiri aim to show that Gogol has come to a new understanding of his cultural and familial identity through his mistakes. It's worth noting that Gogol's very last action is sitting down to read, finally, the short stories of Nikolai Gogol; reading is a sign that he wants to continue to get a better understanding of both himself and the world around him, in this case through approaching an author he knows his father loved dearly. Perhaps the best summary of Gogol's state of mind in Lahiri's novel comes from a discussion shortly before the end, just as his relationship with Moushumi is starting to go sour. After Moushumi reveals the fact that the person their friends know as "Nikhil" was once called "Gogol," Gogol is embarrassed, but in response to the friends finding the name amusing, Gogol blurts out, "There's no such thing as a perfect name. I think that human beings should be allowed to name themselves when they turn eighteen. Until then, pronouns" (Lahiri 2003: 245). While this is certainly not a practical solution to the problem of naming and identity, it does show how Gogol now understands his attempt to rename himself as at best an approximation. In the end, "There's no such thing as a perfect name" is a way of acknowledging that for most people, and for second-generation Indian Americans like himself, identity is always going to be a work in progress.

Chapter 8

"I HAD A PAKISTANI ONCE"

The Reluctant Fundamentalist (2013)
and Nair's Post-9/11 Short Films

While religious identity is not significantly stressed in Nair's adaptation of *The Namesake*, it goes without saying that it has been an extremely important part of diasporic South Asian identity for all major South Asian religious groups—Hindus, Sikhs, Muslims, Christians, Parsis, even the small community of Indian Jews. However, it is mainly in Nair's adaptation of Mohsin Hamid's *The Reluctant Fundamentalist* that we see Nair exploring how South Asian religious identity came to be a flashpoint after the terrorist attacks of September 11, 2001. The protagonist of that film, Changez Khan, follows a trajectory that in some ways resembles that of Gogol Ganguli—he attends a prestigious American university where he meets and falls in love with a white American woman. However, Changez differs from Gogol in that he ultimately reverses his process of acculturation into "Americanness" and reclaims his Pakistani and Islamic identity though a painful experience of progressively deepening alienation. While *The Namesake* can be seen as a film in which Nair sees a new intensification of creative possibilities around the diasporic experience—a deep exploration of cultural, linguistic, and aesthetic hybridity—in *The Reluctant Fundamentalist* those aspirations encounter resistance.

Close followers of Nair's career will be aware that her decision to do a film dealing with the experiences of South Asians in the United States following 9/11 did not come out of a vacuum. For one thing, Nair's husband Mahmood Mamdani has been an outspoken critic of the US "War on Terror," publishing a scathing critique of the United States' role in provoking militant Islamic hostility called *Good Muslim, Bad Muslim: America, the Cold War, and the Roots of Terror* (2005). Mamdani's influence on Nair's work has been quite pronounced in the past, as we have discussed in the analysis above of *Mississippi Masala*, and it seems fair to presume some of Mamdani's trenchant critiques of the War on Terror might influence Nair's own thinking.

Perhaps of greater immediate salience, Nair herself directed two short films not long after 9/11 that began to explore the themes that would finally be given a full-length treatment in her adaptation of Mohsin Hamid's *The Reluctant Fundamentalist*. Both shorts films are fictional, though they are strongly marked by a documentary realist ethos. One is her eleven-minute, nine-second contribution to the film *11'09"01* and a second, called "How Can It Be?" (2008), is included as part of a collection of short films focused on humanitarian issues, called *8*. In *11'09"01*, Nair focuses on the sense of isolation and persecution experienced by an ordinary Muslim family in New York after the terrorist attacks of 9/11. The film is based on a real Pakistani Muslim family in New York, whose son, Salman Hamdani, died trying to assist people trapped in the World Trade Center. Unfortunately, because of their Muslim background and because their son was "missing" after the attacks, the Hamdanis came under suspicion by the FBI as potentially complicit in the attack and were only cleared after the remains of their son were found in the ruins of the towers (indeed, US Congress later recognized Salman Hamdani as a "hero"). In Nair's approach to the subject, her protagonist is Talat Gilani Hamdani (known in the film only as "Mrs. Hamdani"), Salman Hamdani's mother, who is actively mourning the loss of her son while also trying to contend with the sense of alienation experienced as her family comes under suspicion as terrorist-sympathizers in the polarized landscape of post-9/11 New York. In some ways, Nair's *11'09"01* seems to resemble other films about diasporic families who cannot quite find their feet, including especially *Mississippi Masala* and *The Perez Family*. Nair's other short related to South Asian Muslims in New York, "How Can It Be?," also focuses on a mother, here played by Konkona Sen Sharma. Zainab, the orthodox, Burqa-wearing wife of an orthodox Muslim husband, has fallen in love with another man, and decided, with great pain, to leave him and her son. While *11'09"01* describes the unwanted sense of alienation experienced by South Asian American Muslims, "How Can It Be?" focuses on a woman who has, quite on purpose, decided she has to free herself from a restrictive family background. In both films, Nair is careful to suggest that a sense of personal freedom and dignity for women need not be incompatible with an orthodox relationship with Islamic faith.

Alongside the theme of post-9/11 life for cosmopolitan and diasporic Muslims, *The Reluctant Fundamentalist* expands on Nair's rich and highly developed body of work focusing on the lives of South Asian diasporic subjects. To begin with, there are evident connections in *The Reluctant Fundamentalist* to Nair's relatively recent adaptation, *The Namesake*: both films are portraits of young South Asian diasporic men coming of age and charting out a sense of direction in life—and, as mentioned above, both films prominently feature intercultural romances. *The Reluctant Fundamentalist* also intimately depicts the Pakistani (Lahori) equivalent of the urban Punjabi bourgeoisie Nair showed us in *Monsoon Wedding*. And looking further back in Nair's career, we see a set of themes involving the sense of loss in emigration that goes back to her early documentary, *So Far from India*; both that film and *Reluctant Fundamentalist* feature diasporic protagonists who are adrift in New York City. Finally, in between that starting point and *The Reluctant Fundamentalist*, one sees the transgressive multiculturalism of *Mississippi Masala*—a film which was, like *The Reluctant Fundamentalist*, a cross-racial romance set in the context of a historical crisis.

As with *The Namesake*, Nair's process of developing *The Reluctant Fundamentalist* and finding the funds to produce and distribute it were uniquely transnational. In this instance, despite her having lined up a strong cast with experienced and well-known actors in advance, she and her team found securing funding from American investors difficult, with one potential investor in New York indicating that a film about Islamic fundamentalism with a Muslim protagonist would inevitably have only a very limited audience in European and American markets. In the end, Nair secured the nearly $15 million budget for the film from a novel transnational entity, the Doha Film Institute. This healthy budget allowed filming to take place in Atlanta, Delhi, Istanbul, and Manila—again replicating the pattern seen in several of Nair's most powerful works of filming in multiple national contexts (*Mississippi Masala*, *Vanity Fair*, *The Namesake* are three examples of films that use multiple national filming locations in Nair's fictional films). In addition to filming transnationally, Nair returns in *The Reluctant Fundamentalist* to the cross-linguistic method she employed so successfully in *Monsoon Wedding*, with a substantial amount of dialogue in the film occurring in Urdu and Punjabi (the latter language is largely spoken inside the Khan family amongst family members).

As seen in many earlier Nair films, *The Reluctant Fundamentalist* features powerful, diegetically important music, beginning with the Qawwali music by Fareed Ayaz at the opening of the film—suggesting the Indian subcontinent's long tradition of musical fusion as well the heterogeneity of Indo-Islamic devotional practice. Just as the inclusion of "drum and bass"

The Reluctant Fundamentalist. Pakistani TV is spicier than one would think.

tracks by Nitin Sawhney and Midival Punditz in *Monsoon Wedding* and *The Laughing Club of India* signified the shift to a high-tech cosmopolitan urban culture in postliberalization India, the invocation of Sufi Qawwali in *The Reluctant Fundamentalist* is an argument about Islam— namely, that there is more than one way of experiencing the powerful cultural legacy of South Asian Islamic practices and expressive culture. In the case of the music of Fareed Ayaz, Nair presents his performance in the film—which clearly has a strong devotional element—in a secularized setting, with men and women sitting together, dressed comfortably (and not necessarily "modestly"), and alcohol being served to guests. This is a secularized setting–a *mehfil*, not a *madrasa*—where religious devotion and spirituality are understood as part of a liberatory experience, not as a proxy for authoritarianism or theocracy.

Nair also features a moment of self-reflexivity quite early in the film, as the American professor Anse Rainier (played by Gary Richardson) is seen leaving a Lahore cinema with a female companion urgently discussing the value of the controversial contemporary Pakistani film *Bol*, which deals with a religious family's anxiety-ridden response to their transgendered child. That film cannot be considered an aesthetic triumph, but it clearly represents a breakthrough in its willingness to engage topics that have often been taboo in South Asian commercial cinema. Nair's invocation of a popular contemporary film here is part of a tradition in her filmmaking that goes back to *India Cabaret, Salaam Bombay!*, and *Monsoon Wedding*. One significant difference here might be that while citation of popular Indian cinema in those other films was often embedded in a critique of commercial conventions (as I have argued elsewhere in this study), the citation of a contemporary Pakistani film in *The Reluctant Fundamentalist* seems to serve as a kind of horizontal homage.

Another media citation early in *The Reluctant Fundamentalist* references the vibrant, sometimes anarchic new world of Pakistani TV. Here Nair invokes an actual, quite campy Pakistani serial called *Jutt and Bond*, though the footage Nair uses is not from the show itself. Through her allusion to a spicy soap opera featuring a heroine in relatively provocative attire, Nair is reminding international viewers that Pakistan's social values are by no means uniformly conservative or homogeneously "Islamic." Pakistani popular culture has room for more provocative fare, though in the Khan family's amused response to their daughter's participation as an actress on *Jutt and Bond* is a hint that Pakistanis view such fare as more appropriate to the Indian media than to their own. Changez's father (known only as Abu [Father] in the film) jokes with Bina, "Go to India, anything goes there" ("Tu India chale jao. Vaha yeh sab chalta hai").

Both *The Namesake* and *The Reluctant Fundamentalist* engage the "homing desire" of diasporic communities described by Avtar Brah—though they do so in different ways. Changez in *The Reluctant Fundamentalist* returns home to Lahore after growing alienated from his life as a consultant on Wall Street, as well as from his American girlfriend, who humiliates Changez by using his private confessions in an art installation. Changez's turn toward "home" after those experiences reflects his sense that the promise of a hybridized diasporic experience has evaporated for South Asian Muslims after 9/11. By contrast, Nair's *The Namesake* gives both Gogol and Ashima Ganguli routes "home"—for Ashima, returning to Kolkata is a way to rediscovering herself after the death of her husband and the departure of her children, while, for Gogol, traveling through India represents both a path forward for him and a way of reconnecting with the travels earlier undertaken by his father Ashoke. The homing desire in *The Namesake* feels voluntary, possibly even temporary, while in *The Reluctant Fundamentalist* it is something much more immovable and limiting.

As indicated above, both *The Namesake* and *The Reluctant Fundamentalist* involve romantic connections between a diasporic South Asian man and a white American woman. In *The Namesake* there is a palpable sense that

Gogol Ganguli's love interest Maxine represents connection to the good life in the United States—with her parents' wine collection, large parties, and liberal social values contrasting to the rather cramped and puritanical lifestyle of Gogol's own family. Similarly, in Hamid's novel, Erica is seen as connected to an upper-middle-class family, though that status is somewhat deemphasized. By contrast, in Nair's film version, Erica is a niece of Underwood Sampson's CEO ("Mr. Underwood"), making her seem much more directly connected to Changez's career and social aspirations. And yet in some ways she is more like Maxine in Nair's film version of *The Namesake* than she is like the cryptic character in Hamid's novel in that she represents a kind of nonconformist, pleasure-seeking American life that is deeply appealing to Changez given the constraints on his earlier life in Pakistan and his experiences as an ambitious scholarship student at Princeton University.

The divergences between Hamid's novel and Nair's film are quite substantial; as with her adaptations of *Vanity Fair* and *The Namesake*, one sees as much interest in transforming the source material as in closely adhering to the plot and language of the original text. Some of the transformative elements may be designed to help smooth the transition from Hamid's minimalist narrative method to the visual format of film, but the particular use of multimedia installation art in Nair's film contains a reflexive element and a commentary on cultural appropriation that go beyond the scope of Hamid's novel.

In the transition from novel to film script, one sees the sense of uncertainty about both Changez and his American interlocutor that is at the core of Hamid's novel essentially disappear. In a profile in the *New York Times*, the shift is explained as follows: "Ms. Nair made clear that for cinematic reasons, they would have to fill in some of the novel's blanks. They had to establish who these two characters are from the beginning" (Kaplan 2013). Elsewhere Nair has talked about the need for concreteness as a fundamental requirement of cinema: characters, embodied before the viewer in film, have a kind of concreteness that must be recognized by the filmmaker. Liev Schreiber's Bobby Lincoln and Riz Ahmed's Changez Khan may be opaque to each other, but they cannot be played with as much ambiguity for the audience as are the characters in Hamid's novel.

Mohsin Hamid himself collaborated with William Wheeler as a cowriter on the screenplay for Nair's film and spoke about the differences between the novel and Nair's film adaptation, acknowledging that, "in the film, things become much more explicit. People state their politics more clearly. At the same time, the film tries to humanize different political points of view, and also tries play with a degree of ambiguity that doesn't get resolved until the end." (Nair, *The Reluctant Fundamentalist*, 2013, DVD bonus materials)

Another difference between Nair's film and the Hamid novel pertains to the level of detail in the plot. Changez in Hamid's novel is not accused or suspected of any specific crime, while in Nair's film adaptation he is suspected of being directly involved in the abduction of an American colleague at Lahore University, a professor Anse Rainier. In fact, Nair does suggest a possible connection between Changez and the abduction through a series of sequential jump cuts in the opening scene of the film. But that suspicion of involvement, where Changez is shown worriedly conversing on his cell phone in the middle of a raucous family Qawwali party, is quickly diminished as we see police officials searching an office that we soon learn is Changez's own. The reason Changez remains nervous and distant at his family's party is thus made clear. That said, the status of Liev Schreiber's character Bobby Lincoln remains uncertain for much longer in the film than does that of Changez; it is only quite a bit later that Nair reveals that he does in fact work undercover for the CIA (he is in Lahore posing as a journalist).

Nair's film shares with Hamid's novel a certain contingent admiration for American culture and the American way of life. While Nair's script alters the opening chapters of Hamid's novel quite drastically, she does retain Changez's memorable statement that he is "a lover of America." She also adds a female perspective in the form of Changez's sister Bina, who hopes her college-going brother can contrive to have her come along with him to the US, hoping for access to the lifestyle depicted on American television shows like "Sex and the City." Where for Changez the aspiration to life in America is connected strictly to financial mobility and access to American wealth, Bina's perspective on America is more oriented to its cultural symbols: she wants "a loft in Soho, weekends in the Hamptons, and a pair of big, fake, American boobs. . . . God bless America!" Changez's revealing mental retort accepts his sister's comment but redirects it in a direction that will point to his own future career at a prestigious corporate valuations group: "God bless America indeed. God bless its level playing fields. God bless winning."

One of the pervasive themes in Hamid's novel is the idea that the employees of Underwood Samson represent American economic power—they are sent around the world to "downsize" various businesses that are not as profitable as they should be. One of the corporate officers whose job will be affected by Changez's valuation, a man named Juan Batista, goes as far as to compare Changez's role working for transnational American capitalism to the Janissaries, Christian soldiers conscripted to serve and fight for the

Ottoman Empire—a status that often resulted in them killing their own kinsmen in the process. This idea in Hamid's novel, which remains somewhat vague until near the discussion of the Janissaries is introduced near the end of the book, is crystallized almost immediately near the beginning of Nair's film: "I was a solider in your economic army."

One element that is often overlooked in both Nair's film and Hamid's novel is humor. In a scene near the beginning of the film, shortly after Changez has begun to establish himself as a rising star at Underwood Samson, his young colleagues take turns describing where they hope to be in twenty-five years. The aspiring young Wall Streeters say relatively predictable things ("I'm going to be the CEO of a Fortune 500 company"), but when Changez's turn comes he stops the conversation with a deadpan response: "In 25 years, I'm going to be the dictator of an Islamic republic with nuclear capability.... Anyone want a soda?" The same lines are present in Hamid's novel, but at an earlier point in Changez's story (he is still at Princeton). And because of the intermediation of Changez's voice in his memory of the scene, they appear somewhat more ruefully: "The others appeared shocked, and I was forced to explain that I had been joking. Erica alone smiled" (Hamid 2007, 29). In the novel, the joke about becoming the "dictator of an Islamic republic with nuclear capability" suggests a failure of communication, while in Nair's film the line plays somewhat more comically and lightly, set as it is during a Central Park barbecue.

Another somewhat galling moment in Hamid's novel is transformed in Nair's film into a scene of successful, even subversive humor. The scene in question is an encounter in which the CEO of Underwood Samson, Max Underwood, offers Changez a drink and Changez accepts it: "I had a Pakistani working for me once. He didn't drink." "I do." In the novel, that is the end of the interchange, but in Nair's film there is a chance for Erica (in the film she is introduced as Underwood's niece) to indicate to Changez that she knows her uncle's presumption is problematic: "You know, I knew a Pakistani once . . . and he saved me from small talk at a Wall Street party."

The use of humor around cross-cultural miscommunication in Nair's version of *The Reluctant Fundamentalist* is not entirely innocent. Shortly after the scene at the Wall Street party at Mr. Underwood's house, Erica invites Changez over to her apartment and studio, where he sees many photographs of himself. He reads her interest in photographing him as reflecting a possible romantic interest in himself, and he jokes, "This is saying, Changez, throw a burqa on me, confiscate my college degree, and take me home to Mama." As with the earlier miscommunication between Changez and his

Wall Street colleagues at the Central Park barbecue, there is a momentary pause where Erica takes his comment seriously. He is of course joking again (the viewer knows enough about Changez's family—especially through his sexually liberated sister—to know quite clearly that no one in his family wears a burqa). However, given Erica's use of this line later in the film in her art work inspired by her relationship with Changez, we come to see that the joke does not fall so innocently. Rather than helping to debunk Changez's "otherness," it becomes part of an accumulated set of material she can mine to exoticize him in a way that he will find to be quite painful when he sees the words recontextualized in a public art gallery.

By far the most significant deviation from the novel in the psychological plot of Nair's film adaptation of *The Reluctant Fundamentalist* is Nair's choice to have Erica use her relationship with Changez as material for her art installation project. Some of the statements Changez makes to Erica in private, as confessions of his own alienation, are repurposed by Erica as part of a portrait of post-9/11 cross-cultural chaos and alienation. Near the beginning of their relationship, Changez tells Erica, "You know I don't even recognize my own voice anymore. It sounds all tinny and fake, like someone who doesn't come from anywhere." This is the confession of an alienated immigrant whose inner life seems to bely what on the outside looks like a successful acculturation to American norms. Taken out of context, however, the sentence "I don't even recognize my own voice anymore" could also be a somewhat ominous admission of loss of moral bearing. Is the idea of the Pakistani other created in Erica's art show an alien presence or someone intimately known to her (and, by extension, mainstream America)? A similar effect is achieved by the sentence "pretend I'm him." These are words Changez utters in a moment of vulnerability the first time he and Erica sleep together; in context, they are intended to say more about Erica's traumatized psychological state than Changez. But resituated in the abstract context of the art installation, the phrase suggests a desperate disavowing of the self—these sound like the words of a man who has no commitment to owning any authentic self whatsoever. Other key phrases uttered by Changez from earlier in the film are also appropriated by Erica, including "throw on a burqa."

These visual citations of text that the viewer had encountered as spoken utterances before have a disorienting impact; many of the phrases were part of the intimacy that had slowly been building between Changez and Erica. The large crowd of spectators suggest a cosmopolitan public audience, eagerly consuming this exhibit with strong "9/11" and "Islam" themes. Stripped of their personal context, the random phrases suggest a critique from Nair

The Reluctant Fundamentalist. "Throw on a burqa."

(again, going beyond the rhetoric of the novel) of cultural appropriation in the New York City art world. This element of the film might also be seen, in a limited way, as self-reflexive commentary on the part of the filmmaker: Nair's own film might be seen, by a skeptical viewer, as an attempt to appropriate Hamid's text. The implication is that an irresponsible circulation of that text could be damaging to its integrity—a betrayal. Presumably Nair hopes to succeed in interpreting Changez's (and Hamid's) words, even if Erica fails.

There are implications to the appropriation of Changez's words within the diegetic plot of the film as well. Erica is initially bewildered by Changez's anger at her appropriation of materials relevant to their relationship in her art project. She defends her work to Changez as an "expression of love." But he experiences it as a betrayal—the final straw in a series of painful and humiliating experiences that have led him to no longer feel welcome in the country he had hoped to call home. The first of these is his being strip-searched at US customs immediately after 9/11; later he is picked up on the street after being confused for a "crazy Arab" and interrogated by two very flat-footed FBI agents. In effect, this string of humiliations, including the personal betrayal by Erica, makes Changez's decision to return to Pakistan in the film version of *The Reluctant Fundamentalist* somewhat easier to understand than it is in the comparatively more abstract framing of Hamid's novel.

The final point of deviation from Hamid's novel that seems important to note is the filmmaker's decision to rework Hamid's tense, but ultimately somewhat static, narrative method into a kind of action thriller in the second half. The sedate pace of Changez's recounting of his story to Bobby Lincoln gives over to heightened tension as American authorities grow increasingly desperate to track down the kidnapped professor (also a CIA agent). In Nair's film there is the strong implication that Changez will be arrested and interrogated (possibly using torture) at a CIA facility in Peshawar, and also the suggestion of threats against his family in Lahore. And there is a moment of crisis, in which a student protest on the campus of the university threatens to turn violent just as a CIA extraction team moves in to remove Bobby Lincoln from the campus. In the chaos, Bobby accidentally shoots Changez's student Sameer, fatally wounding him. The accident only occurs because Bobby mistrusts Changez and refuses to believe that the text message Changez sends just before word that Professor Rainier has been killed comes through was actually directed to his sister. In effect, Nair's film version of *The Reluctant Fundamentalist* ends with yet another miscue—another instance of an American misreading a Pakistani interlocutor (and potential ally). Admittedly, it is hinted that Bobby Lincoln's crucial failure to understand Changez may be remedied later, as he begins to listen to the recording he had made of their conversation in the final shot of the film. But more importantly, by ending the film with another instance of a miscommunication, Nair ties the failed romantic plot involving Changez and Erica to the "thriller" plot involving the search for an American kidnapped by Islamic militants. In both cases, Americans fail to hear what Changez is trying to tell them, with disastrous consequences for all involved. Changez's warning to Bobby Lincoln at the climactic scene seems very carefully chosen: "You're making a mistake that's going to get us both killed." At this moment, Changez is only too aware that his own life could be ended at any moment at the discretion of US agents; what is perhaps surprising is that he is also aware of, and concerned about, the potential harm that might befall Bobby Lincoln himself.

Unfortunately for Nair as well as for admirers of her work, the commercial reception of the film was poor and critical reception was somewhat mixed. The *New York Times*, for instance, found Nair's approach overly "blunt" (Dargis 2013) while *Film Comment* complained of Nair's "superficial treatment of complex themes" (Slifkin 2013). That said, some critics (Kenneth Turan of the *Los Angeles Times*, for instance) did appreciate the richness and complexity of Nair's approach to the story and admired her use of the film to challenge received notions about the relationship between the Islamic world and the West (Turan 2013). But few really picked up on the novelty of Nair's choice to foreground a Muslim protagonist in the story—rather than the Americans typically figured even in progressive, complex films like Michael Winterbottom's film about the wife of Daniel Pearl, *A Mighty Heart* (2007). Similarly, despite the intense commitment to realism in Kathryn Bigelow's *Zero Dark Thirty* (2011), many progressive viewers (especially non-American viewers) felt that the film only considered one side of the story, focusing only on the nobility and earnestness of the American War on Terror, even the portions of it that have been challenged as abuses of power. Bigelow's film provoked a lively debate over American intelligence agencies' use of torture in which some viewers felt that the film endorsed the use of torture while others defended the film as true to the reality of evolving CIA attitudes and methods after 9/11. By comparison to those other films, *The Reluctant Fundamentalist* goes much further towards enabling the possibility of a critique of the excesses of the War on Terror, and for that reason it seems like a worthy addition to the "postcolonial" body of work Nair has produced from her early documentaries to her films of the 1990s and 2000s. That said, it must be acknowledged that the thriller plot introduced in Nair's film adaptation of *The Reluctant Fundamentalist* does seem to fall a little flat—and in any case it does not mesh as well as one would like with the failed romantic plot that dominates the first half of the film. Many of Nair and Wheeler's deviations from Hamid's novel—especially the introduction of a discussion of cultural appropriation in the art world discussed above—are clearly improvements, but the attempt to render the film as a suspenseful action thriller seems to distort the meditative, reflective tone of Hamid's novel. For all of those reasons, it is perhaps not surprising that, despite its powerful moments and compelling performances (especially from the male leads—Riz Ahmed, Liev Schreiber, and Kiefer Sutherland), *The Reluctant Fundamentalist* did not prove to be a success with audiences.

Chapter 9

"WHERE DO YOU BELONG?":

Returning to Uganda in *Queen of Katwe* (2016)

Nair's most recent film as of this writing, *Queen of Katwe*, marks a turning point of sorts—both a way forward for Nair as a director after the disappointing reception of *The Reluctant Fundamentalist* and an opportunity to return to her documentary realist roots. Admittedly, the film was not, in its inception, a Nair project; it began as an article by Tim Crothers that appeared in *ESPN* magazine in January 2011. Later, Crothers published a book-length version of his report on Phiona Mutesi with Scribner: *The Queen of Katwe: One Girl's Triumphant Path to Becoming a Chess Champion* (2012). The story was optioned by Disney, and the script for the film was written by William Wheeler before Nair herself was ever involved in the project. The fact that *Queen of Katwe* was backed by a large media company, namely Disney, clearly identifies it as a different kind of project than many of Nair's independent pictures. She and her producers did not have to do additional legwork to secure *Queen of Katwe*'s $15-million budget (with *The Reluctant Fundamentalist*, securing the budget was a problem given the film's risky theme and its "fundamentalist" Muslim protagonist). *Queen of Katwe* was also not advertised as a "Mira Nair film" so much as a Disney film. Classical "auteurism" this certainly is not.

That said, while the Disney imprint might suggest some of the limitations of Nair's other "studio" pictures (*Amelia, Vanity Fair, The Perez Family*), in fact Nair's *Queen of Katwe* has much more in common with her early documentary realist films like *Salaam Bombay!* than it does with her other studio-backed projects. Nair and her crew filmed on location in the Katwe slums in Kampala and used many Ugandan street children as extras in filming. As with *Salaam Bombay!*, she and her team set up an acting "boot

Queen of Katwe. Cricketers at King's College Budo, Uganda

camp" to help train the children perform for the camera, which helps the film feel much more authentic. Though the language of the film is English, Nair does include a significant amount of dialogue in the Lugandan language, as well as a certain amount of street slang. The presence of these children is essential to the film's success as a realistic depiction of life in urban slums. Nair also uses David Oyelowo and Lupita Nyong'o, two adult African actors with a pedigree in Hollywood, to anchor the film's major dramatic scenes. The inclusion of Lupita Nyong'o is a feather in the cap of sorts for Nair, as Nyong'o had earlier attended the film academy for young women Nair had created, the Maisha Film Lab. Finally, while Phiona Mutesi does not leave Uganda in Nair's *Queen of Katwe*, spatial displacement and travel are both important themes in the film. Like many other diaspora vérité narratives we have seen in Nair's body of work, once she begins to follow on a journey of personal exploration and liberation—in her case, through playing competitive chess at the international level—she finds it difficult to go "home" to her life in the Kampala slums.

Queen of Katwe is unique as a Disney film set in Africa. Unlike other recent Africa-based Hollywood films, the film is primarily about *humans* (most recent commercial Hollywood films set in Africa, including animated films, deal with animals). There are also no "white savior" figures who enter the picture to give Western viewers a point of relatability (as in *The Last King of Scotland* or *The Constant Gardener*). Indeed, there are no major roles for non-African characters at all in the film. Moreover, the film is unique in that it does not foreground African politics (civil war, genocide, disease— stereotypical "African" themes), but rather the talents and intelligence of a group of African street children. Nair can introduce non-Ugandan viewers to the street life of Uganda as well as aspects of middle class life. We see the flash and glitter of youth street style (especially embodied by Phiona's sister, Night, and her boyfriend Theo); we also get a glimpse of more rarefied settings such as King's College Budo—an expensive residential preparatory school that has educated many prominent members of Uganda's ruling class. Though Phiona Mutesi never emigrates from Uganda, *Queen of Katwe* is nevertheless structured as a diasporic film in the sense that her increasing success as a chess player leads her to feel displaced from her family and the rest of her social milieu. The central tension at the heart of her progress is whether and how she might be able to bring her mother and siblings with her as her chess success gives her a path out of the slum. Initially it seems all but impossible, though by the end of the film she seems to have found a way.

Nair develops the sense of displacement over time using a combination of visual and aural textures. Early scenes in *Queen of Katwe* establish the slum setting—dilapidated shacks with corrugated tin roofs, trash, a sense of chaos. Other scenes (in downtown Kampala) give us market crowds and urban traffic. Throughout these early scenes Nair shows her children, including the Mutesi siblings, in crowd shots, with street noise and Ugandan pop music mixed into the soundscape. The body language of the children is loose; Phiona's brother has a street kid's swagger. Though the specific idioms are different, the way the children gesture with their hands (the distinctive Ugandan "finger snap") and dance recalls the street children Nair showed us in *Salaam Bombay!* nearly thirty years earlier.

The first time the children go to a chess tournament, at an elite private school outside of the city, the bus ride begins in exactly the same way—children singing and laughing, with confidence and well within their comfort zone. That comfort dissipates as the camera locates King's College. The children abruptly stop singing. As they approach the campus, Nair shows the children in isolation, suddenly small against the imposing Victorian architecture. One of Robert Katende's team, the "Pioneers," is shown in silhouette as he is passing through a Victorian arch, as students of King's College play cricket in the background, wearing gleaming white suits. The framing of this image as a window of light bordered by darkness is a visual device Nair uses several times in the film to symbolize the access to new opportunities that chess opens to the children in the film.

Phiona's remarkable success at chess leads her and her coach further and further away from Katwe—first to the national championship and then finally abroad, to compete in international chess tournaments—first in Sudan and then in Russia. The thematics of exile and displacement intensify during this phase of the film in a series of conversations between Phiona and her coach, Katende, between Phiona and her mother, Harriet, and between Harriet and Coach Katende. Shortly before the trip to Russia, Robert Katende says to Phiona, "Sometimes the place you are used to is not where you belong. Where do you belong, Phiona?" Katende is in some ways the initiator and the enabler—the figure urging Phiona to reach beyond her existing boundaries in order to explore her potential. In contrast, Phiona's mother Harriet is worried and resistant regarding what the coach appears to be doing to her children by giving them access to competitive chess. "They will not be able to return to their old lives because they have tasted yours. Not here, not there, like ghosts who cannot rest." In other words, while the coach sees the potential for Phiona to find a new, freer space of belonging, her mother worries that she and her brother might merely end up displaced subjects—where education only succeeds in putting them in exile from their lives. Incidentally, while many of the most memorable bits of dialogue in the film are traceable to moments in Crothers's narrative, the conversation above regarding the worries about displacement are all added in by Wheeler and Nair for the film adaptation. That said, there is all the same a journalistic basis for this anxiety; Crothers's book does describe the sense of alienation experienced by the Pioneers, including Phiona, after their first trip abroad, to Sudan. In Crothers's narrative, Phiona is quoted as describing her return to the Katwe slum after traveling by plane and staying in a luxury hotel abroad: "It felt like I was going back to a kind of prison" (Crothers 2012: 152).

The class and education dynamics in *Queen of Katwe* develop in parallel with the spatial dynamic, where Phiona can travel further and further away from home as she develops her competitive chess-playing skills. This leads to the heartbreaking loss at the world chess Olympiad in Russia, described as a turning point in Crothers's narrative as well as in Nair's film. After her defeat there, she tells Coach Katende (in Nair's film): "But now you see me, see how chess has disturbed me. I will never belong to it—and this will never be my place!" Again, her sense of identity is figured in spatial terms: "This will never be my place!" Against the strong urge to move out and abroad, there is an even greater sense of the need to stay close to "home." Nair's film then returns Phiona to Katwe and reunites her with her family. Unlike many Nair films that feature a diasporic subject who must accept the loss of family and "home" in the interest of gaining access to greater freedoms abroad, in *Queen of Katwe* there is a strong hope that Phiona can grow and change without leaving home and family behind for good. (As a final note, the aftermath of the loss in Siberia is described differently in the Crothers book version of the story.)

In the end, when she sells her story to a foreign journalist (Tim Crothers) and the media company that will option it for a film (Disney), Phiona is able to find a way to get her family out of the slums and into a house with a small garden. She can house her mother and her siblings there as she continues her education. In the closing sequence of the film, Nair makes the unusual move of pairing the actors playing various real people whose stories feature in the film with the people they are playing. This strengthens the sense of authenticity associated with the performances and the approach to the story of Katwe's chess "Pioneers"—most of the actors do resemble younger versions of the people they play. While the framing of the narrative as a competition-oriented underdog narrative (and therefore a "genre" film) does make it difficult to think of *Queen of Katwe* as a straightforward instance of documentary realism, this extended sequence at the end of the film reminds the viewer that chess was ultimately a vehicle through which these children could gain access to an education and a shot at a better life outside of the Katwe slums.

Conclusion

The mix of new experiments and settings with ideas that are clearly well-tried and tested in *Queen of Katwe* is part of a pattern that we have seen emerge as we have followed the development of Nair's career. Nair's filmmaking project has been driven by a strong feminist sensibility that has led her to tell cinematic stories focused on powerful and controversial women characters—from Thackeray's fictional Becky Sharp, to the pioneering pilot Amelia Earhart, to the Ugandan chess master Phiona Mutesi. Indeed, in two of her recent film adaptations, *The Namesake* and *The Reluctant Fundamentalist*, she expanded and deepened the role played by women characters in novels that were largely male-centered (this is especially pronounced in *The Namesake*, where Nair transforms Ashima's character from a relatively marginal position to a starring one). Nair's feminism was especially significant in her early career, when she was one of very few Indian women film directors operating in the international film scene. Many more women directors have emerged since then, though the key decision-making roles in both the commercial and art house cinemas remain heavily male-dominated. Nair's success in this space has undoubtedly made the road a little easier for the next generation of women—directors like Kiran Rao, Zoya Akhtar, and Gauri Shinde.

Nair's feminist sensibility is also evidently postcolonial and diasporic, with women often deliberately setting out on their own as travelers and emigrants eager to escape the confines of rigid social structures and conservative familial arrangements. We saw this postcolonial feminist sensibility in some of her earliest documentaries (*India Cabaret*) and in her middle-period studio films (*Mississippi Masala, The Perez Family, Kama Sutra: A Tale of Love*), and we continue to see traces of it in her most recent film, *Queen of Katwe*. One of the key dimensions of Nair's women-centered narratives of displacement we have explored is the idea that domestic (intranational) displacement can be as challenging as transnational migration. Women like Hansa Seth in *So Far from India* (displaced by marriage), the various internally displaced sex-workers in *India Cabaret*, and Maya in *Kama Sutra* are all shown to be migrants *within* India. (The theme of internal displacement was also important in our reading of *Salaam Bombay!*—though there we see the toll it takes on both Nair's displaced boys and the young Nepali woman who has been the victim of sex trafficking.)

Especially in Nair's more recent films, the choice to leave a difficult home situation does not necessarily mean leaving behind all traces of the past—the roots of one's social identity. Through globalization, today's diasporic communities remain in close, sometimes even constant, contact with friends and family at "home." As we see in films like *Monsoon Wedding* and *The Namesake*, the "homing desire" (i.e., the cultural orientation towards a concept of home that may be far away and removed from one's everyday environment) can remain powerfully formative even for communities that do not actually intend to permanently return to their countries of origin. Especially in these later films, Nair has explored how the complexities of diasporic life can be rich opportunities for creating hybrid cultural identities, rather than spaces of nostalgia for a lost home.

While Nair is very much a South Asian diaspora filmmaker whose Indian origins are important to any serious analysis of her major works, she has done enough work outside of South Asian contexts to justify considering her as a filmmaker in dialogue with larger themes related to migration and socioeconomic inequities on a global scale. We see this, of course, in *Queen of Katwe*—where Nair's confidence in filming in the slums of Kampala comes from sustained engagement with everyday life in Uganda. But Nair also filmed in Uganda in the early 1990s when she made *Mississippi Masala*, and in South Africa, which led to the short film *The Day the Mercedes Became a Hat*. And Nair's fictional film based on the Cuban immigrant experience in the Mariel boatlift, *The Perez Family*, reflects engagement in issues of migration beyond Indian and African contexts. While *The Perez Family* was an uneven effort—perhaps because the filmmaker lacked the long-term exposure to a society that comes from either growing up there (India), or other sustained connection to it through residency—there may be reason to hope that Nair can, in future efforts, continue to explore the many historical and cultural links between East African and South Asian societies.

And finally, throughout her career Nair has been committed to filmmaking that has a documentary realist quality. Early in her career, she expressed that commitment through films that were either documentaries themselves or that addressed specific social issues. But that documentary emphasis has been present even in more recent films such as *The Namesake* and *The Reluctant Fundamentalist*. I have interpreted *The Namesake* as an attempt to document—and serve as a kind of crystallization of—the middle-class Indian immigrant experience from the latter decades of the twentieth century. And for its part, *The Reluctant Fundamentalist* is a response to, and a document of, the ambivalence that many postcolonial writers and intellectuals have felt regarding the American prosecution of the War on Terror. While Nair has, in some of her recent films, drifted away from her documentary realist roots, with *Queen of Katwe* Nair has shown that she is still very much interested in, and capable of engaging with, the powerful themes of street life and poverty in developing nations that first brought her so much well-deserved international critical appreciation thirty years ago after *Salaam Bombay!* While Nair's career has been extensive and impressive, the aggregate number of postcolonial and diasporic stories that have been depicted on screen by her and her peer group remains fairly small; there are still a great many stories left to tell. The hope is that Mira Nair will continue to push the limits of diaspora vérité filmmaking for years to come, giving critics like this one more to write about.

MIRA NAIR'S FILMOGRAPHY

Jama Masjid Street Journal (1979) (Documentary)

Nation: USA
Direction: Mira Nair
Color
Length: 18 minutes

Summary: An episodic documentary depicting street life in the Muslim-majority neighborhood around the Jama Masjid in Old Delhi. The filmmaker uses the observational method, with a high degree of self-consciousness and self-reflexive voice-over commentary. Nair comments on the anomaly of her status as a "woman speaking Urdu holding a movie camera." This early film introduces many of the themes that will be prevalent throughout Nair's career: the concern with documentary realism, the interest in gender, and the problem of documenting life in everyday India as a diasporic subject.

So Far from India (1983) (Documentary)

Nation: USA
Direction: Mira Nair
Cinematography: Mitch Epstein
Editing: Ann Schaetzel
Color
Length: 52 minutes

Summary: Nair explores the tensions experienced by a married couple when the husband, Ashok Seth, is working in New York City, while his uneducated wife through an arranged marriage remains behind in Gujarat. Filmed in parallel in New York and India, the film contains interviews in its second half of various members of the family after Ashok and Hansa are reunited in India. Some of the most telling moments in the film are found in unrehearsed comments made by interview subjects reflecting their doubts and anxieties about the future. The film suggests a picture of emigration as leading to deep social and cultural disruption.

India Cabaret (1985) (TV Documentary)

Nation: India/UK/Canada
Distribution: Broadcast on PBS (USA)
Direction: Mira Nair
Color
Length: 58 Minutes

Summary: Nair's most sophisticated and complex early documentary, produced after the filmmaker spent three months living with a group of nightclub bar dancers in suburban Bombay. Featuring candid and colorful commentary from the bar dancers, nightclub patrons, as well as the owner of the nightclub, the film has a decidedly feminist perspective and remains neutral regarding the dancers' decision to engage in what is only thinly disguised sex work. The dancers are shown as empowered and self-sufficient in the present moment of the film, but with a precarious lifestyle and limited opportunities for the future.

Children of a Desired Sex (1987) (TV Documentary)

Nation: India/Canada
Direction: Mira Nair
Color

Summary: Documentary on sex-selective abortion made for Canadian television.

Salaam Bombay! (1988)

Nation: India
Production: Mirabai Films, Film Four International, NFDC Doordarhsan, Cadrag SA, La Sept
Producer: Mira Nair
Distribution: Cinecom Pictures (USA)
Direction: Mira Nair
Screenplay: Sooni Taraporevala
Cinematography: Sandi Sissel
Editing: Barry Alexander Brown
Music: L. Subramaniam
Cast: Shafiq Syed, Hansa Vithal, Chandra Sharma, Raghubir Yadav, Anita Kanwar, Nana Patekar, Raju Barnad, Anjaan, Amrit Patel, Murari Sharma, Ram Moorti, Sarfuddin Qurrassi, Mohanraj Babu, Chandrashekhar Naidu, Shaukat Kaifi Azmi
Length: 113 minutes

Summary: A young boy named Krishna (Shafiq Syed) is abandoned by the traveling circus where he has been working as a peon. He takes a train to Bombay, where he joins a group of street children living near a red-light district. With help from a teenage drug dealer named Chillum (Raghubir Yadav), he finds work as a tea carrier for a local brothel and is nicknamed "Chaipau" by his friends. He also befriends a Nepali girl nicknamed "Solasaal" (Chandra Sharma) who is being groomed for prostitution work by a pimp and drug dealer known as Baba (Nana Patekar). Baba's girlfriend Rekha (Anita Kanwar) and her daughter Manju also befriend Chaipau. Later the children are separated from the slum and sent to reform centers. Chillum eventually dies after being fired by Baba, leading Chaipau to turn on Baba.

Mississippi Masala (1991)

Nation: USA/Uganda
Production: Studio Canal Souss, Cinecom International, Film Four International, Mirabai Films
Producers: Michael Nozik, Mira Nair
Distribution: Samuel Goldwyn Company

Direction: Mira Nair
Screenplay: Sooni Taraporevala
Cinematography: Edward Lachman
Editing: Roberto Silvi
Music: L. Subramaniam
Cast: Denzel Washington, Roshan Seth, Sarita Choudhury, Sharmila Tagore, Charles S. Dutton, Joe Seneca, Ranjit Chowdhry, Mohan Gokhale, Mohan Agashe, Tico Wells, Yvette Hawkins, Anjan Srivastava, Dipti Sutha, Varsha Thaker, Ashok Lath, Willy Cobbs, Mira Nair, Sahira Nair, Kong Mbandu
Length: 118 minutes

Summary: Jay (Roshan Seth) and Kinnu (Sharmila Tagore) are part of the Ugandan Indian population forced to leave Uganda in 1972 following Idi Amin's Asian Expulsion. After a tense confrontation with Ugandan police, they find themselves in Mississippi, managing a hotel with a sizeable Gujarati expatriate population. They hope to set up their daughter, Mina (Sarita Choudhury) with a nice local Indian boy, but circumstances lead her to fall in love with an African American man named Demetrius (Denzel Washington).

The Day the Mercedes Became a Hat (1993)

Nation: South Africa
Production: Imagine Films
Producer: Mira Nair
Director: Mira Nair
Screenplay: Helena Kriel, Mira Nair
Cinematography: Miles Goodall
Editing: Barry Alexander Brown
Cast: Jennifer Steyn, Russel Savadier, Bess Finney, Sechaba Gulube, Dylan Aspeling, Dolly Rathebe
Length: 10 minutes

Summary: A white family in Apartheid South Africa comes to feel uncertain about its future as it becomes clear that the Apartheid regime is coming to an end, and the black majority will be taking the reins of power. The decision is made to leave the country. This short explores some of the same themes as Nair's *Mississippi Masala*—the ambivalence over exile and the challenges of achieving real cross-racial dialogue given the weight of historical injustice.

The Perez Family (1995)

Nation: USA
Production: Samuel Goldwyn Company
Producers: Michael Nozik, Lydia Dean Pilcher
Distribution: Samuel Goldwyn Company
Direction: Mira Nair
Screenplay: Robin Swicord
Cinematography: Stuart Dryburgh
Editing: Robert Estrin
Music: Alan Silvestri
Cast: Marisa Tomei, Alfred Molina, Anjelica Huston, Chazz Palmintieri, Trini Alvarado, Ceia Cruz, Ranjit Chowdhry, Diego Wallfraff, Ellen Cleghorne, Angela Lanza, Lazaro Perez, Bill Sage, Vincent Gallo, Mira Nair
Length: 113 minutes

Summary: Adapted from Christine Bell's 1991 novel of the same name. Escaping from Castro's Cuba in the Mariel boatlift of 1980, a former political prisoner, Juan Perez (Alfred Molina) and Dottie Perez (Marisa Tomei), a former prostitute, are brought together. They decide to pretend to be a married couple with children to facilitate their immigration process once they arrive in Florida. Meanwhile, Juan Perez's real wife (Anjelica Huston), who has been settled in Florida for more than twenty years, continues to wait for him to appear. Nair adds some provocative touches not present in Bell's source text, including an insightful US immigration officer (Ranjit Chowdhry), but the near absence of actual Cuban actors in the cast weakens the sense of authenticity.

Kama Sutra: A Tale of Love (1996)

Nation: USA
Production: NDF International, Pony Canyon, Pandora Films, Channel Four Films, Mirabai Films
Producer: Lydia Dean Pilcher
Distribution: Trimark Pictures
Direction: Mira Nair
Screenplay: Helena Kriel and Mira Nair
Cinematography: Declan Quinn

Editing: Kristina Boden
Music: L. Subramaniam, Shubha Mudgal, Ustad Vilayat Khan
Cast: Naveen Andrews, Sarita Choudhury, Ramon Tikaram, Rekha, Indira Varma, Ranjit Chowdhry, Khalid Tyabji, Arundhati Rao, Surabhi Bhansali, Garima Dhup, Achala Sachder, Arjun Sajnani, Avijit Dutt, Prabeen Sing, Dinaz Stafford, Maya Krishna Rao
Length: 117 minutes

Summary: Loosely adapted from Wajida Tabassum's Urdu short story "Utaran" (Castoffs), with some text taken from the Richard Burton translation of *The Kama Sutra*. Nair's feminist interpretation of the notoriously male-centered *Kama Sutra* features a princess named Tara (Sarita Choudhury) and a servant, Maya (Indira Varma), who betrays her mistress by sleeping with the princess's new husband. Maya is subsequently exiled, where she meets a dance teacher named Rasa Devi (Rekha) and falls in love with a sculptor (Ramon Tikaram). Maya returns and attempts to help Tara, but the kingdom is troubled on many fronts.

My Own Country (1998) (For TV)

Nation: USA
Production: Showtime Networks, Main Title Pictures Production
Producer: Mira Nair
Distribution: Showtime Networks
Direction: Mira Nair
Screenplay: Jim Leonard Jr., Sooni Taraporevala
Cinematography: Dion Beeb
Editing: Kristina Boden
Music: Jeff Danna
Cast: Naveen Andrews, Glenne Headly, Hal Holbrook, Swoosie Kurtz, Marisa Tomei, Adam Tomei, Ellora Patnaik, Peter MacNeill, Sean Hewitt, William Webster, Sharon Dyer, David Fox, Colleen Williams, Ranjit Chowdhry, Mira Nair
Length: 95 minutes

Summary: Nair made this feature film for the Showtime television network, adapted from Abraham Verghese's nonfiction memoir of the same title. The story is about a young immigrant doctor (Naveen Andrews) who has been forced to leave an African country undergoing conflict. He is hired as an infectious disease specialist at a hospital in rural Tennessee at the beginning of the AIDS epidemic in the early 1980s. Local Tennesseans are forced to confront the fact that HIV is present in their community; gay patients struggle to receive care and attention in light of deep-seated and pervasive homophobia. Nair keeps the essential tension that is at the center of Verghese's book—the challenges faced by a heterosexual immigrant doctor advocating for another group of outsiders (HIV positive gay men) but adds a romantic element not present in the source material.

The Laughing Club of India (1999) (TV Documentary)

Nation: India/USA
Production: Laforest, Mirabai Films
Producer: Adam Bartos
Distribution: Cinemax
Direction: Mira Nair
Cinematography: Adam Bartos
Editing: Barry Alexander Brown
Length: 34 minutes

Summary: After a hiatus of nearly fourteen years, Nair returns to the documentary format with a medium-length documentary largely shot in Mumbai, India. Nair profiles a movement known as "Laughing Yoga," where participants engage in ritualistic laughter-based exercise. Nair interviews participants from different social classes, as well as the originator of laughter yoga, Madan Kataria. The film has self-reflexive elements (Nair herself participates in laughing yoga) as well as a diasporic offshoot with the advent of laughter yoga groups in New York City.

Monsoon Wedding (2001)

Nation: USA
Production: IFC Productions, Mirabai Film, Keyfilms/Pandora Films/Paradise Films, Delhi Dot Com, Baron Pictures
Producers: Caroline Baron, Mira Nair
Distribution: Focus Features (USA)

Direction: Mira Nair
Screenplay: Sabrina Dhawan
Cinematography: Declan Quinn
Editing: Allyson C. Johnson
Music: Mychael Danna
Cast: Naseeruddin Shah, Lillete Dubey, Shefali Shetty, Vasundhara Das, Vijay Raaz, Tilotama Shome, Rajat Kapoor, Kulbhushan Kharbanda, Kamini Khanna, Neha Dubey, Roshan Seth, Ishaan Nair, Randeep Hooda, Sabrina Dhawan
Length: 114 minutes

Summary: Several overlapping narratives and a loose, improvisatory style made this film set in contemporary New Delhi one of Nair's biggest crossover successes. An upper-middle-class patriarch, Lalit Verma (Naseeruddin Shah), is planning a wedding for his daughter Aditi (Vasundhara Das), to a software engineer. Aditi, for her part is in the middle of breaking up with a TV personality (who is not her fiancé). The film also gives significant attention to an aspiring working-class businessman, P. K. Dubey (Vijay Raaz), whose budding romance with a servant gives the film its most conventional romantic plot. Issues of class, changing gender roles, media censorship, diasporization, and the problem of sexual abuse are all themes that figure in this film.

Hysterical Blindness (2002) (For TV)

Nation: USA
Production: Blum Israel Productions
Producers: Lydia Dean Pilcher
Distribution: HBO Films
Direction: Mira Nair
Screenplay: Laura Cahill (based on her play)
Cinematography: Declan Quinn
Editing: Kristina Boden
Music: Lesley Barber
Cast: Uma Thurman, Gena Rowlands, Juliette Lewis, Justin Chambers, Ben Gazzara
Length: 96 minutes

Summary: Nair made this low-budget feature film with a star-studded cast for HBO based on a play of the same name by Laura Cahill. The gritty psychological drama features a young woman named Debby Miller (Uma Thurman) in working-class northern New Jersey who has a personality disorder that makes her repellent to men. With alternative cinema legends Gena Rowlands and Ben Gazzara as an older couple, this film may have been intended as Nair's contribution to the gritty psychological realism of filmmakers like John Cassavetes.

11'09"01 (2002) (Segment: India; Short Film)

Nation: USA
Production: CIH Shorts, Catherine Dussart Productions, Comme des Cinemas, Galatee Films, Imamura Productions, La Generale de Production, Les Films 13, Les Films de la Plaine, MISR International Films, Makhmalbaf Productions, Sequence 19 Productions, Sixteen Films, Studio Canal, Zeta Film
Distribution: Empire Pictures (USA)
Producers: Nicholas Muvernay, Jacques Perrin
Direction: Mira Nair
Screenplay: Sabrina Dhawan
Cinematography: Declan Quinn
Editing: Allyson C. Johnson
Cast: Tanvi Azmi, Kapil Bawa, Taleb Adlah
Length: 11 minutes

Summary: This short film was included in an anthology of films by directors around the world exploring the impact of 9/11 on a range of communities. Nair's contribution focuses on the true story of Salman Hamdani, a rescue worker who died in the Twin Towers on 9/11. Because of his Islamic faith, he and his family were initially viewed with suspicion by investigators and neighbors.

Vanity Fair (2004)

Nation: USA/UK/India
Production: Focus Features presents a Tempesta Films Granada Film Production

Producers: Janette Day, Lydia Dean Pilcher, Donna Gigliotti
Direction: Mira Nair
Screenplay: Julian Fellowes, Matthew Faulk, Mark Sheet
Cinematography: Declan Quinn
Editing: Allyson C. Johnson
Music: Mychael Danna
Cast: Reese Witherspoon, Gabriel Byrne, Romola Girai, Rhys Ifans, Jonathan Rhys-Meyers, Bob Hoskins, James Purefoy, Jim Broadbent, Angelica Many, Ruth Sheen, Lilette Dubey, Tony Maudsley, Deborah Findlay, John Franklyn-Robbins, Douglas Hodge, Geraldine McEwan, Natasha Little, Eileen Atkins
Color
Length: 141 minutes

Summary: Closely adapted from William Makepeace Thackeray's 1847–48 novel of the same name. Nair's adaptation of Thackeray's *Vanity Fair* is very much a postcolonial interpretation of this Victorian classic, emphasizing the importance of India to the financial and cultural landscape of English life in the first decades of the nineteenth century. Many of the India-themed scenes are drawn closely from Thackeray's novel; others reflect a somewhat looser approach to the source text. Nair drastically alters the conclusion of the story, giving Becky Sharp (Reese Witherspoon) a way out of the scandalous situation that is her undoing in Thackeray's version of the story.

The Namesake (2006)

Nation: USA/India
Production: Mirabai Films, UTV Motion Pictures
Producers: Mira Nair
Distribution: Fox Searchlight
Direction: Mira Nair
Screenplay: Jhumpa Lahiri (novel), Sooni Taraporevala
Cinematography: Frederick Elmes
Editing: Barry Alexander Brown
Music: Nitin Sawhney
Cast: Tabu, Irrfan Khan, Kal Penn, Zuleikha Robinson, Jacinda Barrett
Length: 122 minutes

Summary: Closely adapted from Jhumpa Lahiri's novel of the same name. Ashima Ganguli (Tabu) moves to New York to join her husband (Irrfan Khan) after an arranged marriage ceremony in Kolkata. The film dramatizes in slow and elegiac fashion the Gangulis' adaptation to life in America, splitting the focus between parents and their American-born children. Nair's film pays more attention to the lives of the parents than does the source text; gender themes are also prominent.

Migration (2007) (Short Film)

Nation: USA (filmed in Mumbai, India)
Production: Avahan India AIDS Initiative, Bill and Melinda Gates Foundation
Producer: Shernaz Italia, Freny Khodaiji
Direction: Mira Nair
Screenplay: Zoya Akhtar, Vishal Bhardwaj
Cinematography: Jay Jay Odedra
Editing: Barry Alexander Brown
Music: Mychael Danna
Caste: Shiney Ahuja, Tinnu Anand, Raima Sen, Ashok Beniwal, Sameera Reddy, Irrfan Khan, Sulabha Deshbande
Color
Length: 12 minutes

Summary: A short film made to promote AIDS awareness amongst Indian audiences; it played as a short attached to a limited number of commercial Hindi films released in India in 2007–8. A married worker from the countryside contracts AIDS while working in Mumbai, leading to painful revelations when he is reunited with his wife who has remained at home. Explores some of the same themes of internal displacement and rural-to-urban migration Nair has also explored in *Salaam Bombay!*

"How Can It Be?" (2008) from *8*

Nation: France
Production: LDM Productions
Producer: Marc Oberon, Lissandra Haulica
Direction: Mira Nair
Screenplay: Suketu Mehta, Rashida Mustafa
Cinematography: Declan Quinn
Editing: Allyson Johnson

Music: Mychael Danna
Cast: Konkona Sen Sharma, Ranvir Shorey, Birsa Chatterjee
Color
Length: 9 minutes

Summary: Short film included in an anthology. Nair's contribution explores a Muslim woman (played by Konkona Sen Sharma) in a very traditional household in New York who decides to leave her husband. Notable for the involvement of journalist Suketu Mehta as screenplay writer.

New York, I Love You (2008) (Segment 2: Mira Nair)

Nation: USA
Production: Ever So Close Productions, Visitor Pictures
Producers: Emmanuel Benbihy, Marina Grasic
Direction: Mira Nair
Screenplay: Suketu Mehta
Cinematography: Benoit Debie
Editing: Craig McKay
Music: Mychael Danna
Cast: Irrfan Khan, Natalie Portman
Color
Length: 8 minutes

Summary: Nair's section of this film is one of several episodic shorts stitched together for an anthology film by the producers of *Paris, je t'aime*. The script for Nair's segment was written by Suketu Mehta, a fellow diasporic Indian now based in New York City. A Hasidic Jewish woman (Natalie Portman) has an intimate encounter with a Gujarati Jain diamond dealer (Irrfan Khan) in midtown Manhattan that highlights cross-cultural similarities between these communities.

Amelia (2009)

Nation: USA
Production: AE Electra, Fox Searchlight
Producers: Lydia Dean Pilcher, Kevin Hyman, Ted Waitt

Distribution: Fox Searchlight
Direction: Mira Nair
Screenplay: Ronald Bass, Anna Hamilton Phelan
Cinematography: Stuart Dryburgh
Editing: Allyson Johnson, Lee Percy
Music: Gabriel Yared
Cast: Hilary Swank, Richard Gere, Ewan McGregor, Christopher Eccleston, Cherry Jones, Mia Wasikowska, Aaron Adams, Dylan Roberts
Color
Length: 111 minutes

Summary: A biopic based on the life of pioneering aviator Amelia Earhart (Hilary Swank). Nair's film focuses mainly on the time period between Earhart's first transatlantic flight (where she was, it is suggested, more a passenger than a pilot) and her later solo transatlantic flight and eventual death on an attempt to fly around the world. Earhart's complex personal life is also explored, including her troubled marriage to George Putnam (Richard Gere) and her romance with Gene Vidal (Ewan McGregor). Explores themes of fame and Earhart's unique status as a feminist icon; some engagement with non-Western cultures in scenes shot in Africa and southeast Asia during Earhart's final voyage.

The Reluctant Fundamentalist (2013)

Nation: USA/India
Production: Cine Mosaic, Corniche Pictures, Doha Film Institute, Mirabai Films
Producers: Lydia Dean Pilcher, Mira Nair
Distribution: IFC Films
Direction: Mira Nair
Screenplay: Ami Boghani, Mohsin Hamid, William Wheeler
Cinematography: Declan Quinn
Editing: Shimit Amin
Music: Michael Andrews
Cast: Kate Hudson, Riz Ahmed, Kiefer Sutherland, Om Puri, Shabana Azmi, Liev Schreiber
Length: 130 minutes

Summary: Loosely adapted from a novel of the same title by Mohsin Hamid. Changez Khan (Riz Ahmed), a Pakistani student in the United States, gets hired by a financial consulting company and along the way falls in love with Erica (Kate Hudson), an art photographer with a troubled past and the daughter of one of the firm's chief executives. After 9/11, Changez grows increasingly alienated from his life in the United States and from Erica in particular, leading to a breakup and his subsequent decision to return to Lahore. In Lahore, Changez is suspected of involvement with a group of radical students who kidnap a Western journalist. This leads to a confrontation with a CIA agent sent in to try and gather information from Changez.

Queen of Katwe (2016)

Nation: USA/Uganda
Production: Disney, ESPN Films, Cine Mosaic, Mirabai Films
Producers: John B. Carls, Lydia Dean Pilcher
Distribution: Disney
Direction: Mira Nair
Screenplay: William Wheeler, Tim Crothers
Cinematography: Sean Bobbitt
Editing: Barry Alexander Brown
Music: Alex Heffes
Cast: Madina Nalwanga, Lupita Nyong'o, David Oyelowo
Length: 124 minutes

Summary: Based on the true story and adapted from a book by Tim Crothers. Phiona Mutesi (Madina Nalwanga), a young woman from the Katwe slums outside of Kampala, begins studying chess with an inspiring teacher, Robert Katende (David Oyelowo). Though barely literate, she learns the game quickly and becomes the star of the "Pioneers"—a team of children from Katwe slum. She goes on to first national and then international competitions, all the while dealing with the impact of poverty on her family. Lupita Nyong'o, who plays Phiona's mother Harriet, earlier worked for Nair's Kampala-based film school for women, Maisha Film Lab.

NOTES

1. All citations of Nair's films refer to "Mira Nair's Filmography," pp. 197 in this volume, rather than to the main references list.

2. See Nair 1986: 67. "I think this idea about the film presenting a 'male gaze' is basically lifted out of context from Western theorizing about the film and feminism.... In response, I find the fixation on the four minutes of dancing in a sixty-minute film absurdly disproportionate. I must show the dancers dancing because this is what they do to make their living. This criticism is essentially a myopic view because it refuses to confront the dancer and the dance—which is the central fact of their existence."

3. Three of Nair's documentaries, and four of her short fiction films, have recently been released as part of a two-DVD set, the *Monsoon Wedding Criterion Collection* (2009). The documentaries in the DVD set are *So Far from India*, *India Cabaret*, and *The Laughing Club of India*.

4. One prominent exception to the silence about prostitution in Bombay is a photo-essay by a western photographer named Mary Ellen Mark. *Falkland Road: Prostitutes of Bombay* (Mark 1981) contains haunting, gritty, and intimate photographs of the women who work on Falkland Road, roughly the same area as the Kamathipura neighborhood in *Salaam Bombay!* It might be argued that Mark's exploration of the world of prostitutes of varying status and rank verges on a kind of voyeurism—as many prostitutes are photographed nude or partially nude. Nair's film, by contrast, contains no female nudity.

5. According to Mahmood Mamdani, by 1972, there were twenty-three thousand Ugandan citizens of Indian descent, and another thirty thousand had applications for citizenship in process. That left about thirty thousand Indians in Uganda who had not applied for citizenship (Mamdani 1973).

6. For an introduction to the politics of color within the African American community in particular, see Kerr 2006. Of course, colorism is also widespread within the Indian community. For a discussion of skin-tone discrimination amongst Asian Americans in particular, see Rondilla 2007.

REFERENCES

Aengst, J. 2001. "Girl Trafficking in Nepal." Human Rights Advocacy Clinic, University of Denver. http://www.du.edu/intl/humanrights/trafficking.pdf.

Agnes, Flavia. 2008. "Bar Dancer and the Trafficked Migrant: Globalisation and Subaltern Existence." In *Sex as Crime?*, edited by Gayle Letherby, Kate Williams, Philip Birch, and Maureen Cain, 99–117. London: Willan Press.

Aguirre, B. E., Rogelio Saenz, and Brian Sinclair James. 1997. "Marielitos Ten Years Later: The Scarface Legacy." *Social Science Quarterly* 78, no. 2 (June 1997): 487–99.

Allen, Robert C. and Douglas Gomery. 1985. "Case Study: The Beginnings of American Cinéma Vérité." In *Film History: Theory and Practice*. New York: Knopf.

Andrew, Dudley. 1984. *Concepts in Film Theory*. New York: Oxford University Press.

Appadurai, Arjun. 1996. *Modernity at Large: Cultural Dimensions of Globalization*. Minneapolis: University of Minnesota Press.

Appadurai, Arjun and Carol A. Breckenridge. 1991. "Marriage, Migration and Money: Mira Nair's Cinema of Displacement." *Visual Anthropology* 4, no. 1 (1991): 95–102.

Arora, Poonam. 1994. "The Production of Third World Subjects for First World Consumption: *Salaam Bombay!* and *Parama*." In *Multiple Voices in Feminist Film Criticism*, edited by Diane Carson, Linda Dittmar, and Janice R. Welch, 293–304. Minneapolis: University of Minnesota Press.

Badt, Karin Luisa. 2004. "I Want My Films to Explode with Life: An Interview with Mira Nair." *Cineaste* 30, no. 1: 10–15.

Baig, Daniel. 2002. "Interview: Mira Nair." *Counting Down*, May 1, 2002. http://www.countingdown.com/features?feature_id=716479&print=1.

Barrier, N. Gerald. 1974. *Banned: Controversial Literature and Political Control in British India*. Columbia: University of Missouri Press.

Bazin, André. 1982. "Cruelty and Love in Los Olvidados." In *The Cinema of Cruelty: From Buñuel to Hitchcock*, edited by Francois Truffaut, translated by Sabine d'Estrée. New York: Seaver Books.

Beaufoy, Simon. 2008. "Life on the Hard Shoulder." *Guardian*, December 12, 2008. http://www.guardian.co.uk/film/2008/dec/12/simon-beaufoy-slumdog-millionaire/print.

Bell, Christine. 1990. *The Perez Family*. New York: Harper Perennial.

Benson, Sheila. 2004. "Interview: *Vanity Fair* Director Mira Nair." *Seattle Weekly*, September 1, 2004.

Beresford, David. 1997. "Mira Nair Wanted to Introduce India to the Joys of Sex. Her Country's Rulers Had Other Ideas." *Guardian*, June 13, 1997, T8–9.

Bharadwaj, Ashutosh. 2007. "Interview: Praveen Nair." January 24, 2007. http://www.devel opednation.org/interviews/praveen_nair.htm.

Bhatnagar, Rashmi, Renu Dube, and Reena Dube. 2005. *Female Infanticide in India: A Feminist Cultural History*. Albany: State University of New York Press.

Bizeck, J. Phiri. 2005. "Asians: East Africa." In *Encyclopedia of African History*, edited by Kevin Shillington, 112–13. New York: Routledge.

Boltin, Kylie. 2002. "*Monsoon Wedding*: A Discussion of Mira Nair's New Film." *Metro*, Summer 2002, 1–4.

Bose, Brinda. 2006. "Introduction." In *Gender & Censorship*, edited by Brinda Bose, xiii-xlvi. New Delhi: Women Unlimited.

Bose, Derek. 2005. *Bollywood Censored: What You Don't See on Screen and Why*. Bombay: Rupa.

Bovenschen, Silvia. 1977. "Is There a Feminine Film Aesthetic?" Translated by Beth Weckmueller. *New German Critique*, 12 (1977): 111–37.

Brah, Avtar. 1996. *Cartographies of Desire: Contesting Identities*. New York: Routledge.

Bruzzi, Stella. 2006. *New Documentary: A Critical Introduction*. New York: Routledge.

Bumiller, Elizabeth. 1991. *May You Be the Mother of a Hundred Sons: A Journey Among the Women of India*. New York: Ballantine Books.

Butalia, Pankaj. 2002. "*Monsoon Wedding*." *New Internationalist*, March 2002, 32–34.

Chakravarty, Sumita S. 1993. *National Identity in Indian Popular Cinema*. Austin: University of Texas Press.

Chaudhuri, Shohini. 2005. *Contemporary World Cinema*. Edinburgh: Edinburgh University Press.

Cheng, Scarlet. 2003. "Mira Nair: Intoxicated with Life." *World and I*, June 2003, 98.

Corrigan, Timothy. 1999. *Film and Literature: An Introduction and Reader*. New York: Prentice-Hall.

Crothers, Tim. 2012. *Queen of Katwe: One Girl's Triumphant Path to Becoming a Chess Champion*. New York: Scribner.

Damji, Nazneen, et al. 2000. "Progress of the World's Poorest Women." Unifem Biennial Report. New York: United Nations Development Fund for Women.

Dargis, Manohla. 2013. "Dreams Are Lost in the Melting Pot." *New York Times*, April 25, 2013.

Davis, Mike. 2006. *Planet of Slums*. New York: Verso.

De Lauretis, Teresa. 1994. "Rethinking Women's Cinema: Aesthetics and Film Theory." In *Multiple Voices in Feminist Film Criticism*, edited by Diane Carson, Linda Dittmar, and Janice R. Welch, 140–61. Minneapolis: University of Minnesota Press.

Deleuze, Gilles and Felix Guattari. 2009. *Anti-Oedipus: Capitalism and Schizophrenia*. Translated by Robert Hurley. New York: Penguin Classics.

Desai, Gaurav. 2013. *Commerce with the Universe: Africa, India, and the Afrasian Imagination*. New York: Columbia University Press.

Desai, Jigna. 2004. "When Indians Play Cowboys: Diaspora and Postcoloniality in Mira Nair's *Mississippi Masala*." In *Beyond Bollywood: The Cultural Politics of South Asian Diasporic Film*, 71–100. New York: Routledge.
Doniger, Wendy. 2009. *Hindus: An Alternative History*. New York: Penguin.
Doniger, Wendy and Sudhir Kakar. 2002. "Introduction." In Vatsayana, *Kamasutra: A New, Complete English Translation of the Sanskrit Text*, translated by Wendy Doniger and Sudhir Kakar, xi–lxix. New York: Oxford University Press.
Dore, Shalini. 2014. "Retrospective of Brit Director Docs Planned." *Variety*, March 12, 2014. http://variety.com/2014/film/news/gurinder-chadha-to-be-honored-at-new-york-indian-film-festival-1201130239/.
Doss, Joe Morris. 2003. *Let the Bastards Go!: From Cuba to Freedom on God's Mercy*. Baton Rouge: Louisiana State University Press.
Dwyer, Rachel. 2006. "Kiss or Tell? Declaring Love in Indian Cinema." In *Love in South Asia: A Cultural History*, edited by Francesca Orsini, 289–302. New Delhi: Cambridge University Press.
Dwyer, Rachel and Divia Patel. 2002. *Cinema India*. New Brunswick: Rutgers University Press.
Faleiro, Sonia. 2012. *Beautiful Thing: Inside the Secret World of Bombay's Dance Bars*. New York: Black Cat Books.
Foster, Gwendolyn Audrey. 1995. *Women Film Directors: An International Bio-Critical Dictionary*, edited by Gwendolyn Audrey Foster, 277–79. Westport: Greenwood Press.
Foster, Gwendolyn Audrey. 1997. *Women Filmmakers of the African and Asian Diaspora: Decolonizing the Gaze, Locating Subjectivity*. Carbondale: Southern Illinois University Press.
Foster, Gwendolyn Audrey. 2002. "Mira Nair." In *Fifty Contemporary Filmmakers*, edited by Yvonne Tasker, 263–72. New York: Routledge.
Freedmann, Samuel G. 1992. "One People in Two Worlds." *New York Times*, February 2, 1992, H13–14.
Friedman, Thomas. 2005. *The World is Flat: A Brief History of the Twenty-First Century*. New York: Farrar, Strous, and Giroux.
Fuller, Graham. 2004. "Shots in the Dark: More Than a Century and a Half after Her Creation, the Character of Becky Sharp Still Reverberates. A New Film Shows How Social Politics and Social Hunger Have—and Have Not—Changed." *Interview*, September 2004, 132.
Ganti, Tejaswini. 2004. *Bollywood: A Guidebook to Popular Hindi Cinema*. New York: Routledge.
Ganti, Tejaswini. 2009. "The Limits of Decency and the Decency of Limits: Censorship and the Bombay Film Industry." In *Censorship in South Asia*, edited by Raminder Kaur, 87–122. Bloomington: University of Indiana Press.
Ganti, Tejaswini. 2012. *Producing Bollywood: Inside the Contemporary Hindi Film Industry*. Durham: Duke University Press.
Geller, Conrad. 2002. "*Monsoon Wedding*." *Cineaste*, Fall 2002, 43–45.
Gentleman, Amelia. 2006. "Slum Tours: A Day Trip Too Far?" *Guardian*, May 7, 2006. http://www.guardian.co.uk/travel/2006/may/07/delhi.india.ethicalliving?page=all.
Ghosh, Lakshmi B. 2004. "Street Inspires Her." *Hindu* (Delhi), June 12, 2004, 1–3. http://www.thehindu.com/thehindu/lf/2004/12/06/stories/.

Gokulsing, K. Moti and Wimal Dissanayake. 2004. *Indian Popular Cinema: A Narrative of Cultural Change*. London: Trentham Books.

Gopal, Sangita. 2011. *Conjugations: Marriage and Form in New Bollywood Cinema*. Chicago: University of Chicago Press.

Gopal, Sangita and Sujata Moorti. 2008. *Global Bollywood: Travels of Indian Song and Dance*. New Delhi: Orient Blackswan.

Grady, Pam. 2004. "Nair Follows Pulitzer's Trail." *Film Stew*, August–September 2004, 1–2. http://www.filmstew.com.

Hall, Carla. 1988. "Mira Nair and the Faces of India." *Washington Post*, November 10, 1988, B1.

Hamid, Mohsin. 2007. *The Reluctant Fundamentalist*. New York: Harcourt.

Hasan, Ayesha. 2002. "Professor Mira Nair Reflects on Her Film Career During Zora Neale Hurston Lecture." *Columbia News*, August 1, 2002, 3. http://www.columbia.edu/cu/news/02/0/miraNair.html.

Holden, Stephen. 2004. "Becky Sharp Again Weaves Her Wily Web." *New York Times*, September 1, 2004.

Iser, Wolfgang. 1987. "The Reader in the Realist Novel." In *Vanity Fair: Modern Critical Interpretations*, edited by Harold Bloom. New York: Chelsea House Publications.

James, Caryn. 1988. "Mira Nair Combines Cultures to Create a Film." *New York Times*, October 17, 1988. http://www.nytimes.com/1988/10/17/movies/mira-nair-combines-cultures-to-create-a-film.html?scp=2&sq=mira%20nair%201988&st=cse.

Johnson, Donald. 2008. "Arranging a Marriage." In *Through Indian Eyes*, 5th ed., 23–28. New York: Apex-CIPA.

Jorgensen, Jan Jelmert. 1981. *Uganda: A Modern History*. New York: Taylor and Francis.

Kakar, Sudhir. 2008. "The Rediscovery of the *Kama Sutra*." *Little India*, June 12, 2008. http://www.littleindia.com/news/139/ARTICLE/2960/2008-06-12.html.

Kamdar, Mira. 2007. *Planet India: How the World's Largest Democracy is Transforming America and the World*. New York: Simon & Schuster.

Kaplan, Fred. 2013. "Crossing Dangerous Borders: Mira Nair on *The Reluctant Fundamentalist*." *New York Times*, April 19, 2013.

Kapur, Ratna. (1996) 2006. "Who Draws the Line? Feminist Reflections on Speech and Censorship." In *Gender & Censorship*, edited by Brinda Bose, 194–241. New Delhi: Women Unlimited. First printed in *Economic and Political Weekly* 31, nos. 16–17 (April 1996): 20–27.

Kara, Siddharth. 2009. *Sex Trafficking: Inside the Business of Modern Slavery*. Columbia University Press, New York.

Karena, Cynthia. 2003. "*Monsoon Wedding*: Raining on Tradition—Film as Text." *Australian Screen Education*, Winter 2003, 1–4.

Keay, John. 2001. *India: A History*. New York: Grove Press.

Kerr, Audrey Elisa. 2006. *The Paper Bag Principle: Class, Colorism, and Rumor and the Case of Black Washington*. Tallahassee: University of Tennessee Press.

Kishwar, Madhu and Ruth Vanita. (1986) 2006. "Using Women as a Pretext for Repression: The Indecent Representation of Women (Prohibition) Bill." In *Gender & Censorship*, edited by Brinda Bose, 107–115. First printed in *Manushi*, 37 (1986).

Kosambi, Meera. (1998) 2006. "Bandit Queen through Indian Eyes: The Reconstructions and Reincarnations of Phoolan Devi." In *Gender & Censorship*, edited by Brinda Bose, 157–64. New Delhi: Women Unlimited. First printed in *Hecate* 24, no. 2: 37–59.

Lahiri, Jhumpa. 2003. *The Namesake*. New York: Mariner Books.

Lahr, John. 2002. "Whirlwind: Mira Nair." *New Yorker*, December 9, 2002, 100.

Lane, Anthony. 2002. "Making Arrangements: A Wedding in Delhi and a Wake on the English Coast." *New Yorker*, December 9, 2002, 199–201.

Loomba, Ania. 1998. *Colonialism/Postcolonialism*. New York: Routledge.

Lowenstein, Stephen. 2008. *My First Movie: Twenty Celebrated Directors Talk About Their First Film*. New York: Penguin Books.

Macias, Robert. 1995. "The Best & Worst of 1995." *Hispanic* 8, no. 11 (December 1995): 16.

MacKinnon, Catherine A. 2013. "Pornography, Civil Rights, and Speech." In *Sex, Morality, and the Law*, edited by Lori Gruen. Hoboken: Taylor and Francis.

Maira, Sunaina, and Rajini Srikanth. 1996. "Visualizing Three Continents: An Interview with Mira Nair." In *Contours of the Heart: South Asians Map North America*, edited by Sunaina Maira, 136–37. New York: Asian American Writers' Workshop.

Mamber, Stephen. 1976. *Cinema Verite in America: Studies in Uncontrolled Documentary*. Cambridge, MA: MIT Press.

Mamdani, Mahmood. 1973. *From Citizen to Refugee: Uganda Asians Come to Britain*. London: Frances Pinter.

Mani, Bakirathi. 1996. "Moments of Identity in Film." In *Countours of the Heart: South Asians Map North America*, edited by Sunaina Maira, 174–87. New York: Asian American Writers' Workshop.

Mark, Mary Ellen. 1981. *Falkland Road: Prostitutes of Bombay*. New York: Knopf.

Mason, M. S. 2001. "*Laughter* Shows Power of Expressing Joy." *Christian Science Monitor*, August 24, 2001, 19.

Mayne, Judith. 1990. *The Woman at the Keyhole: Feminism and Women's Cinema*. Bloomington: Indiana University Press.

Mazumdar, Ranjani. 2007. *Bombay Cinema: An Archive of the City*. Minneapolis: University of Minnesota Press.

Mazzarella, William, and Raminder Kaur. 2009. "Between Sedition and Seduction: Thinking Censorship in South Asia." In *Censorship in South Asia*, 1–28. Bloomington: University of Indiana Press.

McDonald, Moira. 2004. "English Story Infused with Scents of India." *Seattle Times*, August 29, 2004. http://community.seattletimes.nwsource.com/archive/?date=20040829&slug=mira29.

Mehta, Binita. 1996. "Emigrants Twice Displaced: Race, Color, and Identity in Mira Nair's *Mississippi Masala*." In *Between the Lines: South Asians and Postcoloniality*, edited by Deepika Bahri and Mary Vasudeva. Philadelphia: Temple University Press.

Mehta, Monika. 2008. "What Is Behind Film Censorship? The Khalnayak Debates." In *The Bollywood Reader*, edited by Rajinder Dudra and Jigna Desai. London: Open University Press.

Mehta, Suketu. 2004. *Maximum City: Bombay Lost and Found*. New York: Vintage.
Menen, Rejender. 2001. "The Ironies of Kamathipura." *Hindu Sunday* (Delhi), June 3, 2001. http://www.hinduonnet.com/thehindu/2001/06/03/stories/1303128f.htm.
Mercer, Kobena. 1994. "Diaspora Culture and the Dialogic Imagination." In *Welcome to The Jungle: New Positions in Black Cultural Studies*. London: Routledge.
Mishra, Vijay. 1996. "The Diasporic Imaginary: Theorizing the Indian Diaspora." *Textual Practice* 10, no. 3: 421–47.
Mishra, Vijay. 2002. *Bollywood Cinema: Temples of Desire*. New York: Routledge.
Mody, Perveez. 2006. "Kidnapping, Elopement and Abduction: An Ethnography of Love-Marriage in Delhi." In *Love in South Asia: A Cultural History*, edited by Francesca Orsini, 331–45. New Delhi: Cambridge University Press.
Mohanty, Chandra Talpade. 1984. "Under Western Eyes: Feminist Scholarship and Colonial Discourses." *Boundary 2*, 12–13 (1984): 333–58.
Mookerjee, Ajit. (1966) 1994. *Tantra Art: Its Philosophy and Physics*. New Delhi: Rupa.
Muir, John Kenneth. 2006. *Mercy in Her Eyes: The Films of Mira Nair*. New York: Applause Publications.
Mulchandani, Sandhya. 2006. *Erotic Literature of Ancient India*. London: Mercury Books.
Mulvey, Laura. 1975. "Visual Pleasure and Narrative Cinema." *Screen* 16, no. 3.
Nair, Mira. 1979–2016. Films. See "Mira Nair's Filmography," pp. 197 in this volume.
Nair, Mira. 1986–87. "*India Cabaret*: Reflections and Reactions." *Discourse*, 8 (Fall–Winter 1986–87): 58–71.
Nair, Mira. 2001. "Awards Are Temporary Hype; Mira Nair's Exclusive Interview." *Bengal on the Net*, November 11, 2001.
Nair, Mira. 2002a. "Create the World You Know, Nair Tells Filmmakers." *Variety*, September 30, 2002, 14–15.
Nair, Mira. 2002b. "Interview with Mira Nair." *Netribution Film Network*, 2002. http://www.netribution.co.uk/features/interview/2002/mira_nair/1.html.
Nair, Mira. 2002c. "I Wanted to Make a Film That My Son Could See." Interview by Norman Neil. *Evening Standard* (London). January 3, 2002, 28.
Nair, Mira. 2004. "Eat, Memory." *New York Times Magazine*, November 14, 2004, 125–26.
Nair, Mira, Matthew Faulk, Mark Skeet, and Juilian Fellowes. 2004. *Vanity Fair: Bringing Thackeray's Timeless Novel to the Screen*. New York: Newmarket Press.
Nair, Mira and Jhumpa Lahiri. 2006. *The Namesake: A Portrait of the Film by Mira Nair*. New York: Newmarket Press.
Nair, Mira and Sooni Taraporevala. 1989. *Salaam Bombay!* New York: Penguin Books.
Nichols, Bill. 1991. *Representing Reality*. Bloomington: Indiana University Press.
Parameswaran, Radhika, and Kavitha Cordoza. 2009. "Melanin on the Margins: Advertising and the Cultural Politics of Fair/Light/White Beauty in India." *Journalism & Communications Monographs* 11, no. 3 (Autumn 2009): 213–74.
Pendakur, Manjunath. 2003. *Indian Popular Cinema: Industry, Ideology and Consciousness*. Cresskill, New Jersey: Hampton Press.
Pendakur, Manjunath. 2006. "Censorship." In *Gender & Censorship*, edited by Brinda Bose, 19–30. New Delhi: Women Unlimited.

Peters, Catherine. 1987. *Thackeray's Universe: Shifting Worlds of Imagination and Reality*. New York: Oxford University Press.
Porton, Richard. 2004. "Visualizing *Vanity Fair*: Nair Directs Witherspoon in 19th-Century Classic." *Film Journal International*, September 2004, 16–17.
Rajadhyaksha, Ashish. 2000. "Viewership and Democracy in the Cinema." In *Making Meaning in Indian Cinema*, edited by Ravi Vasudevan. Delhi: Oxford University Press.
Rajadhyaksha, Ashish. 2009. "Indian Cinema." In *World Cinema: Critical Approaches*, edited by John Hill and Pamela Church Gibson, 151–58. Oxford: Oxford University Press.
Rajadhyaksha, Ashish, and Paul Willemen. 2002. *Encylocpedia of Indian Cinema—New Revised Edition*. Oxford: Oxford University Press.
Rajagopal. 2009. *Information Communication Technologies and Globalization of Retailing Applications*. Hershey, PA: Information Science Reference, 2009.
Ramanathan, Geeta. 2006. *Feminist Auteurs: Reading Women's Films*. London: Wallflower Press.
Razdan, C. K. 1975. "Film Censorship in India." In *Bare Breasts and Bare Bottoms*, edited by C. K. Razdan. Bombay: Jaico Publishing House.
Redding, Judith M. and Victoria A. Brownworth. 1997. *Film Fatales: Independent Women Directors*. Seattle: Seal Press.
Rich, B. Ruby. 1994. "In the Name of Feminist Film Criticism." In *Multiple Voices in Feminist Film Criticism*, edited by Diane Carson, Linda Dittmar, and Janice R. Welch, 27–44. Minneapolis: University of Minnesota Press.
Robinson, Andrew. 2005. *Satyajit Ray: A Vision of Cinema*. Calcutta: I. B. Tauris.
Rondilla, Joanne L. 2007. *Is Lighter Better? Skin Tone Discrimination Among Asian Americans*. New York: Rowman and Littlefield.
Roy, Arundhati. 1994. "The Great Indian Rape Trick." *Sunday Observer*, August 22, 1994.
Sarkar, Kobita. 1982. *You Can't Please Everyone! Film Censorship: The Inside Story*. Bombay: IBH Publishing Company.
Sarris, Andrew. 1999. "Notes on the Auteur Theory in 1962." In *Film Theory and Criticism*, edited by Leo Braudy and Marshall Cohen, 515–18. New York: Oxford University Press.
Scanlon, Jessie. 2000. "Making it Morph: Elizabeth Diller and Ricardo Scofidio Want Architecture to Change Everything." *Wired* 8, no. 2 (February 2000). http://www.wired.com/wired/archive/8.02/diller.html.
Schickel, Richard. 1995. "Fresh off the Boatlift." *Time* 145, no. 22 (May 29, 1995): 66.
Seabrook, Jeremy. 1987. *Life and Labour in a Bombay Slum*. London: Quartet Books.
Sellors, C. Paul. 2010. *Film Authorship: Auteurs and Other Myths*. New York: Wallflower Press.
Seshagiri, Urmila. 2003. "At the Crossroads of Two Empires: Mira Nair's *Mississippi Masala* and the Limits of Hybridity." *Journal of Asian American Studies* 6, no. 2 (June 2003): 177–98.
Shah, Amit. 1987. "Mira Nair: A Dweller in Two Lands." *Cineaste* 15, no. 3: 22–23.
Sharma, Alpana. 2001. "Body Matters: The Politics of Provocation in Mira Nair's Films." *Quarterly of Film and Video* 2001, 91–103.
Sharma, Shailja and Gita Rajan. 2006. *New Cosmopolitanisms: South Asians in the U.S*. Palo Alto: Stanford University Press.
Sharpe, Jenny. 2005. "Gender, Nation, and Globalization in Monsoon Wedding and Dilwale Dulhania Le Jayenge." *Meridians: Feminism, Race, Transnationalism* 6, no. 1 (2005): 58–81.

Slifkin, Meredith. 2013. "Review: *The Reluctant Fundamentlist*." *Film Comment*, April 25, 2013.
Srikanth, Rajini. 2004. "Ethnic Outsider as the Ultimate Insider: The Paradox of Verghese's *My Own Country*." *MELUS*, Fall–Winter 2004.
Steritt, David. 1988. "Mira Nair." *Christian Science Monitor*, October 12, 1988, 19.
Stuart, Andrea. 1994. "Mira Nair: A New Hybrid Cinema." In *Women and Film: A Sight and Sound Reader*, edited by Pam Cook and Phillip Dodd, 210–16. Philadelphia: Temple University Press.
Swarup, Vikas. 2005. *Q&A*. New York: Scribner.
Tabassum, Wajida. (1977) 1993. "Utaran." In *Women Writing in India: The Twentieth Century*, vol. 2, edited by Susie J. Tharu, translated by Rasheed Moosavi, Vasantha Kannabiran, and Syed Sirajuddin. Delhi: Feminist Press.
Tankha, Madhur. 2003. "Kaanta . . . Raising A Thorny Storm." *Hindu* (Delhi), July 31, 2003. http://www.hinduonnet.com/thehindu/mp/2003/07/31/stories/2003073100120200.htm.
Taylor, D. J. 1999. *Thackeray*. London: Chatto & Windus.
Thackeray, William Makepeace. (1847–48) 2001. *Vanity Fair: A Novel Without a Hero*. New York: Modern Library Classics.
Tololyan, Khachig. 1991. "The Nation-State and Its Others: In Lieu of a Preface." *Diaspora: A Journal of Transnational Studies*, 1 (Spring 1991): 3–7.
Turan, Kenneth. 2013. "Review: *The Reluctant Fundamentalist* Considers 9/11 Effects." *Los Angeles Times*, April 26, 2013.
Vasudevan, Ravi. (1995) 2006. "Addressing the Spectator of a 'Third World' National Cinema: The Bombay 'Social' Film of the 1940s and 1950s." In *Asian Cinemas: A Reader and Guide*, edited by Dimitris Eleftheriotis and Gary Needham. Honolulu: University of Hawaii Press. First printed in *Screen* 36, no. 4 (Winter 1995): 305–24.
Vasudevan, Ravi. 2010. *The Melodramatic Public: Film Form and Spectatorship in Indian Cinema*. New York: Palgrave Macmillan.
Vatsayana. 1883. *The Kama Sutra*. Translated by Richard Burton. London: Kama Shastra Society. http://www.gutenberg.org/etext/27827.
Verghese, Abraham. 1994. *My Own Country: A Doctor's Story*. New York: Vintage Books.
Verghese, Abraham. 1997. "Last Acts." *New Yorker*, September 22, 1997, 77–79.
Virdi, Jyotika. 1992. "*Salaam Bombay!* (Mis)representing Child Labor." *Jump Cut*, 37 (July 1992): 29–36. http://www.ejumpcut.org/archive/onlinessays/JC37folder/SalaamBombay.html.
Virdi, Jyotika. 2003. *Cinematic ImagiNation: Indian Popular Films as Social History*. New Brunswick: Rutgers University Press.
Williams, Linda. 2008. *Screening Sex*. Durham: Duke University Press.
Williams, Patrick and Laura Chrisman. 1994. "Colonial Discourse and Post-Colonial Theory: An Introduction." In *Colonial Discourse and Post-Colonial Theory*, edited by Patrick Williams and Laura Chrisman, 1–20. New York: Columbia University Press.
Wilmington, Michael. 2004. "Movie Review: Vanity Fair." *Chicago Tribune*, September 1, 2004.
Wood, James. 2001. "Human, All Too Inhuman." *New Republic*, August 30, 2001.
Yabroff, Jennie. 1997. "All About Eros: *Kama Sutra* Director Mira Nair Talks About Sex in 16th-Century India, and What It Means to Us Today." *Salon*, March 7, 1997. http://www.salon.com/march97/970307.html

INDEX

11'09"01 (film), 19, 178; summarized, 205
12 Years a Slave (film), 8
16 Fathoms Deep (film), 43
36 Chowringhee Lane (film), 61

"Aaj Mausam Bada Beimaan Hai" (song), 93–94
ABCD (film), 102
abortion (sex selective), 23
Academy Awards, 59
actors' workshop, 60, 67, 73
adaptations. *See* film adaptations
Aengst, Jennifer, 65
Agnes, Flavia, 24
Ahmed, Riz, 8, 182, 188
Ahmedabad, 41–42
AIDS. *See* HIV/AIDS
Akhtar, Zoya, 193
Amelia (film), 5, 10, 21, 22, 24, 25; summarized, 209
American Chai (film), 102
Amin, Idi, 8, 107–8, 118
Anand, Vijay, 146
Andrew, Dudley, 25, 148, 151, 155
anthropology, 50
Antony and Cleopatra (play), 7
Aparajito (film), 83
Apartheid, 8, 119
Appadurai, Arjun, 17, 50–52, 84
Apur Sansar (film), 168
Aradhana (film), 76
Arora, Poonam, 59, 79

arranged marriage, 166
Asian expulsion from Uganda, 8, 16, 107–11
asylum, 128
auteur theory, 9–10, 189
authenticity, 14–15, 59, 125, 141
awards. *See* Nair, Mira: awards received
Ayaz, Fareed, 179–80

Bachchan, Amitabh, 78, 79
Bandit Queen (film), 27, 102, 144–45
Barthes, Roland, 10
Bartos, Adam, 54
Bazin, Andre, 25, 66, 73
Bell, Christine, 25, 105, 124–27
Bend It Like Beckham (film), 27, 102
Bengali language, 162–64
Bhabha, Homi, 16
Bhaji on the Beach (film), 22, 27, 102
"bhalonaam," 164
bhangra, 92
Bhargava, Prashant, 5
Bhatnagar, Rashmi, 23
"Bhenji brigade," 102
Bicycle Thief (film), 42–43, 66
Bigelow, Kathryn, 22, 187
Biwi No. 1 (film), 28, 83, 93–102
Bol (film), 180–81
"Bollywood," 12, 28–29; in *Monsoon Wedding*, 90–93; in *Salaam Bombay!*, 68–78; in *Vanity Fair*, 149–50, 153
Bollywood/Hollywood (film), 102
Bombay (city of), 11, 45, 53, 60

221

Index

Borden, Lizzie, 5, 22
Boyle, Danny, 58, 63
Brah, Avtar, 18–19, 84
Breckenridge, Carol, 17, 50
Bride and Prejudice (film), 27, 102
British Broadcasting Corporation (BBC), 61
Brown, Barry, 46
Buddha of Suburbia (film), 102
Buñuel, Luis, 57, 66–68
Burton, Richard, 25
Butler, Susan, 25

cabaret (trope in Indian cinema), 51–52
Campion, Jane, 4, 5, 22
Cannes Film Festival, 5, 59, 83
Castro, Fidel, 124
censorship, 22, 23, 56, 71; in *Kama Sutra: A Tale of Love*, 133–35, 141–46; in *Monsoon Wedding*, 87–88
Central Board of Film Certification (CBFC), 133, 142, 146
Chadha, Gurinder, 4, 5, 14, 22, 27, 102
Chetna (film), 72
Children of a Desired Sex (film), 7, 23–24, 30
"Choli ke peeche kya hai" (song), 144
choreography, 97, 153
Choudhury, Sarita, 141
Chowdhry, Ranjit, 127, 129
"Chunari Chunari" (song), 28, 93–101
Chutney Popcorn (film), 102
Cineaste (magazine), 6, 58
cinéma vérité, 30, 33, 34, 51, 57–58, 59; contrasted to style of *Los Olvidados*, 67–68; in Nair's documentary films, 43, 44–45, 46; in *The Namesake*, 169
Cinemax (channel), 53
Clockwork Orange, A (film), 143
colonialism, 15, 107, 147–49, 163
colorism, 113–14
Columbia University, 8
Constant Gardener, The (film), 190
Corrigan, Timothy, 25
courtesans (in Hindi cinema), 72
Crime and Punishment (film), 42
Crothers, Tim, 189
Cuarón, Alfonso, 4

"daknaam," 164
"dance bar" workers, 45–53
Danna, Mychael, 92
Dash, Julie, 5, 22
Day the Mercedes Became a Hat, The (film), 8, 20, 119; summarized, 200
decolonization, 16
De Lauretis, Teresa, 23
Denis, Claire, 5
De Palma, Brian, 126
Desai, Anita, 16
Desai, Gaurav, 107
Desai, Jigna, 113
Devdas (film), 72
Devi, Phoolan, 27, 145
Dharavi (film), 14
Dhawan, David, 28, 93
Dhobi Ghat (film), 58
Dhoom 3 (film), 90
diaspora, 12, 37, 39, 59, 194; as gendered phenomenon, 38, 43–44, 159, 166; in *The Namesake*, 166; "old" and "new" diasporas, 103; in *So Far From India*, 25, 26; in theory, 17–21
"diaspora vérité," 10, 21, 28, 31, 57, 105–6, 132, 133, 195; defined, 4; in *Kama Sutra: A Tale of Love*, 135, 139; in *Monsoon Wedding*, 81, 93, 101; in *The Namesake*, 158; in *Queen of Katwe*, 190; in *Salaam Bombay!*, 57; in *Vanity Fair*, 146–47, 157
Diller, Elizabeth, 170
Dilwale Dulhania Le Jayenge, 92
direct cinema, 34
Dirlik, Arif, 80
Disney, 189–90
Do Bigha Zameen (film), 72
documentary filmmaking, aesthetics of, 3, 30, 32–35, 42–43
documentary realism, 26, 27, 30, 32–35, 53, 57
Dogme 95, 82
Doha Film Institute, 13
Doordarshan, 87
Dube, Reena, 23
Dube, Renu, 23

Dubey, Lilette, 7
Dubey, Neha, 93–102
Dworkin, Andrea, 23
Dwyer, Rachel, 144

Earhart, Amelia, 5, 21
Earth (film), 102
East Africa, 107
editing, 97
Epstein, Mitch, 7, 10, 60, 161
Ethiopia, 120
ethnography, 50–51, 55
exile, 12, 18, 25

Faleiro, Sonia, 24
Fellowes, Julian, 148
female spectatorship, 23
feminism in India, 46
feminist filmmaking, 21–24, 46, 56
feminist film theory, 9
Fiji, 18
film adaptations, 25–26, 133–35, 147, 151, 155, 182, 193
film festivals, 5, 32
Fire (film), 22, 27, 102
Foster, Gwendolyn Audrey, 10–11, 35
Fox Searchlight Films, 13

Ganapati Festival, 77
Ganatra, Nisha, 102
Ganti, Tejaswini, 28, 143–44
Garam Hawa (film), 144
Gay Divorcee (film), 43
Ghai, Subhash, 143–44
Ghatak, Ritwik, 167
Ghosh, Amitav, 16
Ghosh, Nemai, 167
globalization, 84, 101
Godard, Jean-Luc, 9
Gogol, Nikolai, 163–66
Gopal, Sangita, 28, 92
Griswold, Alex, 46

Hamdani, Salman, 178
Hamid, Mohsin, 11, 25, 182–85

Harvard University, 3, 6, 7
"Hawa Hawaii" (song), 76
Helen (film actor), 52
Hindi cinema, 51–52, 83, 87; class biases in, 94; playback singing in, 98; song and dance sequences, 92–95
Hindi language, 41, 89–90
Hinduism, 38–39, 172
Hindustani (film), 95
HIV/AIDS, 65, 105–6, 120–24
Hollywood, 29
home, 19, 159, 181, 190
"homing desire," 19, 84, 181, 194
"How Can It Be?" (film), 19, 178; summarized, 208
Howrah Bridge, 172
Howrah Bridge (film), 68
Hudson, Kate, 8
Hum Aapke Hai Kaun (film), 92
human trafficking, 65
Huston, Anjelica, 130–32
hybridity, 9–12, 14, 17, 39, 103, 119; in *The Namesake*, 166, 169, 174; in *The Reluctant Fundamentalist*, 177
Hyderabad, 45
Hysterical Blindness (film), 10, 32; summarized, 205

immigration, 18, 173, 185
Immigration and Naturalization Service (INS), 127
Iñarritu, Alejandro Gonzales, 4, 13
In-Between World of Vikram Lall, The, 17
indentured laborers, 107
India Cabaret (film), 12, 14, 17, 21, 22–24, 27, 30, 45–53, 54, 58, 59; allusions to commercial Hindi cinema, 51–52; as cinéma vérité documentary, 46–47; depiction of sex workers, 52; as ethnographic work, 50–51; as feminist work, 46; summarized, 198
Indian Administrative Service, 6
Indian censor board. *See* Central Board of Film Certification
Indian film industry, 86–87

Indian film studies, 28
interactive mode of documentary filmmaking, 54
interracial romance, 175, 179, 181–82
intersectionality, 11
intertextuality, 10
Islam, 37, 178–80
It's a Wonderful Afterlife (film), 27

Jama Masjid (Delhi), 31
Jama Masjid Street Journal (film), 7, 30,
   35–37, 54; summarized, 197
Janissaries, 183
John, Barry, 7, 60, 61, 67, 74
Johnson, Allyson, 97
Joyce, James, 172
Jutt and Bond, 181

Kakar, Sudhir, 136
Kalidasa, 140
Kama Sutra (text), 25, 135–37
Kama Sutra: A Tale of Love (film), 5, 7, 8,
   21–23, 25–27, 56, 135–46; censorship
   of, 141–46; derived from Vatsayana's
   source text, 136–37; feminist orientation
   of, 137; influence of Wajida Tabassum's
   "Utaran," 137–39; summarized, 202
Kamathipura, 65, 71
Kamdar, Mira, 85
Kampala, 12, 112
Kanwar, Anita, 73
Kapoor, Anil, 72, 76
Kapoor, Karisma, 94–95, 99
Kapur, Ratna, 145
Kapur, Shekhar, 5, 27, 69, 76, 102, 145
Kara, Siddharth, 65
Karma (film), 72, 143
Kataria, Madan, 54–55
Khajuraho, 135, 140
Khan, Farah, 97, 153
Khan, Irrfan, 13, 169
Khan, Salman, 94–97, 99
Khosla, G. D., 143
Kishwar, Madhu, 23
kissing (in Hindi cinema), 72

Kolkata, 38, 159–60
Kubrick, Stanley, 143
Kureishi, Hanif, 102

Lahiri, Jhumpa, 25
Last King of Scotland (film), 190
Laughing Club of India, The (film), 12, 27,
   30, 31, 35, 53–56; summarized, 203
laughing clubs, 11, 53–56
Lee, Ang, 4, 13
lip-syncing, 98
Loafer (film), 93
Loomba, Ania, 16
Los Olvidados (film), 57, 66–68
Lovell, Mary, 25

Maachis (film), 144
MacKinnon, Catherine, 23
Maisha Film Lab, 8, 190
male gaze, 35
Mamber, Stephen, 34
Mamdani, Mahmood, 8, 105–11, 177–78
Mani, Bakirathi, 113
Manusmriti (text), 136
Mariel boatlift, 11, 105, 124–32
Massey Sahib (film), 61
Mazumdar, Ranjani, 52, 64, 95
Mehta, Anurag, 102
Mehta, Binita, 113
Mehta, Deepa, 4, 5, 14, 22, 27
Mehta, Monika, 144
Mehta, Suketu, 64
melodrama, 57
"Mera Joota Hai Japani" (song), 106, 109–10
Merchant, Ismail, 5, 102
"Mere Sapno Ki Rani" (song), 76
Midival Punditz, 56, 180
Mighty Heart, A (film), 187
migration: domestic, 38–39, 52, 57, 59–60,
   62–65, 168, 194; international, 12, 30–31
Migration (film), 32, 120; summarized, 207
"Migration" (song by Nitin Sawhney), 56
Minh-ha, Trinh T., 5, 22
Mishra, Pankaj, 16
Mishra, Sudhir, 14

Mishra, Vijay, 18, 103
Mississippi Masala (film), 13–14, 16, 18–20, 22, 24, 31–32, 56, 106–19; account of Asian expulsion from Uganda, 112–13; colorism, 113–14; "Mera Joota Hai Japani" song, 106, 109–10; parallels with *From Citizen to Refugee*, 108–11; returning to Uganda, 118–19; summarized, 200
mobile phones, 85
Mohanty, Chandra Talpade, 16, 24
Molina, Alfred, 130
Monsoon Wedding (film), 5–7, 12, 14, 19–20, 24, 26–28, 32, 53, 56, 80–104; actors' workshops in, 82; analysis of "Chunari Chunari" song and dance, 94–101; compared to other South Asian diaspora films, 102–4; compared to *Salaam Bombay!*, 82–83; engagement with commercial Hindi cinema in, 90–93; feminist themes in, 98–100, 102–3; nominated for major awards, 83; languages spoken in, 89–90; sexual abuse in, 102–3; summarized, 204; theme of censorship in, 87–88
Mookerjee, Ajit, 140
Mr. India (film), 28, 69, 72, 76–77
Muir, John Kenneth, 60
Mukherjee, Hrishikesh, 143
"multiplex" film market, 91
Mulvey, Laura, 23
Mundhra, Jagmohan, 5
Muslims, 11, 30, 36–37, 178–80
Mutesi, Phiona, 24, 189–95
My Beautiful Launderette (film), 102
My Own Country (book), 25
My Own Country (film), 5, 18, 19, 120–24; as adaptation of Abraham Verghese's book, 120–21; director's cameo in, 124; parallels between experience of gay/closeted men and immigrants, 123; summarized, 202–3
My Son the Fanatic (film), 102
Mystic Masseur (film), 102

Naipaul, V. S., 16, 17
Nair, Amrit, 6
Nair, Mira: adaptations from fiction, 25–26, 133–35, 158, 193; awards received, 5, 32, 59, 83; biographical sketch of, 6–9; conflicts with Indian censors, 133–35, 141–46; documentary films of, 30–56; education of, 7, 16; as feminist filmmaker, 9–17, 21–24, 26, 193–94; filmography of, 197–210; hybridity of, 14–15; as Indian filmmaker, 14, 194; parents of, 6; period pieces, 26, 134, 148; as postcolonial filmmaker, 9–17, 26, 188; shift from documentary to fiction films, 33, 57–58; short films, 8, 19, 32, 120, 178
Nair, Praveen, 59
Namesake, The (film), 5, 13, 17–20, 25–26, 31, 38, 44, 158–76; as adaptation from Jhumpa Lahiri's novel, 161–66; allusions to Satyajit Ray, 168; bridges as motif, 171–72; names and naming in, 162–65, 169, 175–76; shoes as motif, 173–74; summarized, 206–7; visual motifs, 169–71
Namesake, The (novel), 25, 161–66
National Film Development Corporation, 13, 14, 61
Nehru, Jawarhalal, 85
neorealism, 43, 57, 66
New York, I Love You (film), 208
Nichols, Bill, 34, 54
Non-Resident Indians (NRIs), 90, 92
Nyong'o, Lupita, 8, 190

Obote, Milton, 107
observational mode of documentary filmmaking, 32, 34–35, 43, 54
Odissi dance, 140
Orientalism, 15
Oyelowo, David, 8, 190

Pakeezah (film), 72
parallel cinema, 61
Parama (film), 61
Parmar, Pratibha, 5, 22

Patekar, Nana, 73
Patel, Krutin, 102
Pennebaker, D. A., 7, 44
Perez Family, The (film), 5, 8, 19, 20, 22–25, 31, 124–32; contrasted to *Scarface*, 126; critical reception of, 124–25, 131–32; depiction of Hollywood illusion of "America," 127–28; depiction of Mariel boatlift, 125–26; summarized, 201
Perez Family, The (novel), 25, 124–27
photography, 160–61
Piku (film), 91
Pilcher, Lydia Dean, 10
pornography, 23
postcolonialism, 15–17, 80
postcolonial theory, 15
poverty (in Hindi cinema), 72
poverty, Indian, 85
Prasad, Udayan, 102
prostitution. *See* sex workers
Public Enemy, 116
Punjabi language, 89–90, 179
Pyaasa (film), 64

Qawwali music, 179–80
Queen (film), 91
Queen of Katwe (film), 3, 8, 13, 21, 24, 26, 34, 189–95; as adaptation of Tim Crothers's book on Phiona Mutesi, 189, 191–92; budget and financing, 189; summarized, 210; theme of exile and displacement in, 190–91; visual motifs in, 191
Quinn, Declan, 10, 141

racism, 12, 113, 162, 178
Radhakrishnan, R., 16
Rafi, Mohammed, 56
Rai, Raghu, 161
Rajadhyaksha, Ashish, 28
Rajan, Gitja, 20, 103
Rajan, Rajeswari Sunder, 17
Ramayana, 38
Rao, Kiran, 5, 58, 193
Ray, Satyajit, 61, 83, 167–68
refugees, 18
Rekha, 139

Reluctant Fundamentalist, The (film), 5, 8, 12, 13, 37, 177–88; as adaptation of Mohsin Hamid's novel, 182–87; allusions to contemporary art, 185; citations of commercial cinema and TV, 180–81, 183; compared to earlier Nair films, 179, 181; critical reception, 187–88; funding of, 179; locations, 179; music, 179–80; summarized, 210; use of humor, 184
Reluctant Fundamentalist, The (novel), 25, 177–88
Rich, B. Ruby, 23
Rome, Open City (film), 66
Roy, Arundhati, 145
Roy, Bimal, 72
Rushdie, Salman, 16, 17, 80, 141

Safran, William, 18
Salaam Baalak Trust, 6, 8, 59
Salaam Bombay! (film), 21–22, 24, 26–28, 32, 52, 57–80; amateur cast in, 73; authenticity as Indian film, 78–80; compared to *Monsoon Wedding*, 82–83; compared to other Indian art cinema, 61–62; critique of commercial Hindi cinema in, 68–78; depiction of sex workers, 63–64; influence of Buñuel on, 66–68; as narrative of domestic migration and displacement, 59–60; representation of poverty in, 78–79; summarized, 199; use of actors' workshop in, 67, 73–76
Sangari, Kum Kum, 16
Sarkar, Kobita, 144
Sarris, Andrew, 9
Satanic Verses, The, 17, 141
Sawhney, Nitin, 56, 180
Scarface (film), 126
Schreiber, Liev, 182, 188
Scofidio, Ricardo, 170
Seabrook, Jeremy, 64
self-reflexive mode of documentary filmmaking, 35–37, 56
Sellors, C. Paul, 9–10
Sen, Aparna, 22
Sen, Sushmita, 94–97, 99
Seth, Roshan, 82

Sex and the City, 183
sexual abuse, 102
sex workers, 12, 22, 24, 45–53; in commercial Hindi cinema, 63–64, 72; in *India Cabaret*, 46–50; in *The Perez Family*, 125–26; in *Salaam Bombay!*, 60, 65, 71–72
Shah, Amit, 46
Shah, Naseeruddin, 13, 82
Sharma, Konkona Sen, 178
Sharma, Shailja, 20, 103
Shinde, Gauri, 193
Shree 420 (film), 72
Shyamalan, M. Night, 5
Singh, Maharajah Duleep, 151
Singh, Raghubir, 161
Singh, Tarsem, 5
Sippy, Ramesh, 143
Sissel, Sandi, 60
slavery, 16
Slumdog Millionaire (film), 58, 63, 72
social realism, 32
So Far from India (film), 18–20, 24, 26, 30, 35, 37–45, 54, 58, 60; allusions to European art cinema, 42–43; gendering of emigration, 38, 43–44; Hinduism, 38–39; summarized, 198; as work of cinéma vérité, 44
software industry, 81
South Africa, 8, 119
Soyinka, Wole, 16
Spivak, Gayatri Chakravorty, 16, 79
Sridevi, 76
Such a Long Journey (film), 144
Sutherland, Kiefer, 188

Tabassum, Wajida, 25, 135–39
Tabu, 13
Tagore, Sharmila, 106, 146, 168
Tantric art, 135, 139–40
Taraporevala, Sooni, 7, 59–60, 75, 105, 115
Thackeray, William Makepeace, 5, 11, 134; connections to India, 153–54
Thakur, Divya, 170
Theater Action Group, 7, 60
Tikaram, Ramon, 139

Tololyan, Khachig, 18
Tomei, Marisa, 132
transgendered individuals, 70
Truffaut, Francois, 9
Tyabji, Khalid, 7, 139

Uganda, 8, 11, 106–13; Asian expulsion from, 107–11; in *Queen of Katwe*, 189–95
University of Delhi, 7, 16, 17
UTV Motion Pictures, 13

Vachani, Nilita, 74–75
Vanita, Ruth, 23
Vanity Fair (film), 5, 18, 21, 22, 24–27, 146–57; choreography, 153; colonial themes, 149–51; compared to earlier adaptations of the novel, 147, 157; as "diasporic" film, 147, 157; as feminist film, 155–56; historical fidelity of, 156–57; realism of, 148; settings, 151; summarized, 206; as "transformative" adaptation of Thackeray's novel, 155
Vanity Fair (novel), 11, 16, 25, 134, 146–57
Vassanji, M. G., 16, 17
Vasudevan, Ravi, 28, 92
Vatsayana, 135–37
Venice Film Festival, 5, 83
Verghese, Abraham, 25, 120–24
violence (on screen), 67
Virdi, Jyotika, 17, 59, 79
von Trier, Lars, 82

Wheeler, William, 182, 189
Winogrand, Garry, 161
Winterbottom, Michael, 187
Witherspoon, Reese, 146
Wolcott, Derek, 16
women-centered stories, 24
women's cinema, 23
Working Girls (film), 22
World of Apu (film). See *Apur Sansar*

Yadav, Raghubir, 61, 73
yoga, 32, 54–55, 82

Zero Dark Thirty (film), 187